Understanding Street Drugs

Companion volume

Understanding Drug Issues
A Photocopiable Resource Workbook
Second Edition
David Emmett and Graeme Nice
ISBN 1 84310 350 8

of related interest

Listening to Young People in School, Youth Work
and Counselling
Nick Luxmoore
ISBN 1 85302 909 2

Supporting Parents of Teenagers
A Handbook for Professionals
Edited by John Coleman and Debi Roker
ISBN 1 85302 944 0

Understanding and Supporting Children with Emotional
and Behavioural Difficulties
Edited by Paul Cooper
ISBN 1 85302 665 4

Adolescence
Assessing and Promoting Resilience in Vulnerable Children
Brigid Daniel and Sally Wassell
ISBN 1 84310 019 3

Helping Adolescents and Adults to Build Self-Esteem
A Photocopiable Resource Book
Deborah Plummer
ISBN 1 84310 185 8

Just Schools
A Whole School Approach to Restorative Justice
Belinda Hopkins
Foreword and Introduction by Guy Masters
ISBN 1 84310 132 7

Deliberate Self-Harm in Adolescence
Claudine Fox and Keith Hawton
Child and Adolescent Mental Health Series
ISBN 1 84310 237 4

Understanding Street Drugs

A Handbook of Substance Misuse for Parents, Teachers and Other Professionals

Second Edition

David Emmett and Graeme Nice

Jessica Kingsley Publishers
London and Philadelphia

First published in 2006
by Jessica Kingsley Publishers
116 Pentonville Road
London N1 9JB, UK
and
400 Market Street, Suite 400
Philadelphia, PA 19106, USA

www.jkp.com

Library of Congress Cataloging in Publication Data

Emmett, David.
    Understanding street drugs : a handbook of substance misuse for parents, teachers and other
professionals / David Emmett and Graeme Nice.— 2nd ed.
        p. cm.
    Revised editions of: Understanding drugs, published in 1996.
    Includes index.
    ISBN-13: 978-1-84310-351-6 (pbk. : alk. paper)
    ISBN-10: 1-84310-351-6 (pbk. : alk. paper) 1. Drug abuse—Study and teaching—Great
Britain. 2. Drug abuse—Treatment—Great Britain. 3. Youth—Drug use—Prevention. I.
Nice, Graeme. II. Emmett, David. Understanding drugs. III. Title.
    HV5840.G7E55 2006
    392.29'0941—dc22

                        2005025926

British Library Cataloguing in Publication Data
A CIP catalogue record for this book is available from the British Library

ISBN-13: 978 1 84310 351 6
ISBN-10: 1 84310 351 6

Printed and bound in Great Britain by
Athenaeum Press, Gateshead, Tyne and Wear

With special thanks to Jean Emmett
and the late Alan 'Deano' Dent

*Human history becomes more and more a race
between education and catastrophe.*

H.G. Wells
The Outline of History (1920)

Contents

List of figures

Chapter 1

Introduction

Since we set about writing the first edition of this book in 1996, much has changed in and around the drug scene in the UK. Drug usage has soared. There are an estimated five million regular users of illegal substances in the UK. A million of these have used cocaine within the past 12 months, a drug that is rapidly becoming a major part of the drug-using landscape and whose use has quadrupled within the past ten years. There are now also an estimated four million cannabis users in the UK, despite the drug being heavily implicated in concurrent mental-health and drug-misuse problems in patients that we see on an almost daily basis, the phenomenon known as 'dual diagnosis'. Yet the UK government has seen fit to reclassify cannabis from class B to class C, despite these well-established health concerns. Overall spending on drugs has now risen to an estimated £8 billion annually, despite most drugs having fallen in price. For example, in 1970 a gram of cocaine would have cost the equivalent of £300 in today's economic climate, but in 2004 it could be bought for as little as £30. Rap music, enjoyed by so many young people, often extols the virtues of drug usage and glorifies dealers, talking of rags-to-riches lifestyles full of easy money, easy women and glamorous living.

Among all this bad news, it is pleasing to note that many new services funded by central government have come into being in order to reduce drug-related deaths, stem drug-related crimes and increase treatment choices for those who wish to reduce or stop their drug usage. But, despite these new measures, we must also do whatever we can, both as individuals and in groups, to try to dissuade or divert young people from trying drugs in the first place or intervene at an early enough stage to save them from possible future legal, health and social problems. Therefore, we must continue to deliver education and prevention programmes, for they are still our best weapons in the fight against drugs.

One of the questions people often asked us during our work with young people is whether we have ever taken any illegal drugs. Indeed, it is often thrown out as a sort of challenge: 'How can you talk about drugs? Have you ever tried them?' The short answer is a simple 'No, never.' This is not because we have ever made any conscious choice about it but simply because no-one has ever offered us illegal drugs, and so we have never had to choose. We suspect that this is common to many adults. We, ourselves, were lucky enough to grow up at a time and in a place where drugs simply were not so readily available. We never spoke of drugs with our friends, never thought about taking drugs and, as far as we know, never knew anyone who did. Drugs simply were not part of our world picture. Young people today are not growing up in the same world that many of us did; their culture is very different. The majority of young people will have to make a choice about drugs. They will make that choice because someone is likely to offer them drugs. It is difficult enough, as most adults know, to understand the mind of an adolescent. How much more difficult it is to understand the mind of an adolescent who is making a decision that many of us have never been, and may never be, challenged to make. We are protected by our age and will never be called upon to choose. We are too old. We are past it. We are no longer members of the customer generation; it is our children who are, or will be.

Our personal experience of illegal drugs therefore does not come from ever having tried drugs but from our work over many years with the subject in all its forms. This work has taught us countless things about the subject, and it is worth outlining a few of them for you.

It is our view that the problem of substance misuse represents the biggest single social danger that affects our society today. We believe that this problem is potentially going to do more damage to our society in the next 25 years or so than anything ever has in our national history. If you think that is an exaggeration, then simply look around the world at the places where drug misuse is especially high. Look in particular at what is happening in the USA. There are parts of some US cities that have become hostile to non-drug-taking people. There are areas where the ordinary things of life do not go on, where it is difficult to get a taxi or a bus, where it is impossible to get someone to come and fix your television or your heating. There are even areas where the US mail service does not operate. This is because no-one will venture in there. To do so is simply unsafe. If one were to blunder in to such a place, it would not be a matter of the inconvenience of being lost; it could be a matter of survival. We may consider ourselves lucky just to get out alive. We could be mugged or murdered for the shoes on our feet or simply to be seen to fall down. One of the biggest single causes of death in US males under the age of 25 years is being shot in a drug-related incident. What happens in the USA often happens in the UK a few years later. One only has to keep an eye on the media to see stories almost daily of the untimely deaths of young people, the destruction of families, the turning of estates into drug-infested areas, rising crime, inter-gang shootings and so on – all related to drugs.

These problems belong to today's young people. Most adults have no problem around drugs, but many young and some not quite so young people do. The decisions that adults make about drugs may have limited effect. It is the decisions that young people now and in the future make that count. They are directing the drug scene. They are deciding what level illegal substances should occupy in the society that they are inheriting.

The current problem of drugs is one that adults have given to today's young people. When we, ourselves, were young, the drug scene was at an almost insignificant level, but as the second half of the twentieth century went by it slowly developed and grew around us. Our society did nothing, because we were unaware that we had a problem brewing, or we had no idea what to do about it, or we did not care because we thought it would not affect us personally. Maybe we had ill-conceived ideas about what should be allowed and what should not. Now we have handed over the problem to today's younger generation, most of whom in turn will become the concerned parents of tomorrow. Our greatest worry is that today's young people will do just what we did – nothing – and let the problem continue to escalate. If they do that, then they will pass on the problem to their own children in due time. By then, it may have developed into a crisis of such a magnitude that their children will inherit a society more problematic than we have today, which they will not thank us for.

As well as inheriting the problem, we believe very strongly that young people today have the power to do something about it. They have something that most adults have very little of: they have influence over each other. We learned a long time ago that the influence of parents, teachers and indeed all adults over young people is insignificant compared with the influence that they wield over each other.

Surveys across the UK still show that the majority of young people state that they have not taken, and do not intend to take, drugs. Indeed, if we pushed them a little further, many would say that they are opposed to drugs. We would like to pose some questions to those anti-drug young people: What are you doing about it? What have you done about it today? It is those anti-drug young people, not those who welcome drugs and see them as being fashionable and desirable, who can affect things.

Let us try to illustrate this point by looking at two different examples. Consider first adult cigarette-smoking, which is now regarded by many people as antisocial and unacceptable. Cigarette smokers may be looked down upon as being people who damage their own and others' health. A few years ago, if you held a party in your own house, even as a non-smoker you felt obliged to put out ashtrays for the guests. After they had gone home, you might open all the doors and windows and

complain about the smell of tobacco smoke. These days, if someone lights up a cigarette in a non-smoker's house without permission, they are liable to find themselves
removed into the garden. Most workplaces are now non-smoking environments due
to the health issues surrounding smoking, and it is common to see small groups of
people huddled outside office blocks smoking, because they are banned from doing
so inside. As a result of this public disapproval and peer pressure, the number of
adult smokers is dropping rapidly. It was not the influence of smokers that brought
this about; it was the influence of non-smokers. Smokers did not state that smoking
was unacceptable, that it polluted the air; it was non-smokers who felt liberated to
have their say – and what a difference they have made.

Now let us look at a young person's example. At the beginning of the 1980s,
we, ourselves, were involved in dealing with a major outbreak of the sniffing of solvent glues by children on a large housing estate. The craze lasted for three years;
during that time, five young people died as a result of their sniffing. If one paid a
visit to the estate during that period, one got the impression that the problem was
out of control: young people, some as young as nine years of age, were sniffing everywhere. But then, during the summer of 1983, something very remarkable happened.
In the space of a few short weeks, the problem simply faded away and disappeared.
It went away not as a result of the efforts of the many teachers and other adults who
became involved in trying to deal with it but simply because it went out of fashion.
What had been in favour was now outmoded. If you talk about glue sniffing with
the majority of young people on that estate now, they will explain that it is for losers.
In the early 1980s, it had been considered cool; if you were not sniffing, you had no
street credibility. But by the end of 1983, you had no street cred if you *were* sniffing.
It was not the influence of the sniffers that brought this about; they did not go
around telling people that glue sniffing was for losers. It was the non-sniffers who
brought about the change; as a result, the problem disappeared, and to date it has
not returned to that estate as a major visible problem. Everything that we do in drugs
education must be geared towards unlocking this weapon of positive influence, a
weapon that can change the world.

In recent years, many adults have taken to thinking that young people's influence over their peers is mostly bad. Perhaps it is time we started to recognise the immense power of positive influence. We need to be reinforcing the decisions of
non-drug-taking young people and to strengthen and empower them in the use of
that influence. It is, after all, their society now that substance misuse is likely to damage. It sometimes seems that we are banging our heads against an enormous problem
that is slowly overwhelming us, but drugs can be overcome. There can be a light at
the end of the tunnel. We cannot see that light yet, as it is around the corner, and
there may be more corners after this one, but it is there waiting for us. It is there because many people who are concerned about the problem are starting to work to-

gether. Parents are beginning to learn about drugs when previously they felt helpless and unable to have any sensible or useful discussion about the subject with their children. Parents are starting to acquire the necessary knowledge to make a real contribution to their children's education about these issues. Similarly, teachers are receiving the necessary training to enable them to work with this subject, and, in the UK, all schools are now required by law to have workable integrated drugs policies and education programmes for pupils. These programmes not only deliver information but also lead to an understanding of the issues affecting our society that go along with drug use. The police in many areas are getting involved in schools' drug education programmes and bringing their unique experience of the subject into lessons and discussions. In addition, health authorities and the prison service are putting more resources and well-trained personnel into prevention, education and treatment.

In 1995, the UK government funded the setting up of local drug action teams and drug reference groups under its Tackling Drugs Together initiative. The government is also funding well-conceived and expertly presented awareness-raising campaigns and supporting the efforts made by a whole range of other agencies. This strategy has developed and grown in the years since its inception and continues to demonstrate the UK government's commitment to the problem.

Only by working together can we enable future generations of young people to begin to influence the problem. We as adults may not be able to change it, but young people can. Our job is to enable and support them to do so.

At the end of the Battle of El Alamein, the first major Allied victory of the Second World War, Winston Churchill said: 'This is not the end. It is not even the beginning of the end. But it is, perhaps, the end of the beginning.' We believe that this is where we are currently in the war against drug abuse. The beginning is over and we have engaged the enemy. A few years ago, the majority of people did not even know there was a war to be fought, much less a war they had to become personally involved in. But now we can all be involved, and because of this we need not fail. We must not fail, for even to contemplate failure is to think the unthinkable.

Chapter 2

A Brief History of Drug Use and a Snapshot of the Current Drugs Situation in Britain

Until recently, Western Europe has had very little history of drug use. It is necessary to look only at the geographical position of the region to see why. The climate does not bring enough in the way of hot weather or bright sunlight (even with global warming), and therefore none of the major drug-producing plants have evolved here. No opium poppies, coca bushes or mescaline cacti occur naturally. Similarly, cannabis of drug-producing quality does not occur naturally in the UK, although it has been introduced illicitly on a small scale.

Historically, the only drug that occurred naturally in Western Europe was based on hallucinogenic mushrooms. In certain parts of Scandinavia and northern Russia, there was substantial use of these fungi for recreational and religious purposes. While there is little doubt that early residents of the remainder of Europe knew of the properties of the various 'magic mushrooms', their use remained largely restricted to a few pagan religious leaders and soothsayers. The Romans had knowledge of opium through their dealings with the Middle and Far East and used several different preparations of the drug for pain relief. They undoubtedly took supplies of these preparations with them during their occupation of other countries, but there is no evidence of the use of opium as a mind-altering substance by the indigenous populations. When the Roman occupation ended as the empire retreated, the use and knowledge of opium was lost for many hundreds of years.

It was not until the European nations began to create their own empires and send their forces around the globe that their populations began to come into contact with the major plant-based drugs. Opium and cannabis reached Europe through contacts with Africa and Asia, and then coca arrived from the new world. Non-medical use of these drugs was restricted largely to sailors, travellers and a small number of wealthy people who were able to afford to import them. The use of such drugs by 'ordinary' people, and in particular by young people, was to remain almost unknown until after the Second World War. In the years that followed, people's incomes began to rise slowly and to provide them with a little more in the way of disposable funds that could be used for recreational activities. Simultaneously, young people throughout the world began to seek their own cultures and identities. It has often been said that until the 1950s, there was no such thing as a 'youth culture' or a 'youth market'. Young people started to have money to spend, and others began to provide commodities for them to spend it on. The same thing had been happening for some years in the USA, and drugs had become one of the commodities that many young people had taken to. This soon spread throughout Western Europe and other developed countries, and by the beginning of the 1960s we began to see an increase among certain sectors of young populations in the use of cannabis; this was followed, inevitably, by the use of other illegal substances. Many people have the idea that drugs, and particularly cannabis, were in use by the majority of young people during the 1960s. The authors were both young men during these times and can say, based on their own experience, that nothing could be further from the truth. The vast majority of young people had no contact with drugs. This picture remained static throughout the 1970s, and indeed many countries even saw a decline in the use of certain drugs at that time, but all that has now changed sadly.

Within the past 15–20 years, the worldwide drug culture has evolved in dramatic and alarming ways. The reasons for these worrying changes stem from two developments. First, the major customer generation has shifted sharply towards the young, especially adolescent and young adult males. Second, the availability of drugs has become very widespread indeed, to the point where whole nations, from inner-city areas to suburban towns and even sleepy country villages, seem to have become affected, and this greater availability has led to falling prices.

Even class A drugs have become much more affordable and well within the reach of greater numbers of people who may wish to try them. Add to this scenario the advent of new venues of drug use that have permeated the commercial social scene, such as raves, dance clubs and pubs, and appear to have become accepted by many young people as an integral part of their relaxation and pleasure, and you will appreciate that drug-taking is no longer viewed as an antisocial activity carried out by a small number of 'losers' and by some people is not even considered illegal.

Drugs supply is now a major international business that nets billions of pounds each year for the producers, importers, suppliers and dealers. For these people, the name of the game is money, influence and power, and their greed feeds upon the exploitation of others. They will not lose sleep by worrying about the misery they cause to so many people or the potentially destructive nature of the goods that they peddle. There will always be new recruits to replace those who escape their clutches or who damage their health or lose their lives through overdose or accident.

Despite the fall in drug prices, the development of tolerance and dependence by users towards their drugs still leads many of them to turn to crime to fund their increasingly expensive habits. In the UK, it has been estimated that many billions of pounds' worth of property crime is committed each year for this reason. Add to this the legally available funds and goods used to acquire drugs and you can appreciate the very lucrative nature of this multinational industry. Many users are tempted to take risks and deal drugs themselves in order to make quick and easy money. Several court cases have involved drug dealers who were above their country's state retirement age.

Some of these street drugs, especially cannabis, crack and amphetamine, can be produced in private homes, although by far the greater proportion are imported. Most of the countries in Western Europe, Asia, the Middle East and South America have become major producers and exporters of various illegal substances, and there is growing evidence that suppliers in some former Eastern Bloc countries have also cashed in on the trade in order to attract much sought-after foreign currency.

An illustration of this trend can be seen in *World Drug Report* by the United Nations Office on Drugs and Crime in 2004, which reports that although the majority of detected methylamphetamine-production facilities are still found in the USA, there is an increasing trend towards production in Eastern Europe, with the highest number of production facilities (104) found in 2002 in the Czech Republic, up from 28 in 2001.

Street drugs today are not so much pushed as pulled. Dealers no longer have to put themselves at risk by trading on the streets, as most hide behind the geographic anonymity offered by their mobile phones. Users will now seek out dealers to acquire supplies of their chosen drug or drugs. At an even more basic level, some users may supply drugs to their friends and acquaintances in order to pay for their own drug habit. They will buy in bulk, often through contacts made on the Internet, and then sell the drugs on in small quantities at a good profit.

For young people today, the way is open for more freedom of choice, opportunity and experience. Consequently, illegal drugs have infiltrated their world, maximising that choice of experience.

One of the most well-known of these drugs, a drug that at times receives a great deal of media attention, is ecstasy. Ecstasy itself is not new: it was available in the early part of the twentieth century for use in the treatment of certain psychiatric disorders. It has merely been repackaged and relaunched to potential users as a relatively harmless substance that, due to its stimulant and hallucinogenic properties, will enable you to dance for hours, make friends easily and have heightened sensory experiences. It is estimated that around two million ecstasy tablets are used each week in the UK. It is used mostly by young people in a commercial social setting, such as dance clubs, raves and parties. Ecstasy is used by an estimated 250,000–500,000 people on a regular basis, mostly at the weekends.

To keep the interest of the young drug-using public, and the money rolling in, old established drugs are sometimes repackaged and given other identities to appear new and more exciting. Or some previously mostly unknown substances emerge on to the scene to offer potential users more extreme or unusual sensations and experiences. One of these is ketamine, a general anaesthetic used mostly in paediatric medicine and in veterinary medicine for sedating animals. Known on the street as 'special K' and 'vitamin K', ketamine can be taken by mouth, injected and snorted. It can induce mixed feelings of euphoria, detachment and remoteness from surroundings, hallucinations, depersonalisation and even 'near-death' and 'out-of-body' experiences, which some users actively seek to attain. Ketamine is also implicated in some cases of date rape, because it has the potential to interfere with memory. The dangers of ketamine are obvious: anaesthetics should always be administered under close medical supervision due to the possibility of overdose and adverse reactions.

Another drug increasingly in use by young people is cocaine and its smokable form, known as crack. This powerful stimulant drug, like so many others, has become more readily available to young people as its powder form (for snorting and injection) has substantially reduced in price. Like other stimulants, both cocaine and crack will increase the user's confidence, enhance energy levels and make them feel euphoric. These effects, however, may last for only 10–20 minutes, depending on the form in which the drug is taken. Habituation can develop very quickly, and the user may use the drug more often in an attempt to keep the short-lasting effects of cocaine active over very much longer periods. This will have inevitable implications for cost. Indeed, one crack user reported to us that he was spending as much as £2800 a week to fund his habit, with the money coming from the sale of his house. There have been reports of school-age pupils using the drug during the morning and lunch breaks, and escaping detection because of the brevity of the drug's effects.

Ecstasy, ketamine and cocaine today are linked closely with young peoples' social scenes. Thankfully, only a small percentage of users will ever suffer any permanent or discernible harm, such is the resilience of the human body. The effects of long-term regular use over a period of years are not understood clearly, however, and it could be considered that every person using these drugs on that basis are taking part in one of the largest drugs trials that the world has ever seen.

As well as these three street drugs, there is another drug, this time a depressant with mild hallucinogenic properties, that is in regular use across the world by an even greater number of people of all ages. This drug is cannabis. Cannabis was recently reclassified in the UK from a class B to a class C drug, leading to much confusion and misinformation. A conservative estimate based on a national survey in Britain indicated that cannabis was in use on an occasional to regular basis by more than 7.5 per cent of the adult population, some four million-plus individuals, thus making it the most popular illegal drug of abuse in this country.

Due to the high level of international demand for cannabis, the bulk of its supply still comes from countries with a climate more favourable for intensive cultivation of the plant from which it is produced. Increasingly, however, it is being cultivated on a semi-commercial basis in the countries where it is in demand. An ever-increasing quantity of cannabis is being produced with the use of highly sophisticated hydroponic growing methods and artificial sunlight under factory-like conditions, in converted rooms or in some cases whole houses or other premises totally devoted to the process.

Some individuals also grow their own plants for personal use on window ledges at home, in gardens and at work. One innovative user grew cannabis plants alongside a busy motorway, until they were put out of business by a sharp-eyed traffic policeman.

Home-growing of cannabis has increased simply to help fulfil the heavy demand. Cannabis seeds are easy to obtain from other growers, from websites and from centres such as Amsterdam, where visitors can see whole shops devoted to the cultivation and use of the plant. Indeed, there may even be specialist shops in your local high street where you can buy cannabis seeds, for it is illegal only to germinate them, not to buy them. It is likely that the popularity of cannabis will continue to rise in the years to come, and the legalisation debate is now being considered in many countries, even in government circles. This debate is being promoted and influenced by the pro-cannabis lobby that has sprung up in various countries. Their ultimate aim is to see cannabis made legal or, at the very least, de-criminalised, as it is in the Netherlands. We have no doubts that the real reason behind the actions of many who wish to see the drug legalised is that they stand to make a great deal of money cultivating and marketing the drug to an ever-increasing customer population.

The wide acceptance of cannabis use can also be noted from some of the many logos and slogans that can be found on a wide range of young people's fashion garments and accessories. Caps, jeans, jackets and T-shirts sporting a variety of pro-cannabis symbols are available from market stalls, Internet suppliers and even many leading stores.

Apart from these four drugs, which seem to have become an integral part of the international mass youth culture, we still have to contend with the menace of another substance, heroin. In general, heroin originates from outside of the main user countries. Despite record seizures by customs and police officers each year, enough slips through the defences to supply the requirements of the countless users throughout the world. Happily, the number of users is still smaller than those who at present favour cannabis. However, despite only a small percentage of adult populations using heroin, the social problems and crime associated with it easily outweigh those created by any other illegal drug.

The addictive nature of heroin must never be underestimated. One 20-year-old addict related to us his experience of heroin use as like 'living under water and having to buy air to breathe', outlining his total dependence on the drug simply to feel normal and to be able to carry out his everyday functions. Of those who succumb to heroin, few can ever totally give up their need for the drug. Relapse among former users can almost be considered normal behaviour. The psychological attraction to its use, even after years of abstinence, can be overwhelming, even though users' expectations may never be fulfilled by actual use of the drug.

Addiction to heroin is the root cause of much property crime today. Most of these crimes are burglary, street robbery and opportunist theft, but much worse deeds may be perpetrated to fund habits that, in extreme cases, may cost the user as much as £100 per day, or £35,000 per year. It is accepted that much of the property stolen may realise as little as only 10 per cent of its true value and that a heavy user may therefore be faced with obtaining property of the value of £350,000 every year. This figure is for just one user and for just one drug.

On top of all of this must be added the further costs to society in providing increasing social and medical intervention services and substitute drugs, such as methadone and buprenorphine, to existing and former heroin users. The current UK government drug strategy document states that drug misuse in the UK gives rise to between £10 billion and £18 billion a year in social and economic costs, almost all of which are accounted for by problematic addicted users.

In contrast to heroin, fewer cases of addiction to cocaine are reported. Its much talked about derivative, crack cocaine, does not seem to have swept other countries as it did in some parts of the USA and was feared and predicted to do worldwide. Currently, pockets of high crack usage are confined mostly to inner cities and areas of high social deprivation, but use is spreading.

We must at this point introduce a degree of perspective among all this doom and gloom and state quite categorically that there is evidence to show that many people will still never use any illegal drugs. Of those who choose to do so, only small numbers will ever become permanently dependent or suffer irreversible adverse effects. Many young people will still make the decision that drugs are not going to form a significant part of their lives. If we can only harness the power of this group, we may still be in a position to firmly reject and eject from our society illegal drugs.

To complete this snapshot of drug use today, we must now concentrate on three other types of substance in common usage that are currently all available from legal sources.

The sniffing and inhaling of volatile substances has been with us for many years, and there are some indications that the habit has experienced something of a revival in popularity among sometimes very young people. The use of solvents is changing constantly and today it seems that a wider and much more dangerous variety of products is being used. The use of solvent glues for inhalation has in many countries given way to the spraying of liquid petroleum gas and other lighter fuels or aerosols directly into the mouth and throat. As a consequence, there are many instances of death in young people through asphyxiation and associated problems due to this type of substance misuse.

Tranquillisers and sleeping pills are still much misused. Millions of genuine prescriptions for these are written by doctors every year, although there is a move to reduce this. A proportion of these prescribed drugs, together with those obtained by fraud, theft and importing, form the basis of a thriving street trade. Many users of other drugs will seek out tranquillisers in order to cope with the adverse effects of their more usual drug or to alleviate the come-down effects they experience when their usual drug is unavailable to them. Others will use them simply for the numbing, stress-relieving and sleep-inducing effects for which they were designed. The sleeping pill temazepam, for example, is misused by many people. It proved to be a particular problem within some communities in Scotland, where, in its previous gel capsule form, it had been used intravenously. This practice ceased when new government restrictions prevented its distribution in this form. However, tablet forms of temazepam remain available, and these can easily be crushed and mixed with water in order to be injected. The majority of doctors are much more aware nowadays that certain prescription drugs can be misused and are now more reluctant to supply them, favouring alternative treatments or drugs that do not cause dependency and that cannot be misused so easily.

The final group of drugs that we need to be aware of, because of their increasing popularity, especially among some young males, are steroid drugs manufactured for oral use or injection. Anabolic-type steroids are used in conjunction with regular heavy exercise and certain diets to build muscle bulk. They should be used only under strict medical supervision, as incorrect use can lead to potentially dangerous side effects. Despite these dangers, many people involved in weight-training and body-building, together with some people in the rave and dance club scenes, use anabolic steroids to resculpt their bodies. This is done in order to raise their self-esteem as a result of having bodies that they perceive as being more masculine or sexually attractive. As in all areas of drug use, there are, of course, unscrupulous suppliers. Many of the so-called steroids available on the streets are of spurious quality or not even steroids at all, while others come from very questionable sources such as veterinary surgeries and are intended solely for use in animals.

Many countries operate needle-and-syringe schemes, originally set up to combat the spread of human immunodeficiency virus (HIV) and hepatitis infection among injecting drug users. Many of these schemes are now reporting a steady increase in the numbers of younger male steroid users who are making use of their services, where they can obtain clean injecting equipment and correct information and advice concerning their steroid use. It is hoped that governments will introduce controls to try to stem the improper supply and use of these very dangerous drugs, but it remains to be seen whether proposed controls will merely drive the problem further underground.

To summarise this picture of drug use and availability today, it must be realised that the whole range of drugs and other substances, both legal and illegal, that can be misused is available throughout the world. There are some local and regional variations in availability, due to preference, financial circumstances and the age range of the using populations, but the 'fab four' favoured especially by young users – cannabis, cocaine, ecstasy and heroin – appear to be universally available. Due to the sheer popularity of these drugs, a vast international network of manufacturers and suppliers has grown up to service this great demand.

If societies are unable or unwilling to stem the supply of illegal and dangerous substances on the streets, then we have only education and harm-reduction measures to resort to as a means of averting a further escalation of the problems that we already face as a result of drug misuse.

Part I

Part 1

Chapter 3

Cannabis

Delta-9-Tetrahydrocannabinol

Cannabis: quick reference guide

Source

Plants of the genus *Cannabis*, particularly *Cannabis sativa*.

Forms and appearance

Herbal: dried plant material, similar to a coarse-cut tobacco-like mixture. Usually greenish brown in colour. Sometimes the mixture has been compressed into blocks; occasionally it is seen wound with thread around a thin stick.

Resin: dried and compressed resinous sap, found in blocks of various sizes and shapes. Ranges in colour from black or grey, through every shade of brown, to a pale honey colour. Ranges in consistency from hard and brittle, for hard and dense, to soft and oily, to dry and crumbly.

Oil: extracted from the resin form by the use of a chemical solvent. Seen as a thick heavy oil ranging in colour from dark green or dark brown to jet black and with a distinctive smell like rotting vegetation.

Marketing

Sold by the ounce or as fractions of an ounce in a variety of packaging and sometimes with no packaging at all. Available in every city, town and village in the UK, in public houses and clubs, on the street, outside schools and colleges – indeed, anywhere that young people gather.

Cost

Between £40 and £125 per ounce for the herbal and resin forms. The more potent form of cannabis known as 'skunk' can retail for anything up to £200 an ounce. There is no fixed price for the much rarer oil.

Legal position

Class C controlled substance under the Misuse of Drugs Act 1971.

Methods of use

Commonly smoked in a variety of ways. Can be put into food or made into drinks. Occasionally eaten on its own.

Effects of use

Relaxation, happiness, congeniality, increased powers of concentration, sexual arousal, loss of inhibitions, warmth, increased appetite, talkativeness.

Adverse effects

Loss of short-term memory, impaired judgement, impaired driving skills, dry mouth, lethargy, decreased blood pressure, bloodshot eyes, dizziness, confusion, anxiety, panic, paranoia, psychosis, depression, schizophrenia, potential for causing cancers and breathing disorders.

Tolerance potential

Tolerance develops rapidly with continued use.

Habituation potential

True physical habituation is rare, but most users will develop a strong psychological habituation with continued use.

Withdrawal effects

Disturbed sleep patterns, anxiety, restlessness, irritability and aggression, nausea and cramping.

Overdose potential

It is not thought to be possible to fatally overdose with cannabis.

Cannabis: in-depth guide

Introduction

Cannabis is without any doubt the most commonly abused illegal drug throughout the world, particularly the developed world. It is imported into the UK in vast quantities – so vast that the amounts seized by the police and customs are officially recorded in metric tonnes.

Source

All plants of the genus *Cannabis* produce a complex chemical called delta-9-tetrahydrocannabinol (THC). Three varieties of the plant produce THC in significant amounts: *Cannabis sativa*, *Cannabis indica* and *Cannabis ruderalis*. Of these, *C. sativa* produces THC in the highest concentrations and therefore is the preferred source of the drug. *C. sativa* occurs wild in subtropical countries and is cultivated extensively in many of those countries for export to the rest of the world. It is grown in the UK, but it does not flourish here unless it is provided artificially with the high light levels, extended daylight hours and warm temperatures that it is used to. *C. indica* and *C. ruderalis* produce lower levels of THC but are more tolerant of the climatic conditions of northern Europe and are grown both under artificial conditions and in the open. In recent years, all three varieties have been hybridised to produce varieties that will provide high THC levels and grow well in the UK. The plant has two distinct forms, a male and a female; both produce THC, but the female produces higher levels.

Forms and appearance

Herbal

Herbal, or vegetable, cannabis has in the past few years slipped in popularity in comparison with the resinous varieties. Herbal cannabis now accounts for perhaps 45 per cent of the UK market. It is produced by drying and chopping the leaves of the cannabis plant into a coarse-cut tobacco-like mixture. The finest-quality herbal cannabis is produced by drying and chopping the flower, known as the bud, of the female cannabis plant. This preparation, known on the streets as sinsemilla and sinsy, contains the highest levels of THC in herbal form, but it is rare and relatively expensive.

Drug producers are more interested in the quantity of drugs that they can produce rather than the quality, and so the vast majority of herbal cannabis that finds its way on to the streets of the UK generally is of poor quality. It consists of a mixture of chopped leaves of all sizes from both female and male plants, thin stems, small quantities of flower buds and some seeds. Most samples of herbal cannabis are greenish brown in colour, although rarely, pale green and golden samples are seen.

Herbal cannabis can easily be mistaken for various forms of tobacco due to their similar appearances, (see Figure 3.1) and many parents and teachers have accused young people of illegal possession of cannabis only to find out later that it was nothing of the sort. Close examination of the sample should prevent this mistake. Most samples of tobacco have been produced by chopping dried plugs of tobacco leaves that have been formed from several leaves of different tobacco varieties layered together and cured. This layering can be seen in the form of strata of differing colours in the small shreds of tobacco. Cannabis has no such layering. Round seeds about 5mm in diameter are often found in herbal cannabis; tobacco contains no such seeds. Tobacco often has a strong aromatic smell, whereas herbal cannabis simply smells a little musty.

Figure 3.1 Examples of cannabis in herbal and resin form

Resin

The leaves and stems of both male and female cannabis plants are covered in a coating of fine hairs. In bright sunlight, as the plant approaches maturity, each hair begins to exude a sticky resinous sap. This exudate is collected and then dried and compressed to produce the finest forms of cannabis resin. As with the herbal variety, modern producers are intent upon producing the drug in large quantities without being concerned about quality; therefore, rather than wait for the plant to exude its own resin, producers often crush the sap from the whole plant in commercial-size crushing machines.

Cannabis resin now accounts for approximately 55 per cent of the UK market. No cannabis resin is produced in the UK; all of the resin that we see is imported from countries with generally warmer climates than our own. Morocco, Lebanon, Pakistan, Turkey, India, Nepal and Afghanistan are major producers of the cannabis resin that reaches the UK.

Cannabis resin is seen in a wide variety of colours, consistencies and forms (see Figure 3.1). The variations in colour and consistency are mostly a result of differences in climate and production methods. The colour can vary from the deepest black, through slate grey and every imaginable shade of brown, to pale honey. Some black forms are hard, shiny and brittle and can be snapped like old-fashioned liquorice. Dark-brown resins tend to be hard and dense and very difficult to break up. The user normally has to heat the block with a flame before being able to crumble it. This process of heating is called 'roasting' or 'toasting'. Many of the paler resins are soft and dry and crumble easily in the fingers.

Oil

Cannabis oil is produced by dissolving the flowering parts of the cannabis plant or its resin in a powerful commercial solvent, filtering out the fibre content and then evaporating off the solvent to leave behind a viscous heavy oil that contains a very high level of THC. The oil varies in colour from dark green or dark brown to black. It has a very powerful smell similar to that of a rotting cabbage or bag of Brussels sprouts. This oil is either dribbled onto hand-rolling cigarette tobacco or smeared with a matchstick onto the sides of commercially made cigarettes.

Note

Despite the differences between the various forms of cannabis, in essence they are all simply THC. Whatever it is called and whatever it looks like, it is all the same. Many users claim that they use only one sort or another and never touch the other forms.

This is nonsense: whatever form they use, it is THC that they are putting into their bodies.

Marketing

Cannabis is smuggled into the UK through a wide variety of entry points and by a vast range of methods. The majority of imported cannabis enters in large consignments, each weighing many tonnes, through entry ports and across isolated beaches all around the country. It also enters in small- to medium-sized amounts in light aircraft and in cars and goods vehicles via the English Channel and North Sea. Add to this the not inconsiderable quantities that are smuggled in individually small amounts in the pockets and baggage of travellers and tourists, and you have a picture of smuggling on a vast scale. It is impossible to give an accurate figure of the amount of cannabis that enters the UK. In 2002, the Independent Drugs Monitoring Unit estimated that the UK cannabis market was worth around £5 billion annually, which gives some idea of the magnitude of the trade.

Much of the cannabis that enters the UK is packed in individual amounts that weigh many pounds. It then needs to be broken down through the distribution chain into smaller and smaller quantities, so that it reaches the streets in amounts that are convenient to the distributor and user in terms of both size and price.

Curiously, cannabis is the only one of the many street drugs in use in the UK to be sold by the ounce or fraction of an ounce; all other street drugs are sold in metric measures.

Herbal cannabis is sold at street level in small plastic bags, commonly press-seal bags, sometimes printed with the image of a cannabis leaf; less commonly, it is sold in bags issued by banks for holding coins.

Resinous cannabis is sold in blocks of various size, which are often wrapped in clear plastic film. The resin will have been cut up by the dealer to suit the particular market that he or she is supplying. Common quantities when selling to young people are a sixteenth of an ounce – known on the street as 'a Louis' or 'a teenth' – and an eighth of an ounce – known as 'a Henry' or simply 'an eighth', although other sizes will also be available. As with most commodities, there are savings to be made by buying in bulk, and young people will often pool their resources in order to buy larger amounts and get a cheaper deal.

Cannabis oil is usually sold in small bottles in fractions of a fluid ounce. Rarely, it is sold contained inside a condom. Oil is still a rare drug on the streets, as it is a very specialist article. It is unlikely that young people will be offered it, but it will be available by special order from many dealers.

Cost

The price of herbal and resin cannabis fluctuates wildly, according to the amount available in any one location. Price follows closely the laws of supply and demand; when cannabis is in good supply, the price will fall dramatically. In times of shortage – known by users as 'droughts' – usually following local raids by the police, the price will move rapidly upwards. A price of between £40 and £125 per ounce is common in the UK. An average user would require less than £2 worth of herbal or resin cannabis to provide one smoke of good strength. However, special prices are often agreed when a supplier is opening up a new market, particularly among young people. We have seen low-grade cannabis sold to school pupils for as little as 50p for sufficient cannabis to provide one smoke.

Cannabis oil is still so rare and difficult to obtain that no fixed price exists. The supplier is able to ask almost any price for it, and many users will be willing to pay a high price just for the experience of trying it before returning to their more usual form of the drug.

Legal position

Cannabis in its various forms is a class C controlled substance under the Misuse of Drugs Act 1971. At the time of writing, it has no legally recognised medical use. This situation may change in the future, as a number of research projects into the medicinal use of cannabis are ongoing. All drugs under class C carry the same penalties:

- *Simple possession*: maximum penalty on indictment – two years' imprisonment plus an unlimited fine. Unlike other substances controlled under class C of the Misuse of Drugs Act, possession of cannabis carries a police power of arrest.

- *Possession with intent to supply to another*: maximum sentence on indictment – 14 years' imprisonment plus an unlimited fine and seizure of drug-related assets.

- *Supplying to another*: as above.

- Cultivation of cannabis plants: as above.

Another offence that is worth mentioning is one that concerns people in control of premises in which cannabis is smoked. Any person who allows the premises of which they are in control to be used for the smoking of cannabis commits an offence that is punishable on indictment by a maximum of 14 years of imprisonment. Many thousands of parents in the UK are either conned or intimidated by their children into allowing them to smoke cannabis at home; these parents run the risk of prosecution for this offence. In the eyes of the law, the controller of any premises has to take all steps possible to prevent cannabis being smoked there. It is not sufficient for a parent to say that he or she forbade their child to smoke cannabis at home: they have to positively prevent it, even to the point of calling the police.

In January 2003, the UK government changed the classification of herbal and resin cannabis from class B to class C, while specifically retaining the power of arrest for simple cannabis possession. At the same time, it published guidance for police officers as to the way the law in relation to cannabis was to be enforced. This guidance made it clear that people over the age of 18 normally would not be arrested for simple possession but would be dealt with by way of an instant warning and confiscation of the cannabis. Exceptions to this non-arrest policy were to be made for people flagrantly smoking cannabis in public places, for known repeat offenders, where the use of the drug had public-order implications, and for people in possession in or near any place where young people are present, such as schools and youth clubs. The guidance stated that people under the age of 18 found in simple possession should be arrested and taken to a police station, their parents summoned, and then dealt with by means of a reprimand or warning. Young repeat offenders would not normally qualify for further warnings but would be charged and dealt with through the courts. Such an appearance in court could then lead to a conviction and the beginning of a criminal record.

A reprimand or warning is not a criminal conviction and does not result in a criminal record. A criminal record for a drugs offence is still an immensely powerful conviction and can seriously affect a young person's eligibility for entry into a career in most government services, the armed forces and the police services. Many countries will not issue residential or work permits to people with such convictions. Such restrictions could have an extreme effect on a young person's life and prospects and can perhaps be viewed as being too severe for an act of rashness carried out in adolescence. The use of a police reprimand or warning for possession of cannabis allows a young person to be given a second chance and an opportunity to learn that possession of drugs is not a game and can bring very serious consequences. In deciding whether a person qualifies for a reprimand or a warning, the police have to be satisfied that the amount of cannabis found in the person's possession can rightly be called a small amount for personal use. No fixed figure is used; it is the circumstances that count. The UK Association of Chief Police Officers (ACPO) in its guidance to operational police officers, issued in December 2003, reiterated this point, commenting that if a fixed amount is set, then street dealers will simply carry just under that amount and carry on dealing. A person who lives in a place where there is a ready supply of cannabis can buy whenever they want, and so the amount would need to be small, whereas a person living in a place where cannabis is difficult to obtain would be able to buy only at more irregular intervals and would need to purchase larger amounts each time. Young people often believe that possession of small amounts such as an eighth of an ounce would qualify for a warning, while larger amounts would result in a prosecution. This is dangerous nonsense: it is the circumstances of the offence that are important, not just the amount of drug found.

Methods of use

Cannabis is most commonly smoked, with the lungs carrying the active ingredient, THC, into the bloodstream. It can be smoked in many ways, but whatever way is chosen, there are several practical problems for the user to overcome. First, herbal cannabis is a dry and short-stranded product, unlike tobacco, which is moist and long-stranded. Therefore, cannabis does not cling together in the way that tobacco does and it is not an easy substance to roll into cigarettes. Second, cannabis burns at a much higher temperature than tobacco, and if the user does not take some measures to deal with that degree of heat, then it will burn the lips and the tongue. Third, cannabis contains much higher levels of tar than tobacco: the average street sample of cannabis contains some three to five times the amount of tar found in the highest tar-rated commercially available tobacco.

The most common method used to smoke cannabis is to roll it in a hand-rolled cigarette, known in the UK as a 'joint', 'spliff' or 'splith' (see Figure 3.2). The old name for such cigarettes, 'reefer', appears to be making a comeback and is now used regularly on a number of popular drug-oriented websites and, perhaps as a consequence, by young people. If the smoker is using herbal cannabis, then usually it will be rolled without the addition of tobacco. If the resin is used, then it will be crumbled or chopped and added to tobacco before rolling. The tobacco for mixing with cannabis is often obtained by splitting open commercially made cigarettes. The remains of such cigarettes, usually in the form of clean unused filters attached to some strands of paper, are a good indicator of cannabis-smoking.

The smoker will often use one of the commercially produced king-size cigarette rolling papers to build a joint. Many thousands of packets of these papers are sold in the UK every week allegedly for the hand-rolling tobacco-smoker, but we have yet to meet a tobacco-smoker who uses such papers: all of the users of king-size papers that we have come across use them for cannabis. It is worth recounting here an incident that happened recently to one of us. We use a drug paraphernalia kit in our education work with parents and teachers and we needed to replace our packet of king-size papers that had become dog-eared. Visiting a small convenience store in a tiny, sleepy English village, a request was made to one of the two mature female

Figure 3.2 Cannabis joints and rolling equipment

assistants for 'a packet of king size' from the tobacco stand behind the till. The female assistant commented on the large size of the cigarette papers. Her colleague remarked that she sold lots of them: 'They're the ones all the kids buy.' If the smoker does not use such papers, then a number of smaller papers are used together, commonly two laid side by side and a third across the top.

Before sealing the cigarette, the smoking mixture is added, and a small cylinder called a 'roach' or 'roach end' is inserted at the mouth end. This cylinder is made from a small piece of cardboard, usually torn from the cigarette-paper packet cover, which is rolled up tightly and then allowed to relax. It forms into a spiral, which serves two purposes: first, it acts like a mesh to keep the smoking mixture inside the cigarette and stop it coming out into the smoker's mouth; second, it places the burning end of the cigarette a little further away from the smoker's mouth and thus alleviates the heat problems. In practice, it is doubtful whether the short length of most roaches can have any real effect on the temperature of the smoke, and it seems likely that it is more a question of fashion with most users; indeed, we have seen an increasing use of roaches in recent years in hand-rolled tobacco cigarettes. The use of a roach end is perceived to be the correct way to construct a cannabis cigarette and gives the smoker status as someone who is familiar with the drug. The opposite end of the joint is twisted together to prevent the contents spilling out.

The cigarette-paper packet cover is capable of providing only a small number of roaches before it falls apart. There will normally be several cigarette papers left in the packet at this stage, and they are often found, still interleaved together, on the floor. The presence of such papers is a good indicator of the use of the area by cannabis smokers.

Over the past ten or so years, we have come across an increasing number of 'roach cards': these are usually colourful advertisements for a commercial product or an upcoming music event printed on a postcard-sized piece of thin card that has been pre-perforated into perfect roach-size oblongs so that the user can read the advertisement and than use it to build their joints.

There is a fashion among many smokers for making their joints in extravagant shapes and sizes. Large joints are built using five or even seven papers; some are as large as corona cigars and are used as 'party joints' intended for several people to share. Some smokers stain their cigarette papers with colouring agents first; cold tea is often used to give a yellowish brown colour. Curious shapes are sometimes constructed, often with more than one burning end. There are a number of freely available publications and websites that give instructions to users in building such strange creations.

The traditional way of smoking cannabis using a water pipe is still very popular. Expensive hand-crafted and decorative hookah pipes made from the finest materials are to be seen for sale in most European countries and on a vast number of Internet websites. Also available from such websites, commonly called 'head shops', is a vast array of well-made modern versions of the traditional hookah, made from ceramic, glass, acrylic, wood and even stainless-steel. While they all operate on the same principles, they can be very ingenious in their construction.

An Internet search using the phrase 'cannabis pipes' will reveal a vast selection. It is still common for many young people to construct a crude version called a bong using a wide assortment of different watertight objects (see Figure 3.3). At its simplest, such a pipe can be constructed from a plastic one-litre drink bottle. A hole is pieced in the side of the bottle about halfway up, and a tube is inserted at a downwards angle until its end is close to the bottom. A waterproof seal is then made between the side of the bottle and the tube with chewing-gum or similar. The tube may be made from plastic, glass, wood, rubber or metal. A smoking bowl is fixed to the other end of the tube. This bowl may be constructed from tin-foil punctured with holes or a bottle top, although more robust smoking bowls are often made from mechanics' sockets with holes drilled in the base. Water is poured into the bottle until the lower end of the tube is covered. The bong is then ready for use. The smoking bowl is filled with cannabis, which is lit while the smoker inhales through the neck of the bottle. By doing so, the smoker creates a partial vacuum over the water and smoke is drawn from the burning cannabis down the tube to bubble up through the water to the smoker's mouth.

Figure 3.3 Home-made 'bong'

There are many variations on this basic design. We have seen bongs made from all sorts of bottles and containers: brandy bottles, chemical retorts (glass flasks used in school laboratories), ball-valve floats, buckets and, on one occasion, a dustbin.

Bongs are often abandoned by users when smoking is finished. It is not uncommon to find numbers of bongs in places where young people gather, and they provide good evidence of the use of cannabis in that area. Users of bongs claim that this is a healthier way of smoking cannabis as the water cools the smoke and removes most of the tar from the cannabis. The tar is certainly removed – the water in the vessel goes dark brown during use and tar is condensed in large quantities on the inside of the bong – but their claim to healthier smoking is unfounded. By cooling the cannabis smoke and removing a lot of the tar, bong-users make the smoke much less irritating to the lungs and so are able to inhale it more deeply and to retain it in their lungs for longer. They thus absorb higher levels of THC than they would if smoking cannabis in a joint. Bong-users may well avoid the dry mouth and burnt throat, but the higher levels of THC potentially will lead to more serious problems.

Bongs made in the Far East from poor-quality materials are sold legally and very cheaply on market stalls and in shops in the UK. Many are also brought back into the country as innocent holiday souvenirs.

Many users of cannabis have taken to using special pipes called 'chillums' to smoke their drug (see Figure 3.4). Chillum pipes are usually purchased ready-made, but they can be home-made. The main feature of a chillum is a drilling made straight through the stem from the mouthpiece under the bowl to open at the front of the pipe. The bowl has an opening at its base, which leads directly to this drilling. The

Figure 3.4 Carved wooden 'chillum' pipe

smoker places a finger over the front opening of the drilling and is thus able to close or open this hole to allow air to be drawn into the smoke coming from the bowl to both cool and dilute it. Chillum pipes are sold openly in the same way as bongs.

A more recent addition to the range of cannabis-smoking implements is a variety of high-tech pipes. These are often made from metal and take a number of forms from something the size of a rather thick credit card to a finger-sized cylinder. All feature extended internal smoke passages leading from the burning bowl to the mouthpiece. This extended pipe work allows the hot cannabis smoke to cool down. Many of these modern designs would not be recognised by an uninitiated person as being connected to any form of drug use. Again, an Internet search for 'cannabis pipes' will educate the reader in what to look out for.

Another form of pipe used for the smoking of cannabis is the 'toke' or 'toke can' (see Figure 3.5). These remain popular with many young people as they take only a few seconds to prepare. The user takes an empty drink can and uses their thumb to make a depression in the side of the can near to the base. This depression is made in line with the ring-pull opening and on the same side of the can. A few holes are punctured in the base of the depression and the pipe is complete. The user places a small quantity of herbal or resin cannabis in the depression and lights it while sucking at the ring-pull opening. The large metal body of the can provides sufficient cooling of the smoke. When finished, the can is simply thrown away and a new one made when required. Most people see discarded drink cans simply as litter, but a careful look at such cans will often provide a clue as to whether a place is being used for the smoking of cannabis. As with other cannabis paraphernalia, ready-made toke

Figure 3.5 Toke can

cans are available, often with hand-painted cannabis leaves decorating the sides and with reinforced smoking bowls.

Another form of cannabis pipe, known as a 'lung', is sometimes used by young people (see Figure 3.6). A lung is manufactured from a small plastic drink bottle. The bottom is cut off and replaced with a plastic bag fixed to the bottle with sticky tape. A simple smoking bowl is constructed at the open top of the bottle with metal foil punctured by a number of holes. Herbal or resin cannabis is added to the bowl and lit. The plastic bag is pumped up and down to draw the smoke into the bottle and bag. The smoking bowl is then removed and the user pumps the plastic bag to drive the smoke back out of the bottle into the mouth. The lung may be passed round a group until all the smoke has been used up before the process is repeated.

Cannabis smokers are ingenious people and have discovered all sorts of other ways in which to indulge in their pastime. In 'hot-knifing', a knife is heated with a match or cigarette lighter until it is very hot and then pressed against some herbal cannabis or a piece of resin, which will immediately begin to smoke. The smoke is then collected with a cupped hand or using a funnel made from the top of a lemonade bottle and breathed in. Sometimes the sleeve from a box of matches is used to collect the smoke; the matchbox sleeve is known as a 'mouth organ', and using it in this way is called 'playing the mouth organ'. Another variation is to pick up a piece of cannabis resin between the blades of two hot knives, collecting the smoke as before. The possession of a knife with a blade stained by heating is a good indicator that the owner is smoking cannabis. There is almost no other reason to burn a knife blade, for such treatment spoils the sharpness of the edge.

Figure 3.6 'Lung' filled with smoke

A further smoking variation is known as 'spotting'. A small piece of resin is impaled on the end of a pin; sometimes the pin at the back of a badge is used. The resin is then ignited with a match or lighter and the smoke allowed to fill a glass, often a beer glass. When full, the glass is passed around a group, with each member 'drinking' some of the smoke.

Smoking cannabis is by far the most popular method of using the drug, but it can also be taken by mouth. Herbal or resinous cannabis can be eaten on its own, but more usually it is used as an ingredient in various forms of cooking: cannabis pies, stews, pizzas and quiches are very popular. Cakes containing the drug – called 'hash cakes' and 'space cakes' – are regular fare at parties. A drink can be prepared by infusing herbal cannabis in boiling water to make a form of tea, also popular at parties. Eating or drinking cannabis introduces the THC into the body via the stomach. The effects are much the same as with smoking cannabis, but they take longer to occur.

Also available is a wide range of cannabis confectionery. Cannabis-laced sweets and lollipops, known as 'fun candy' and 'hemp suckers', are sold on a large number of Internet 'head shops' and specialist confectionery websites. All of these products contain cannabis in various strengths. They give the user the usual cannabis effects while carrying out an apparently innocent act of eating sweets.

This raises an important point for young people who attend parties. They need to take care about what they eat and who prepares the food or supplies such things as cakes and sweets. Many cases exist of young people being badly affected by cannabis taken inadvertently by eating food prepared by someone who sees the 'spiking' of it as some sort of joke – a joke that could have disastrous consequences.

Effects of use

The effects of using cannabis, and the duration of those effects, vary greatly from person to person and according to the strength used and the expectations and mental state of the user. An inexperienced or irregular user can expect the effects of one cannabis cigarette of medium strength to produce effects that will last for between two and four hours, with the effects tapering off after that.

Most users will experience a feeling of bodily warmth, which is a purely physical reaction to the drug. The small blood vessels close to the surface of the skin dilate and suffuse with blood. This gives the skin a flushed appearance and makes it warm to the touch. It also leads to the characteristic cannabis user's bloodshot eyes known as 'cannabis red eye'.

Users often report a feeling of relaxation, happiness and congeniality, with them taking a great deal of pleasure from the company of other people around them. If these other people are also using cannabis, then there is the potential for very pleasurable experiences. Many cannabis users make use of the drug in order to give themselves confidence in social situations and find that it helps them to mix with others and to make friends. Cannabis users often become very talkative and report that the drug has opened their minds and given them such insights that they are able to have the most wonderful conversations with other cannabis users about all sorts of subjects, including the big questions of life, love, religion and death. The truth of this is very different: we have listened many times to these conversations as sober observers and have found them to be utter drivel and to make no sense at all. A common feature of these conversations is the 'unfinished sentence effect', otherwise known as the 'ums', in which the user will forget the subject of their conversation halfway through and the sentence will tail off in an extended 'um …'.

Some users claim that cannabis in low doses temporarily increases their powers of concentration, and many young people use it as an aid to studying and revision. They feel that the drug enables them to study for longer periods without fatigue.

Most users will lose their inhibitions and do things that they would never dream of doing when sober. In some users, cannabis raises sexual awareness; this, together with the loss of inhibitions, may lead them to have unprotected sex, sometimes resulting in unplanned pregnancy or the transmission of various diseases.

Adverse effects

Short-term effects

At low or infrequent doses, the adverse effects of cannabis are fairly mild; many users report few if any adverse effects. Some users suffer from dryness of the mouth and throat if the cannabis has been smoked, and some will suffer bouts of nausea and dizziness. An increase in appetite is experienced by most users. Many users experience 'the munchies', during which they consume large quantities of food, often stripping the refrigerator on their return home of anything edible, even things that they would not normally eat.

At comparatively low levels of use, many users suffer from short-term memory loss, with no retention of any clear memory of events occurring during and immediately following their use of the drug. This makes a nonsense of the use of the drug as an aid to studying. Such users may well have the powers of concentration that learning requires, but the drug prevents them retaining much of what they have been studying. We have had a great deal of contact with students in our work and have often been told by them of their realisation, sometimes too late, that their use of cannabis while studying had a deleterious effect on their grades.

Even at these low levels, cannabis has a powerful effect on the judgement and information-processing skills required to perform complex tasks such as driving a car or even riding a bike. In 2000, the UK Department for Transport published a research report into the effects of cannabis on driving.[1] They concluded that cannabis impairs driving in many of the same ways as alcohol does but that many cannabis users adopt a more cautious driving style than those affected by alcohol. Thus, the adverse effects of cannabis use can, to a certain extent, be mediated by a change in driving style.

Many cannabis users who make regular use of the drug report that time appears to run at a different rate than normal. This 'cannabis time' runs much more slowly, with minutes feeling like hours. Some users report that they feel that they are walking in slow motion when under the influence of the drug. As the dose increases, many users begin to suffer the onset of many of the more unpleasant side effects of cannabis. THC is a moderately powerful hallucinogenic substance, and users will

---

1   Department for Transport (2000) *Cannabis and Driving: A Review of the Literature and Commentary (No.12)*. London: HM Government.

begin to experience an altering of their perception of the world around them. Their hearing may be enhanced and low-level sounds may be exaggerated until they reach unpleasant or even frightening proportions. Light levels and colours may change, causing confusion, disorientation and nausea. The initially pleasant feeling of relaxation and happiness may be replaced by anxiety, panic and eventually paranoia. Many users report that they feel trapped inside what they are still able to recognise is a false reality created by the drug and feel that it is never going to end.

Although rare, full-scale hallucinations are possible with high doses of cannabis. These 'trips', unlike those induced by some other hallucinogenic drugs, are almost always unpleasant and can be positively terrifying.

Long-term effects

Trying to make sense of all of the available information about the long-term effects of regular cannabis use is very difficult. Our current state of knowledge can be likened to the position that society was in some years ago with our knowledge of the health problems associated with the smoking of tobacco. Research had revealed some very serious problems, such as lung cancer and heart disease, but as time went on further research was to reveal much more. Medical research of a similar nature into cannabis use is still in the early stages, but it is beginning to reveal some worrying evidence.

Perhaps the most concerning effect of regular cannabis use by young people is that their use of it as a way of dealing with the ups and downs and the stresses and strains of modern life means that they fail to learn the necessary coping skills to deal with such problems in the real world. Such coping skills can be learnt properly only when a person is young – trying to learn them effectively during adulthood is difficult if not impossible. If a young person fails to learn those skills, they will have great difficulty in dealing with adult life, and many will find that they can cope with the pressures of life only by using drugs – and often potentially much more dangerous drugs than cannabis.

Many regular users of cannabis demonstrate a loss of basic motivation, sometimes called amotivational syndrome. It seems clear to us from having dealt with many such young people that it is not possible to place the blame for this solely on the use of cannabis. Many of these unmotivated young people were performing badly at school and demonstrating similar forms of unmotivated behaviour before they were using cannabis, and, at worst, the cannabis simply exacerbated a pre-existing condition. It is not uncommon for such young people to drop out of school or college, to give up work and to opt out of life in general. Most will have no goals – and see no point in having any. Their lives may be characterised by drift and increasingly will become built around their drug use.

Cannabis is certainly cancer-causing. The smoke produced by burning it contains about 50 per cent more known carcinogens than the same volume of cigarette-tobacco smoke and deposits around four times as much tar in the lungs and bronchial passages of the smoker. This is not as straightforward as it seems at first glance. Most people who smoke only tobacco consume much greater amounts of their chosen drug than do people whose choice is cannabis. Having said that, it is not so unusual now as it once was to find people who use amounts of cannabis that approach the amounts of tobacco consumed by many cigarette-smokers. There are also important differences in the way users smoke cannabis. Most users of cannabis will inhale much more deeply than most tobacco-smokers do and will, in order to extract the maximum effect from it, retain the cannabis smoke in their lungs for much longer. This means that the smoke will be in contact with the membranes of the throat and lungs for a greater period of time than is usual with cigarette-smoking. The picture is confused further by the facts that most cannabis is smoked mixed with tobacco and that most cannabis-smokers also smoke tobacco cigarettes. What is clear is that there are growing numbers of documented cases of throat, mouth and lung cancers that appear to be connected directly to the smoking of cannabis. A 2005 review of cannabis-related health risks by the drugs information charity DrugScope (see Appendix 2) drew attention to a number of cases of cancers of the digestive tract found in young adults with a history of heavy cannabis use. These forms of cancer are not common in people under the age of 60 and further highlight the carcinogenic potential of cannabis.

There can be serious problems for the fetus growing in the womb of a woman who uses cannabis. Cannabis crosses the placental barrier and enters the bloodstream of the unborn infant, who will be affected in the same way as the mother, but to a much greater extent. Put bluntly, when a pregnant woman is stoned, so is her child. The developing fetus is very delicate and susceptible to damage caused by the actions of drugs taken by the mother. Firm evidence on this issue is difficult to come by and can be contradictory. Female users of cannabis during pregnancy will, in our experience, often use a range of other substances, including tobacco and alcohol. Such multi-drug use can make it difficult to separate the causal agents of any subsequent health problems in the baby. What does seem clear is that use of cannabis on any regular basis during pregnancy can lead to reduced birth weight and a range of problems during the child's early years, including attention, memory and cognitive functioning deficits.

Cannabis has an effect on the level of the hormone testosterone in males. This is the hormone that provides masculine characteristics. As soon as a male begins to use cannabis, his testosterone level reduces. If he stops using the drug, the level will return quickly to normal. The real problems occur in males, particularly those with a predisposition to sperm-production problems, who continue to use cannabis on a regular basis and over an extended period. Research indicates that in some males, the reduction in testosterone level becomes permanent and the level becomes so low that problems are then experienced in achieving or maintaining an erection and performing sexual intercourse. It would seem to us that these things are of some importance to most young males and something they ought to consider. One of the most worrying aspects of chronic use of cannabis by young people is the link between such use and its potential adverse effects on mental health. In our conversations with many hundreds of young cannabis users over the years, it has become clear to us that this aspect of the health issues surrounding cannabis is the one that concerns them most. Cannabis in high doses can precipitate an acute psychosis in some users. This manifests itself in anxiety, confusion, agitation, hallucinations and delusions. What is also becoming apparent is a link between cannabis use and schizophrenia. Although it remains unclear as to whether cannabis use alone can cause schizophrenia in otherwise mentally healthy young people, the drug does seem to precipitate schizophrenia in people who may already be vulnerable to the illness. The conclusion seems to be that any young person with a family history of schizophrenia would be extremely unwise to make cannabis use a part of their lifestyle.

This research is ongoing, and it seems likely that much more information will be revealed yet. What can be said with certainty at this stage is that cannabis is not a harmless herb, as some would have young people believe, but a powerful drug that no-one should underestimate.

Tolerance potential

As with the majority of drugs, cannabis users can quickly develop tolerance, such that they require larger doses to achieve the same effects. The pattern of tolerance is somewhat confused in new users by another of the drug's characteristics. THC is very persistent and is absorbed by the brain and the fatty tissues around many of the body's soft organs. From here, it leaches back into the bloodstream over a long period. This steady leaching maintains a level of THC in the bloodstream; if further doses of cannabis are then taken, they add on to the drug already there and the user appears to experience a sort of reverse tolerance, with the full effects of the drug being reached with lower doses. This phase soon passes as bodily tolerance grows, until a more normal pattern is reached with ever-increasing doses being required to achieve what the user is seeking.

Habituation potential

When considering the habituation potential of any drug, we need to be clear as to what terms such as 'addiction' and 'habituation' mean. A true addiction is normally taken to mean some form of chemical dependence on the substance being taken. The addicted person requires further doses of the substance to stave off physical symptoms of withdrawal. Their body has adapted physically and requires the substance to continue to operate. Drugs such as heroin, cocaine and nicotine are powerful producers of chemical addictions.

Habituation is more often a purely psychological phenomenon. The user becomes dependent mentally on their substance. It can be likened to the habit of biting one's nails. Is the nail-biter addicted to the calcium in their nails or maybe the substances under them? No: nail-biting is a purely mental thing. The nail-biter chews away out of boredom, to relieve stress or merely to derive some comfort from it. This is a psychological habituation but it is no less difficult to deal with than chemical addiction. Anyone who has tried to break a child out of the habit of nail-biting will know how difficult it can be. Sometimes parents put thick gloves on the child's hands or paint evil-tasting products on the child's nails, but the child carries on biting, often until the nails and fingers are left bleeding and painful.

Many users of cannabis claim that the drug is not addictive; for the vast majority of users, this will be true. It is very rare for anyone to become chemically dependent on cannabis in the same way that users of drugs such as heroin and cocaine become dependent. Cannabis does produce in many of its users a very powerful psychological habituation, however. This dependence is purely mental, and users may start to rely on the drug to deal with the everyday processes of their lives. We know of many users who feel unable to get out of bed in the morning without first using cannabis and who then go on to use the drug regularly throughout the day to enable them to cope.

Withdrawal effects

There are very few purely physical symptoms following the cessation of use of cannabis; most withdrawal effects are psychological. The symptoms that any particular user will experience depend on the amount of the drug that they have been using and the period over which they have been using it. A person who has used only on an occasional basis or over a short period will experience very little in the way of withdrawal symptoms, but as the amount used increases or the period of use becomes extended, some users will experience great difficulty in giving up.

Some users will experience problems with sleep when they try to give up cannabis, becoming restless and suffering insomnia. Sleep deprivation can be difficult to cope with, and the temptation to use the drug once more to induce sleep will be very powerful. Other users suffer panic attacks and experience feelings that they are unable to cope alone with the ordinary trials of day-to-day life. Others may experience bouts of nausea and cramping of varying severity.

These symptoms can be overcome by giving the user support, counselling and, in some cases, medication, but it is often a difficult and rocky road to be overcome before the user is truly able to operate without the substance.

Overdose potential

It is not thought possible to fatally overdose on cannabis. It is possible to take such a high dose that the user falls into a stupor, during which they may be at risk of having an accident or being sick and inhaling their own vomit.

Street names

Herbal: Grass, marijuana, puff, blow, wacky baccy, herb, bush, Skunk, home-grown, dope, draw, weed, tips, buds

Resin: Pot, hash, shit, black, gold, soap, dope, draw

Oil: Oil, hash oil, diesel, honey

Slang associated with use

Joint, spliff, reefer – Hand-rolled cannabis cigarette

Bong – Water pipe for smoking cannabis

Chillum – Clay or wooden pipe for smoking cannabis

Skinning up, building – Making a cannabis cigarette

Henry, an eighth – One-eighth of an ounce of cannabis

Louis, a teenth – One-sixteenth of an ounce of cannabis

Toking – Smoking cannabis

Toke can – A pipe made from a drink can for smoking cannabis

Hash cake – Cake made from cannabis

Fun candy, hemp suckers – Cannabis-laced sweets

Head shop – Place where cannabis paraphernalia can be purchased

Cannabis: benefits and drawbacks

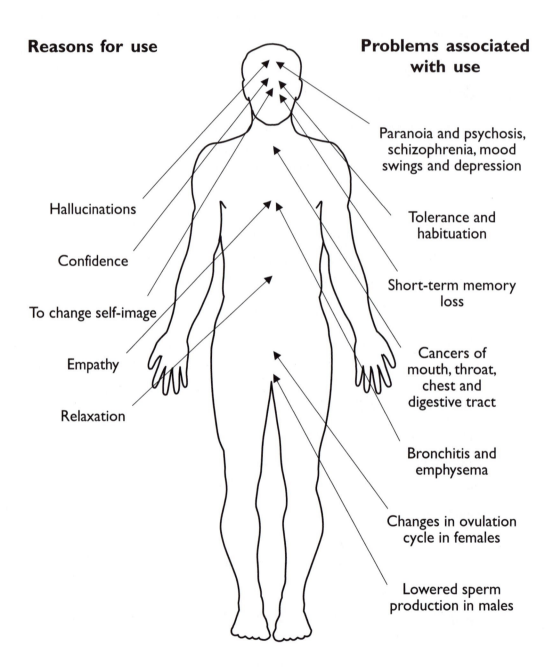

Reasons for use

Hallucinations

Confidence

To change self-image

Empathy

Relaxation

Problems associated with use

Paranoia and psychosis, schizophrenia, mood swings and depression

Tolerance and habituation

Short-term memory loss

Cancers of mouth, throat, chest and digestive tract

Bronchitis and emphysema

Changes in ovulation cycle in females

Lowered sperm production in males

Chapter 4

Stimulants

Amphetamine (amphetamine sulphate)

Amphetamine: quick reference guide

Source

Totally synthetic product.

Forms and appearance

Seen as a rather coarse powder. Usually off-white or, very occasionally, pink or yellow in colour. Also seen in 'base' form, which is a similar colour to the powder but is moist and has a putty-like consistency. Also available in tablets and capsules of various colours, sizes and shapes, although this is becoming less common.

Marketing

Both the powder and the 'base' form are usually sold by the gram or half-gram, commonly wrapped in paper packets made from a small square of carefully folded paper or in small press-seal plastic bags. Tablet forms of the drug are sold loose and priced by the tablet. Amphetamine is available all over the UK in public houses, night clubs, dances and raves, on the street and from local small-time drug suppliers.

Cost

The street price of amphetamine in the UK has varied by only a small amount over the past ten years and is now somewhere between £8 and £15 per gram for powder and perhaps a little more for 'base'. There is no fixed price for individual tablets and capsules.

Legal position

Class B, schedule 2 controlled substance under the Misuse of Drugs Act 1971. Class A penalties apply if the drug is prepared for injecting.

Methods of use

The powder form most commonly is taken orally by dissolving it in a drink or licking it off a finger; more rarely, the powder is rubbed into the gums. 'Base' is commonly wrapped in cigarette paper in the form of a 'bomb' and swallowed. Powder amphetamine can be sniffed up the nose (snorting), mixed with tobacco or cannabis for smoking, or smoked straight off tin-foil. It may also be dissolved in water for injecting.

Effects of use

Increase in energy, strength and powers of concentration. Feelings of euphoria and elation. Increase in confidence, suppression of appetite and reduction in the need for sleep.

Adverse effects

Increase in blood pressure and concomitant increased risk of stroke, dry mouth, diarrhoea, increased urination, disturbance of sleep patterns, tiredness, loss of appetite and consequent weight loss, immune-system impairment, restlessness, mood swings and agitation, depression, delusions, panic, paranoia and psychosis. Vein collapse, gangrene and ulcers if injecting. Blood-borne diseases such as HIV infection and hepatitis if sharing injecting equipment. Damage to nasal passages if snorting.

Tolerance potential

Tolerance develops rapidly with continued use.

Habituation potential

Physical dependence is rare, but psychological dependence develops quickly in most regular users.

Withdrawal effects

No physical symptoms. Mental agitation, depression, panic and feelings of being unable to cope.

Overdose potential

Fatal overdose is possible with amphetamine. This could occur at low doses in inexperienced users.

Amphetamine: in-depth guide

Source

Amphetamine sulphate is a manufactured product. It was first produced in Germany in the 1880s and used medically as a stimulant, tonic and appetite suppressant. Its value was quickly recognised by military authorities all over the world, and the drug was regularly given in tablet form to troops engaged in battle or when long periods of physical activity without pauses for rest or food were required. During the Second World War, some 72 million amphetamine tablets were issued to British troops. From the 1950s onwards, as people became more weight-conscious and with the increasing fashion for slimming, large quantities of amphetamine were prescribed as an aid to weight loss. Its use for these purposes was not without risks and has now largely ceased. Some varieties of amphetamine are still used medically in the treatment of hyperactivity in children and, more rarely, for the treatment of certain sleeping disorders.

The manufacture of illicit amphetamine is not difficult and takes place in both the UK and continental Europe. It requires only a basic knowledge of chemistry and very little in the way of equipment to produce the drug in substantial quantities.

Forms and appearance

Most commonly, amphetamine is seen in the form of a coarse crystalline powder. This will usually be a rather dirty off-white to cream colour. It is coarse in constituency, containing crystals of different sizes and small lumps of coagulated powder. This form will be only 8–12 per cent pure amphetamine sulphate, with the remainder being made up with all sorts of other substances. If the user is lucky, these mixing or 'cutting' agents may be caffeine, milk powder, glucose, vitamin C powder or bicarbonate of soda. For less fortunate users, the adulterants may be chalk, talcum powder or a medicinal drug such as paracetamol or aspirin.

Powdered forms are sometimes seen in different colours. These coloured varieties usually are pink or yellow and have been produced by crushing pharmaceutical amphetamine tablets. Amphetamine powder produced in this way is usually more pure and of a much higher strength. However, it is not unknown for ordinary, crudely produced amphetamine to be mixed with coloured powders to attract a higher price.

Varieties of amphetamine are produced by the pharmaceutical industry for medical use in tablet and capsule form. The tablets are most commonly pink, white or yellow; the capsules come in a wide range of different colours. Small quantities of home-made tablets are also available on the streets from time to time. The amphetamine used in the manufacture of such tablets is usually of a reasonably high grade and is coloured to imitate the commercially produced varieties.

The 'base' or 'paste' form of amphetamine is produced at an earlier stage in the manufacturing process than the powder form. As such, its purity levels can be much higher, perhaps as high as 50 per cent. However, it is becoming increasingly common for the purity to be 'cut' back towards that of powder amphetamine. It is seen as a dirty white, almost grey putty-like substance, often with a slight smell of ammonia. Ordinary powder amphetamine has been sold moistened with water to make it look like 'base' and thus attract a higher price.

Marketing

Amphetamine in both powder and 'base' form is commonly dealt on the streets in individual doses of half a gram or one gram. Each dose is usually contained in a carefully folded paper envelope called a 'wrap' or a 'deal' (see Figure 4.1). These envelopes are made from a square piece of paper measuring about 5 cm by 5 cm. The paper is commonly from glossy magazines. Glossy paper is preferred because it repels moisture a little better than plain paper, but damp-proofing is sometimes reinforced by adding a layer of clear plastic film around the paper wrap. We have, on occasion, also seen both powder and 'base' dealt in wraps made entirely from clear plastic film. Once folded, a half-gram paper wrap will measure about 1 cm by 2.5 cm. A wrap is a very efficient container for powder drugs such as amphetamine: it is virtually leak-proof and can be concealed easily. Users may hide wraps under the tongue when being searched by the police; they may even conceal them by inserting the wrap into the anus or vagina. When unfolded, the paper wrap has a characteristic pattern of criss-cross fold lines across it, making it instantly recognisable. The finding of such pieces of paper is a very good indicator of the use of amphetamine or other powder drugs. Individual wraps are sometimes seen bundled together in small packages of 20 or so, secured with an elastic band. These bundles are commonly called 'decks' or 'bindles'; two bundles will fit easily inside a 20-cigarette packet.

Some drug suppliers also make use of more modern packaging when dealing amphetamine. The drug is often sold in small plastic bags, each approximately 3 cm square, with a press-seal opening; larger bags are used for bulk supplies. Amphetamine in tablet form is commonly sold one tablet at a time and with no wrapping.

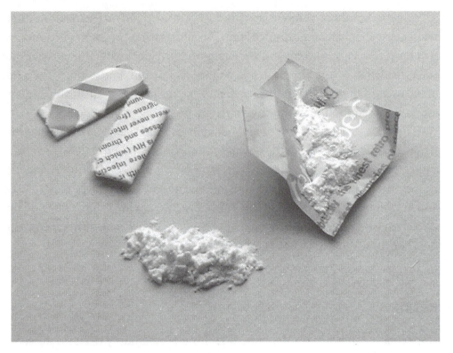

Figure 4.1 Amphetamine with open and folded 'wrap'

Cost

The street price of amphetamine varies considerably depending upon the availability of supplies in any one area and on what the supplier believes their particular market will bear. Low-grade amphetamine in powder form will sell for between £8 and £15 per gram, while 'base' sells for £10–20 per gram. As with all drugs, discounts are available for purchases in larger quantities. A beginner buying half a gram to try out the drug will expect to pay at least £5. Many users will pay higher prices for pink and yellow amphetamine powder in the belief that they are buying crushed tablets and therefore a purer and stronger form of the drug, and prices as high as £20 per gram of such a product are not unusual.

Amphetamine in tablet form is sold at prices that vary to an even greater extent. Single tablets will sell for anything from £2 to £15 depending on the circumstances of the sale. Tablets bought on the street will be cheaper than the same product bought in a pub; even higher prices will be achieved for tablets sold at parties and raves.

Legal position

Amphetamine sulphate is a class B, schedule 2 controlled substance within the Misuse of Drugs Act 1971. As a class B drug, offences concerning amphetamine carry the following penalties:

- *Simple possession*: possession of amphetamine for personal use carries a maximum penalty on indictment of five years' imprisonment plus an unlimited fine. If the amphetamine has been prepared for injection, the maximum penalty increases to 14 years' imprisonment plus the fine.

- *Possession with intent to supply*: possessing the drug with the intention of supplying it, either by sale or by gift, to another person carries a maximum penalty on indictment of 14 years' imprisonment plus an unlimited fine, plus seizure of drug-related assets. Possessing injectable amphetamine in the same circumstances increases the maximum imprisonment term to life.

- *Supplying to another*: as for possession with intent to supply.

- *Importation or manufacture*: as for possession with intent to supply.

The inclusion of amphetamine in schedule 2 of the act recognises that there are some limited medical uses for the drug. Its use by doctors therefore is permitted under very strict control.

Methods of use

Most amphetamine is taken orally. The powder is usually dissolved in a soft or alcoholic drink and swallowed. We have seen users who prefer their amphetamine in a cup of tea and others who take it mixed with neat spirits. Dosage may vary from as little as half a gram to several grams at a time, depending on the user's tolerance levels.

Another common method of taking the powder drug is known as 'dabbing', using a wet finger to pick it up and transfer it to the mouth. Some users will use the wet-finger technique to pick up the drug and then rub it into the teeth and gums. This method is called 'washing', and some users employ it as a way of checking the quality of what they have bought. Good-quality amphetamine will produce a tingling sensation in the teeth when it is rubbed in, and the degree of sensation will tell an experienced user the approximate strength of the sample. Both the powder and the 'base' form are also taken orally by wrapping the drug in thin paper, such as cigarette-rolling paper, into a small bomb-shaped package and swallowing it. This method is preferred by most 'base' users, as this form of amphetamine has a bitter unpleasant taste.

Less commonly, powder amphetamine is snorted or inhaled through the nose. The powder can be snorted directly from the paper wrap or placed in the hand or in a spoon held up to the nose. The practice of snorting amphetamine is less common than it once was. The poor quality of most street samples and the uncertainty of what has been used to cut or dilute the product has put off many users, as many of the cutting agents used can cause a great deal of painful damage to the nasal membranes.

Amphetamine is sometimes sprinkled onto cannabis or tobacco and smoked in hand-rolled cigarettes or bongs. Amphetamine burns readily. The smoke produced carries the drug into the body through the lungs. Heating amphetamine powder on a piece of tin-foil by applying a match, candle or lighter underneath it will also cause the drug to burn, producing a light-coloured smoke with a harsh acrid smell. The smoke is then inhaled through a rolled piece of card or a matchbox sleeve.

The powder can also be dissolved and injected. A common agent for dissolving amphetamine is water to which has been added a few drops of lemon juice. There is a belief among some users that the addition of lemon juice enhances the effect of the drug. Certainly injecting any drug will increase the immediacy of the 'hit' or 'rush' that it produces. Tablet forms of the drug are usually taken orally, but good-quality pharmaceutical products are often crushed between two spoons and dissolved for injection.

Effects of use

The time interval between taking the drug and the onset of its effects is very short. If injected, the effects will be almost instant, the rush occurring within a few seconds of the drug entering the bloodstream. If the drug has been taken orally, it will have to pass through the stomach wall in order to reach the bloodstream, and then on to the brain, which can take between 10 and 20 minutes, according to the contents of the stomach. The rush produced will be slower to build and less pronounced.

The short-term effects of the drug may last for several hours. The exact duration will vary greatly from person to person and will depend on the amount of drug taken and how much experience the user has of the drug. Each person's physical makeup is different, and many factors will have an influence on the drug's effects, such as body weight and gender. An inexperienced or irregular user can expect the effects from a single medium-strength dose of amphetamine to last for three to four hours. The rush that amphetamine produces gives its users a great feeling of wellbeing and even euphoria. Feelings of fatigue, stress, anxiety and fear will be swept from the mind. Most users experience a considerable increase in energy and a feeling of strength.

Along with the energy comes an increase in the ability to concentrate and a substantial increase in self-confidence. Many users who normally are shy and feel socially awkward will use amphetamine to give themselves the necessary self-confidence to enable them to mix with others and have a good time. Other people use the drug simply to give them the increase in energy needed to party the night away.

Amphetamine, like most stimulants, provides no energy of its own. Its action is to increase the user's metabolic rate, so that they consume their own blood sugar at a faster rate. The more of the drug that is taken, the faster that consumption will occur. When the blood-sugar levels drop to a point at which the user cannot sustain the activity they are engaged in, they will 'crash' and experience great fatigue and loss of strength.

Along with an increase in available energy, amphetamine suppresses the body's need for sleep, and so users are able to 'keep going' for long periods. As a result, it is often used for this purpose by young people attending all-night parties and raves.

Amphetamine is also a very powerful appetite suppressant, and many users take the drug as an aid to slimming. The increase in energy burns off calories at a high rate; in combination with its appetite-suppression effects, this means that rapid weight loss is inevitable.

Adverse effects

Amphetamine sulphate is a very powerful drug whose position in class B of the Misuse of Drugs Act 1971 belies its potential for causing real harm to its users. Indeed, this potential was alluded to in the report produced by the Advisory Council on the Misuse of Drugs led by Professor Sir Michael Rawlins in 2002, which recommended to the UK government that cannabis be reclassified from class B to class C.[1] Part of the reasoning in that report was that the potential for harm through amphetamine use was markedly higher than for cannabis and consequently cannabis should be downgraded. Cannabis reclassification was thus proposed to avoid users believing falsely that the potential for harm of both drugs was equal, leading to an increase in the use of amphetamine. It seems to us that an equally powerful and valid argument could have been made for reclassifying amphetamine to class A.

1   Advisory Council on the Misuse of Drugs (2002) *The Classification of Cannabis under the Misuse of Drugs Act 1971*. London: HM Government.

The physical problems that amphetamine causes for users are few but can be significant. Of much more importance is amphetamine's real potential for causing profound psychological problems. Both of us have had a great deal of first-hand experience with amphetamine users who have become badly damaged psychologically through their use of this drug. It is not an exaggeration to say that it is a drug that has the power to destroy a person mentally.

Physical effects

Amphetamine increases blood pressure and raises the temperature of the body. The energy produced by using the drug may result in strenuous physical activity, which will also have the effect of further raising the blood pressure and body temperature. If the user has any underlying (perhaps unknown) defect or weakness within their circulatory system, then this increase in pressure will find it out: there are many documented cases of users – often first-time users – suffering stroke and heart failure. Most users will experience dryness of the mouth and an increased thirst; if this thirst is not satisfied, the user runs the risk of dehydration and collapse.

The sudden onset of tiredness and loss of strength experienced when the stimulating effects of the drug wear off can be very unpleasant and can be dealt with only by allowing the body to rest and to regain its strength naturally. The temptation is to take more of the drug in order to keep going. This has the effect of burning up what little reserves of blood sugar remain and will result in an even greater crash at the end. The powerful sleep-suppressing effects of amphetamine may prevent the user obtaining the rest that is needed to refresh the body and rebuild reserves of strength; as a result, the general condition of the body will be reduced. The appetite-suppression effects may well mean that the body is prevented from taking in the necessary fuel it needs to return the blood-sugar levels to normal. These two effects taken together mean that many users lose a great deal of weight and their general health and body condition become very poor. The immune system in some users may be damaged, leaving them prone to a whole range of illnesses.

Psychological effects

It is in this area that amphetamine causes its most profound and distressing problems. Most people can understand and feel able to cope with a physical illness or infirmity, but a mental illness is a different thing. It is perhaps the fear of the unknown that makes mental illness so frightening, but all users of amphetamine should clearly understand that they are taking a drug that has a real potential for releasing latent mental illnesses, which may be very difficult if not impossible to treat successfully.

It is very rare for people to suffer adverse psychological effects with their first experience of amphetamine or if their use is only occasional. The potential for mental problems becomes more apparent with continued or heavy use. Many such users become depressed and lethargic when they are not actually under the influence of the drug and feel that life without the drug is simply not worthwhile. With continued use, this depression can move very easily into paranoia, with the sufferer feeling that everyone and life in general is against them. Complicated and well-constructed delusions can result, with the user believing that people around them are part of a complex plot that is being hatched against them. Long-term and heavy users may move into a drug-induced psychosis in which these delusions become the basis of their lives. These delusions can be deep-seated and difficult to treat and can result in the sufferer requiring inpatient treatment in a psychiatric hospital.

Tolerance potential

Most users of amphetamine rapidly develop a tolerance to the drug. The body becomes familiar with the drug and adapts to its effects, so that the usual dose rapidly becomes insufficient to achieve the effects that the person is looking for, and much larger doses are required. It is not uncommon for users of amphetamine who have been involved with the drug for any length of time to be using as much as two or three grams at a time, several times a day.

Habituation potential

Without doubt, amphetamine has a potential for the development of a powerful dependence. There is little evidence of users developing a true physical addiction to the drug; the major risk lies in the development of a profound psychological dependence. Amphetamine pushes away the problems of life, makes the user feel good, and provides the user with energy and confidence to face up to all the problems and stresses that life can produce. As the user comes down from the drug, they will experience physical tiredness and loss of strength, typical of the use of stimulants, and therefore feel even less able to cope than they did before using the drug. There is clearly a temptation to continue use in order to cope. With the added complication of the onset of amphetamine-induced mental illness such as psychosis, the user may be terrified to give up using the drug. This habituation can be so intense that it becomes very difficult to deal with, and the user may require expert professional treatment by a regime of medical drugs and supportive counselling if they are to have any real hope of recovery.

Withdrawal effects

The withdrawal effects of amphetamine use vary according to the amount that the user has been taking and the duration and regularity of the use. Most inexperienced users who have taken only a small to moderate amount of amphetamine will experience a period of tiredness and loss of strength. This can be dealt with by allowing the body to rest, sleep being the best way of doing so. If the use of the drug has been at a much higher level or over an extended period, the withdrawal effects will be much more severe. Many such users will find it extremely difficult to cope with the feelings of anxiety, panic, paranoia and insomnia that withdrawal brings. Anyone attempting to give up the use of amphetamine after heavy or prolonged use is advised to seek the advice and guidance of a professional drugs service.

Overdose potential

There is a real possibility of overdosing on amphetamine. The amount needed to overdose is high in most users, but an inexperienced person could reach overdose at quite low levels of the drug. The main risks lie in pushing up the body temperature to such a high level that the brain is unable to cope, leading to convulsions. In some cases, these convulsions can lead to the death of the user. An additional danger is posed by the substances used to dilute or 'cut' the drug, particularly if the drug is injected. Ingesting large and regular doses of cutting agents, such as paracetamol, carries very real risks for the user.

Street names

Speed, buzz, whiz, Billy whiz, white, amphet, sulph, dexie, base, paste

Slang associated with use

Wraps or deals – Folded paper packets containing the drug

Decks or bindles – Bundles of wraps secured with an elastic band

Snorting – Sniffing the powder up the nose

Rubbing or washing – Rubbing the powder into the teeth or gums

Dabbing – Licking the drug from a finger

Hit or rush – The effects felt as the drug reaches the brain

Amphetamine: benefits and drawbacks

Reasons for use

Problems associated with use

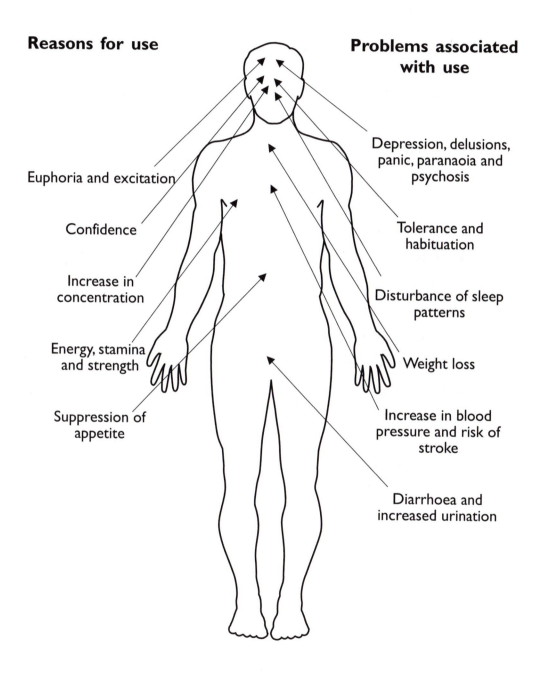

Euphoria and excitation

Confidence

Increase in concentration

Energy, stamina and strength

Suppression of appetite

Depression, delusions, panic, paranaoia and psychosis

Tolerance and habituation

Disturbance of sleep patterns

Weight loss

Increase in blood pressure and risk of stroke

Diarrhoea and increased urination

Methylamphetamine (methylamphetamine hydrochloride)

Methylamphetamine: quick reference guide

Source

Totally synthetic drug, closely related to amphetamine sulphate.

Forms and appearance

Most commonly, the drug is seen in the form of clear crystals of various sizes, the largest being about 1 cm across and having the appearance of clear ice or glass. It is also seen in the form of crystalline powders of various colours, white, yellow and light brown being the most common. Occasionally, it is seen in the form of tablets of varying sizes, shapes and colours.

Marketing

Methylamphetamine in powder form is sold on the streets in the same half-gram and one-gram packaging as amphetamine sulphate. The crystal form is sold, usually wrapped in clear plastic film, by the gram or fraction of a gram or sometimes by the crystal. Tablets are sold loose and without packaging.

Cost

The street price in the UK of the powder form of the drug has come down considerably in the past ten years or so, and it now sells for about £30–50 per gram. The crystal form is currently selling for between £15 and £30 per crystal, depending on size. No established price structure exists for tablets, due to their rarity.

Legal position

Class B, schedule 2 controlled substance under the Misuse of Drugs Act 1971. If prepared for injection, class A penalties apply.

Methods of use

Methylamphetamine is used in similar ways to amphetamine. The powder and tablet forms can be taken orally in drinks. The powder can also be taken from a wet finger, by sniffing into the nose, by burning and inhaling the fumes, or by injection. The crystal form is used almost exclusively by burning in a special pipe or heating on metal foil and inhaling the fumes.

Effects of use

Feelings of euphoria, great strength and energy, and ability to sustain high levels of activity over extended periods without rest or food. Some users also report an increase in sexual arousal.

Adverse effects

Increase in blood pressure and body temperature with concomitant increased risk of stroke and heart failure, dehydration, dry mouth, diarrhoea, increased urination, severe disturbance of sleep patterns, lethargy, loss of appetite and consequent weight loss, restlessness, aggression, violent mood swings, agitation, visual and auditory hallucinations, depression, delusions, panic, paranoia, psychosis and bizarre psychotic behaviour.

Tolerance potential

Tolerance builds up very rapidly with continued use.

Habituation potential

Profound psychological dependence develops quickly in most users. Physical dependence can also occur.

Withdrawal effects

Severe cravings for the drug may be experienced, with high levels of mental agitation, depression, panic and feelings of being unable to cope.

Overdose potential

Serious risk of fatal overdose at very low levels in some people.

Methylamphetamine: in-depth guide

Source

Methylamphetamine is a synthetically produced stimulant. It is similar in formulation to amphetamine sulphate and is produced commercially for use in certain pharmaceutical preparations. Very little of the legally produced drug reaches the street market. Most forms of the drug found on the streets are produced in illicit facilities, which are found all over Europe and the USA.

The *World Drug Report* 2004, published by the United Nations Office on Drugs and Crime, reports that although the majority of detected methylamphetamine production facilities are found in the USA, there is an increasing trend towards production in Eastern Europe, with the highest number of production facilities (104) found in 2002 in the Czech Republic. The drug enjoyed a period of popularity in the UK in the early 1970s in its tablet and powder forms, but its high level of unpleasant side effects and the violence that is often associated with use of the drug made its popularity short-lived. It has returned in its crystal form to the streets of the UK since the beginning of the 1990s, and it has established itself in the drugs market as a part of the club scene. Contrary to many fears expressed in the mid-1990s, its use in the UK has declined in recent times. This picture is not true in the USA and some Asian countries, where its use is common and increasing.

Forms and appearance

The powder form of methylamphetamine is similar in appearance to amphetamine sulphate. Methylamphetamine is often of a higher purity and the powder will have a more even appearance, with greater uniformity of particle size. The colour varies widely, but creamy white, pale yellow and light brown varieties are by far the most common.

Methylamphetamine tablets are rare, although they are available at some raves and dance clubs. Some of these tablets are produced commercially by the pharmaceutical industry under various brand names and in a variety of shapes and colours; home-produced tablets are characterised by their crudeness of manufacture and uneven colouration. One particular tablet form that is seen occasionally is white and imprinted with the words 'speed king'. Since the late 1980s, a crystalline form of the drug has appeared on the streets of the UK. By processing the basic drug with other chemicals, it has been possible to form it into clear glass-like colourless crystals of various sizes. Most of these crystals are quite small and have the appearance of fine-grade rock salt, but many of them are much larger, with some individual crystals measuring 1cm or more across.

Marketing

The powder forms of methylamphetamine are sold in much the same way as ordinary amphetamine and are usually seen in paper wraps or plastic press-seal bags containing half or one gram. The tablet forms, when available, are sold by the individual tablet, with no particular packaging.

Crystal or 'ice' methylamphetamine is sold by weight or by individual crystal. The small crystals are sold in plastic bags containing a gram or a fraction of a gram. Larger crystals are sold individually, with the price being set according to the weight. Users are prepared to pay a premium for the largest crystals in the belief that their use will achieve the most powerful effects. Individual crystals are usually wrapped in a twist of clear plastic film or more rarely in a single cigarette paper. This type of packaging is sometimes called a 'bomb' because of its shape.

Cost

Because of the irregular nature of the supply of methylamphetamine in powder and tablet form, street prices in the UK vary widely, with suppliers able to ask whatever they think the market will bear. Many first-time users will be prepared to pay very high prices to experience the drug. A more steady market price has become established for the crystal form of the drug. Many users believe that the crystalline forms are less likely to be adulterated with other substances, and so the crystalline forms are preferred when available. Crystal methylamphetamine has maintained a steady but low level of popularity at the wealthier end of the UK rave and dance club scene. Prices of around £30–50 per gram for the smaller crystals are common, with larger crystals achieving prices of between £15 and £30 each, according to size. A single £15-crystal would be enough for one hit lasting up to 16 hours.

Legal position

Methylamphetamine is a class B, schedule 2 controlled substance within the Misuse of Drugs Act 1971. As such, it attracts the following penalties:

- *Simple possession*: possession of methylamphetamine for personal use carries a maximum penalty on indictment of five years' imprisonment plus an unlimited fine. If the drug has been prepared for injection, the maximum penalty increases to 14 years' imprisonment plus the fine.

- *Possession with intent to supply*: possessing the drug with the intention of supplying it, either by sale or as a gift, to another person carries a maximum penalty on indictment of 14 years' imprisonment, plus an unlimited fine, plus seizure of all drug-related assets. In the same circumstances, methylamphetamine prepared for injection increases the maximum imprisonment term to life.

- *Supplying to another*: as for possession with intent to supply.

- *Importation or manufacture*: as for possession with intent to supply.

The inclusion of methylamphetamine in schedule 2 of the act recognises that there are some limited medical uses for the drug. Its use by doctors therefore is permitted under very strict controls.

Methods of use

Methylamphetamine is used in similar ways to amphetamine sulphate. The powder forms are mostly used orally, taken in a drink, dabbed from a wet finger or rubbed into the gums and teeth. Much smaller quantities of the drug are needed than amphetamine sulphate and users will experiment until they find the right quantity for them to achieve the effect that they desire. The powder can also be sniffed up the nose, but this use is rare. The powder form or crushed tablets can be mixed with water and a mild acid such as lemon juice and injected intravenously. Injecting provides a much more instant and intense hit, and an increasing number of users are favouring this method. Methylamphetamine powder can be mixed with tobacco or cannabis and smoked in the same way as ordinary amphetamine; however, this is not popular, as the high temperature reached in the burning cigarette, particularly in a cannabis cigarette, can damage the drug and reduce its effects. The crystal or 'ice' form of methylamphetamine is most commonly smoked on its own. In this form, the high temperature does not seriously reduce the drug's effects. The ease of this method makes it very popular. A few small crystals or a single larger crystal are placed in the smoking bowl of a glass or metal pipe and heated with a match or cigarette lighter, causing the drug to melt and slowly vaporise. Alternatively, the crystals are placed on a piece of metal foil and heated in the same way until they vaporise. The vapours are then inhaled deeply and the drug is carried into the bloodstream via the lungs. This is a very efficient way of using the drug, providing a hit with a speed of onset and intensity second only to injecting.

Effects of use

The effects of methylamphetamine are similar to, but much more intense than, those of ordinary amphetamine. The user will experience feelings of supreme euphoria, great strength and energy. These feelings will be particularly intense if the drug has been injected or smoked. The hit or rush felt by such users has been described by many as the most intense of any drug. The effect achieved is particularly long-lived, lasting between 2 and 16 hours, depending on the amount taken. The user will feel able to dance or take part in other strenuous activities for very long periods without rest or food. Many users report that the drug also causes a tremendous increase in sexual appetite, which, together with its energy-giving properties, may lead them to engage in long sexual sessions.

Adverse effects

As with the desired effects, the adverse effects of methylamphetamine are similar to those of ordinary amphetamine, but to a more intense degree. The same feelings of great fatigue and physical weakness will be felt when the drug has run its course. Blood pressure, body temperature and heart rate are raised by the drug, reaching dangerous levels in some people. These physical effects are nothing, however, com-pared with the potential of the drug for causing psychological problems and exacer-bating existing mental conditions. Methylamphetamine users often report the experience of powerful visual and auditory hallucinations. Many of these hallucina-tions are frightening and unpleasant and can lead to the user becoming extremely violent to people around them; the user may appear to have little or no little control over their emotions. This aggression and lack of control, coupled with the increase in sexual appetite, has led to many male users becoming involved in serious acts of sexual assault and rape.

The onset of psychiatric problems can be very rapid with methylamphetamine, and regular use over the course of only a few weeks can lead to the exhibition of bi-zarre behaviours and the development of deep paranoia, complex delusions, psy-chosis and schizophrenia-like symptoms.

Tolerance potential

Tolerance to methylamphetamine develops very quickly with continued use. Most users will use only a very small amount of the drug at their first experience. Amounts of around a twentieth of a gram are not uncommon for beginners. This will very soon rise as the user feels they are not getting the sensations they are seeking. The amount of each dose and the frequency of use will increase until the person may be using as much as half a gram or even more a day. They will very soon reach the position of having acquired a seriously expensive habit.

Habituation potential

Physical dependence on the drug can occur within a very short time with regular use, and severe cravings for the drug will result. Even more powerful will be the deep psychological dependence that soon develops. Most regular users will reach a point very quickly of being totally unable to face their lives without the drug.

Withdrawal effects

Along with severe cravings for the drug, a regular user who is trying to withdraw will experience high levels of mental agitation, depression, panic and feelings of being unable to cope. These feelings, together with the likelihood that the user will be suffering from a range of psychological problems, will make withdrawal a fraught process. No-one who has used methylamphetamine regularly should attempt to withdraw from using the drug without professional help.

Overdose potential

It is impossible to say with any degree of accuracy what amount of methylamphetamine will lead to overdose. In certain people, this level can be very low. Factors such as a person's physical size and their previous experience with methylamphetamine will make a difference. A person taking an overdose of the drug can suffer severe convulsions, leading to coma, with the possibility of respiratory and cardiac arrest and ultimately death.

Street names

Crystal form: Ice, meth, crystal, cristy, glass, crank, Nazi crank, yaba, ice-cream

Powder or tablet form: Meth, methedrine

Methylamphetamine: benefits and drawbacks

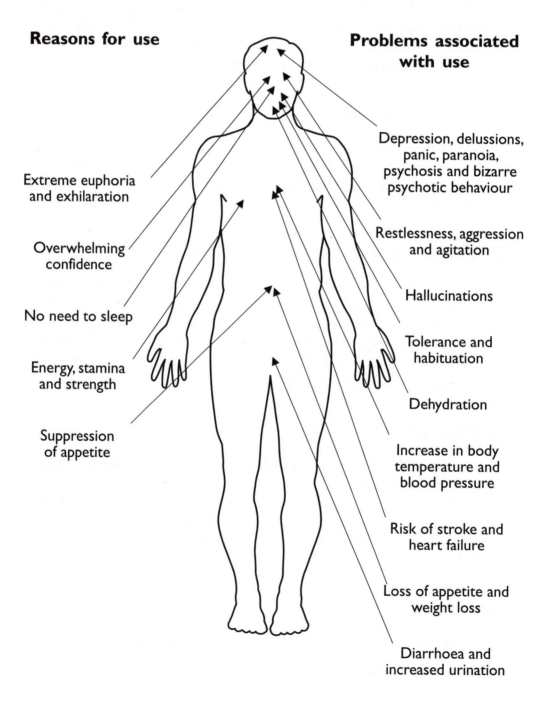

Reasons for use

Extreme euphoria and exhilaration

Overwhelming confidence

No need to sleep

Energy, stamina and strength

Suppression of appetite

Problems associated with use

Depression, delussions, panic, paranoia, psychosis and bizarre psychotic behaviour

Restlessness, aggression and agitation

Hallucinations

Tolerance and habituation

Dehydration

Increase in body temperature and blood pressure

Risk of stroke and heart failure

Loss of appetite and weight loss

Diarrhoea and increased urination

Cocaine (cocaine hydrochloride)

Cocaine: quick reference guide

Source

Derived from the leaves of the coca bush, *Erythroxylum coca*.

Forms and appearance

Commonly seen as a white crystalline powder with a sparkling appearance. Very occasionally seen in its paste form known as 'basuco'.

Marketing

Sold by the gram or fraction of a gram. The usual form of packaging is a paper wrap similar to that used for amphetamine. Also seen in small plastic press-seal bags. Coca paste is so rare that there is no recognised form of packaging. Cocaine is available from street drug dealers in almost every town and city in the UK.

Cost

The street price of cocaine in the UK has fallen in the past ten years. It varies greatly from one place to another but costs between £30 and £70 per gram for the powder form. There is no established street price for coca paste.

Legal position

Cocaine and coca paste are class A, schedule 2 controlled substances under the Misuse of Drugs Act 1971.

Methods of use

Cocaine powder is commonly sniffed through the nose. The paste form can be smoked in a pipe or, less commonly, mixed in a hand-rolled cigarette with tobacco or cannabis. Powder and paste sometimes are dissolved in water and injected, either into the veins or under the skin.

Effects of use

Feelings of energy, strength, exhilaration, euphoria, confidence and wellbeing are often reported following cocaine use. Users often become very talkative.

Adverse effects

Agitation, panic and feelings of persecution or threat often follow cocaine use. Regular use can damage the nasal passages and cause exhaustion and weight loss. Injection can lead to collapsed veins or skin ulcers at the injection site. Larger doses may lead to delusions and violent behaviour.

Tolerance potential

Tolerance develops rapidly with continued use.

Habituation potential

Cocaine users often rapidly develop both physical and psychological dependence on the drug.

Withdrawal effects

Feelings of anxiety, depression and panic, with a severe craving for continued use.

Overdose potential

It is possible to overdose fatally on cocaine.

Cocaine: in-depth guide

Source

Street cocaine is derived from the leaves of the coca bush, *Erythroxylum coca*, which grows both wild and under cultivation in high-altitude areas of South America, especially Columbia, Bolivia and Peru. It also occurs in parts of South-East Asia, India and Africa, although these areas are not considered to be major sources for the cocaine trade.

The leaves of the coca bush have been chewed by native South American people for many thousands of years for its stimulating effects and to reduce the effects of hunger and cold that were often a feature of their high-altitude existence. Visitors to high-altitude parts of South America, such as the Andes, are often offered coca leaves or coca tea as a remedy for altitude sickness. Statues and carvings dating from 3000 BCE have been discovered that show the chewing of coca. Each leaf contains about 2 per cent cocaine, which is locked into chemical compounds within the structure of the leaf. Repeated chewing of the leaf is enough to release small amounts of cocaine, which can be absorbed by swallowing. The early users discovered that chewing the leaf with an alkaline substance released much more of the cocaine. The traditional alkaline used in South America is lime produced by burning and then pulversing the shells of crustaceans. This fine powder was kept in a hollowed-out gourd hung from the user's waistband together with a pouch used to store a supply of coca leaves. The top of the gourd was plugged with a stick that reached down into the lime powder. The user would lick the stick, pick up a little lime with it and place it in the mouth with a handful of coca leaves. By chewing the two together, cocaine was released from the mixture and absorbed by the tissues of the mouth, tongue and gullet. The addition of lime also helped to sweeten the normally bitter taste of coca leaf. So common was the habit that it was normal in some South American native cultures for a boy, on reaching his twelfth birthday, to be presented with his own coca pouch and lime gourd by his proud parents.

When the Spanish conquistadors reached South America, they found the use of cocaine to be almost universal among the native people. Priests travelling with the conquistadors noticed that many of the users had become dependent upon the drug and sought to forbid its use. The Spanish authorities agreed at first, but then the more commercially minded of them began to see that this was a trade they could take over profitably. The growing of coca became a monopoly of the occupying forces, and the plants produced were either sold to the locals or used as payment for manual work done for the Spanish.

The chewing of coca leaf by indigenous peoples in most of the South America cocaine-producing countries is still lawful and continues to this day.

In 1859, the active ingredient of coca was isolated. Shortly after, a technique was invented to extract it. This technique involves putting the coca leaf through a series of processes that produce first coca paste and then cocaine hydrochloride, the compound we know as cocaine.

Cocaine has useful properties as a local anaesthetic and its use provided the foundation of modern pain-free dentistry. Its stimulant properties were recognised at an early stage, and it was used in a wide range of tonic and energy-providing medicines, food and drink: Coca-Cola®, when first marketed, contained a very small dose of cocaine to give the drink its stimulating properties, and an invigorating wine called Vin Mariani that contained cocaine was awarded a medal of quality by the Pope. A form of cocaine hydrochloride tablets called Forced March were used by the members of Sir Ernest Shackleton's expedition to Antarctica in 1909 to provide energy and protection from the cold. It is reported that the drug was used openly during training by athletes taking part in major international events, including the Olympic Games, around the beginning of the twentieth century. One of the teams that relied on cocaine as an essential part of their preparation was the Canadian ladies lacrosse team, which won many international titles at that time. Many European heroin and opium addicts were given cocaine by their doctors in order to help them stave off the debilitating effects of heroin and opium withdrawal. The technique was successful but often turned the heroin or opium addict into a cocaine addict.

These original uses of cocaine as a stimulant were based on the belief that it could be used without danger. This soon proved to be false, and many people became dependent on cocaine-containing products. No legal use is now made of cocaine for its stimulating properties, although it continues to be used on a small scale as a local anaesthetic.

Forms and appearance

The majority of cocaine is used in the form of cocaine hydrochloride powder. This is a pure white crystalline powder. The crystals are small and even and sparkle when exposed to the light. Cocaine is usually about 85 per cent pure at the end of the manufacturing process, and it is in this form that it enters the UK. It is 'cut' or diluted further as it passes down the dealer network, before it reaches the streets, and it may be reduced to as little as 30 per cent purity, although samples are seen that are up to 60 per cent pure. The most commonly used agents for cutting the imported cocaine are various forms of glucose and lactose, although on occasions other local anaesthetics such as lignocaine are used. The purpose of adding other local anaesthetics is that they give the same numbing effect as good-quality cocaine to the tongue of anyone testing the street drug.

Marketing

The production and distribution of cocaine from South America has become an enormous industry whose tentacles reach out into every country in the developed world. In Columbia, Bolivia and Peru, cocaine plays a significant part in the economy, and the growing of the coca bush has replaced the growing of food crops in a large way. There are fantastic profits to be made through the production of cocaine, and this has led to a great deal of violence, often reaching war-like proportions, as the various growers fight with each other for control of the trade. The legitimate governments in those countries, acting under pressure from countries on the receiving end of cocaine distribution, are fighting an endless and expensive war on the industry. Those in control guard their empires with great ferocity, but recent years have seen significant inroads made into cocaine production. The United Nations Office on Drugs and Crime *World Drug Report* 2004 states that the estimated production of dry coca leaf in Colombia, Boliva and Peru fell from a peak total of 358,700 tonnes in 1996 to 235,890 tonnes in 2003; the production of cocaine hydrochloride powder fell from 950 tonnes to 650 tonnes over the same period.

Cocaine is smuggled into the UK in a wide variety of ways. Very large consignments, often of many hundreds of kilograms at a time, enter the UK through sea ports. Smugglers use a great deal of imagination to import the drug, and UK customs officers have to show the same degree of ingenuity. Cargo containers, which often have arrived by very circuitous routes, have been found with false bottoms and sides, and apparently innocent imports often conceal packages of compressed cocaine. Another method of smuggling cocaine into the UK is by light aircraft flying from airfields in continental Europe. There are hundreds of small and disused airfields in southern and eastern England, where there is little control over what arrives. If no landing strip is available, smugglers will drop consignments over open country for waiting accomplices to collect. Significant amounts of cocaine are smuggled in within the stomachs of couriers arriving by air. Fifty grams or so of cocaine can be placed in a condom and then swallowed just before departure. On arrival, the traveller simply allows nature to take its course, and the condom passes out of the body to be recovered. At UK airports, some couriers with as many as 200 such condoms in their stomach have been detected. These couriers are referred to in the drugs trade as 'mules' because they are acting as beasts of burden for the drug importers. Many mules are women from impoverished backgrounds. They are recruited to the trade with offers of large cash sums and are willing to take the associated risks. Tragedies have occurred when the condoms have split in the courier's stomach, causing a massive overdose of cocaine and almost certain death.

As soon as one smuggling method is detected and closed down, the distributors find another way to bring in the drug, so lucrative is the trade. Recently, more than 6kg of cocaine had been dissolved and impregnated into the clothing contained in the suitcase of a traveller.

Once in the UK, the drug is divided into smaller and smaller amounts as it passes through the dealer chain that now exists nationwide. As it does so, it steadily increases in price, until, by the time it reaches the streets, a lot of people have made very large sums of money from it. At street level, cocaine is normally sold in small paper wraps in the same way as amphetamine. The standard wrap will contain half a gram of cocaine, but wraps of other sizes are available. Cocaine is not as easily obtainable as cannabis and amphetamine, but it is not difficult to find in any UK city or town. It is still one of the more expensive street drugs, which restricts its use to people with ready access to fairly large sums of money and those prepared to raise large sums of money through activities including crime.

Cost

Cocaine powder currently costs between £30 and £70 per gram in the UK. The common half-gram wrap costs between £20 and £40. As with all drugs, there are economies to be made by buying in larger quantities. Enough cocaine to provide one hit to an inexperienced user costs around £5.

Legal position

Cocaine and coca paste are class A, schedule 2 controlled substances under the Misuse of Drugs Act 1971. As with all class A drugs, offences involving it carry the following penalties:

- *Possession for personal use*: the possession of an amount of cocaine for personal use is punishable on indictment by a maximum sentence of 14 years' imprisonment plus an unlimited fine.

- *Possession with intent to supply*: possession of cocaine with intent to supply the drug by sale or gift to another person is punishable on indictment with a maximum sentence of life imprisonment, plus an unlimited fine, plus seizure of all drug-related assets.

- *Supplying*: as for possession with intent to supply.

- *Importation*: as for possession with intent to supply.

The position of cocaine within schedule 2 of the Misuse of Drugs Act 1971 means that it is permitted for doctors to use it for medical purposes under strictly controlled circumstances.

Methods of use

Most users of cocaine in its powder form 'snort' the drug, sniffing it sharply into the nose, which allows the drug to be absorbed into the bloodstream through the membranes inside the nose. The drug is placed on a smooth hard surface such as a mirror or china plate and then arranged into a thin line by the use of a razor blade or credit card (see Figure 4.2). The amount of cocaine in each line will vary from user to user; in the UK it is typical to get 10–20 lines from each gram of cocaine. Using a razor blade or credit card is also a very efficient way of dividing an amount of cocaine into equal parts so that more than one person can share it, without having to use scales to divide a sample of powder. Having arranged the powder into a line, the user places a small tube into one nostril and closes off the other nostril with a finger. They then place the end of the tube at one end of the powder line and sniff sharply, thus drawing the powder into the nose. As they do so, they move the tube along the line sniffing up the powder. The tube may be purpose-made from glass, plastic or metal. It may even be 'Y'-shaped so that an end can be placed in each nostril at the same time. More commonly, a temporary device created from a rolled-up bank note or piece of paper is used. The inhaled powder adheres to the surface of the mucous membranes of the nose and is readily absorbed into the bloodstream.

In some circles, there is a fashion for snorting cocaine from a small specially shaped spoon. This spoon is often very ornate and may well be made from solid silver, with the bowl set at right-angles to the handle. It is filled with cocaine powder and held up to one nostril for snorting. When not in use, the spoon may be seen hanging from a silver chain around the neck of its owner, like a status symbol.

Some users of cocaine rub the drug into their gums with a finger. The cocaine is absorbed rapidly into the bloodstream, which allows more of the drug to reach the brain than when it is snorted. However, the drug has a very bitter taste, which limits the popularity of this method. Occasionally, cocaine is dissolved in a drink or added to cold food. This is not a particularly efficient way of getting the drug into the bloodstream and has few followers.

In recent years, there has been a significant increase in the number of users who inject cocaine. The drug is injected either into a vein or into the fat layer just below

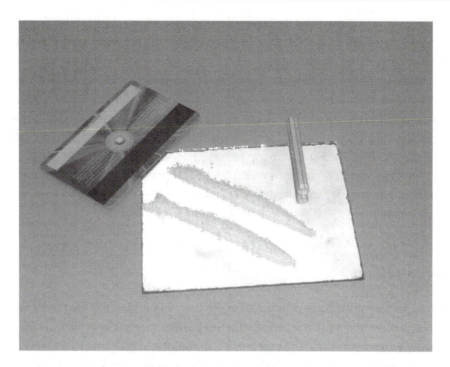

Figure 4.2 Lines of cocaine ready for 'snorting'

the surface of the skin, a process known as 'skin popping'. Injecting cocaine into the veins provides the most rapid hit, as the drug reaches the brain in high concentrations within a few seconds. Skin popping is much slower, as the drug has to find its way into the many minute blood vessels in the fatty layer beneath the skin and from there move into the main bloodstream.

Coca paste is rarely available in the UK and when seen is treated by users as a curiosity. The normal method of using coca paste is to smoke it. The efficacy of cocaine in this form is easily damaged by high temperatures, and so a normal tobacco pipe with its enclosed bowl is not favoured. The paste is normally smoked in a small version of the cannabis water pipe (bong) or in a pipe (chillum) with ventilation holes that provide a supply of cool air into the smoke. The few examples of coca paste that reach the UK are usually of a high purity level and contain around 60 per cent cocaine. This, together with the efficiency of smoking as a method of getting the drug into the bloodstream, makes this a potent way of using cocaine.

Effects of use

The hit provided by cocaine is felt rapidly. The brain takes up the drug easily, and the user will begin to feel the effects of its use within a few seconds of taking it. The effects are very short-lived, however; depending on how much of the drug is used and the previous experience of the user, the effects will last from a few minutes up to two or three hours at the most.

Most users report feelings of euphoria and overpowering feelings of wellbeing, energy and strength. They experience great clarity of mind and feel that they have been given deep insight into their lives. The drug gives users feelings of confidence and freedom from anxiety and stress. Cocaine users often become very excitable and talkative and are unable to keep still, wanting to be actively involved with other people.

In many users, cocaine increases the sexual appetite and desires; such users may well become engaged in episodes of casual sex with other users who have been affected similarly.

Adverse effects

What goes up must come down, and many users of cocaine pay for the energy and feelings of wellbeing that it gives by then experiencing equally powerful feelings of lethargy and depression. The user may become agitated and panicky and feel threatened by people around them. If the user has been taking very high doses of cocaine, this coming-down period can lead to bizarre and often violent behaviours.

Prolonged or heavy use of cocaine can lead to poor body condition and substantial weight loss. Some high-dose users experience severe disruption of their normal sleep patterns and may suffer from chronic insomnia. Male users may become impotent and incapable of achieving or maintaining an erection. Some long-term heavy users become paranoid and may even exhibit symptoms of clinical psychosis.

The practice of snorting cocaine powder into the nose can lead to problems with the membranes and lining of the nasal passages. One of the immediate effects of cocaine is constriction of the blood vessels that it enters. This may lead, especially in the minute blood vessels found in the nose, to them closing down completely. This results in the tissues fed by these blood vessels becoming starved of the blood supply necessary to keep them alive. The tissues begin to die and cannot be replaced by normal processes at a fast enough rate to keep up with continued use of the drug. The membranes often perforate, causing ulcers to form within the nasal passages; it is not uncommon for the septum, the membrane that separates the right and left nasal passages, to perforate completely. Infection within these nasal ulcers is common, and the user may require medical treatment to deal with the damage.

Injection of cocaine can also cause physical problems. The drug causes constriction of the veins into which it is injected, with a risk of the veins collapsing and becoming blocked. Such a blockage can lead to the blood supply being cut off to tissues normally fed by that vein, which can lead to disorders such as gangrene; if left untreated, this can cause septicaemia, the loss of limbs and even death. Because of this danger, many injecting users prefer to inject subcutaneously – that is, just beneath the skin – by the process known as skin popping, with small amounts of liquid being injected into the layer of fat that lies just below the skin. The thigh and the upper side of the forearm are favourite sites for this. The amount injected into any one site is between half and one millilitre of liquid. If larger amounts are being administered, several sites are used. The liquid causes a small bubble to form just under the skin, which disappears as the drug is absorbed into the tissues. Because of the vein-constricting properties of cocaine, these sites often become ulcerated and painful. Infections at the injection sites are common and can lead to serious problems unless treated medically.

People who share needles and syringes with users who have infections run the risk of acquiring the same infection, such as HIV, septicaemia and hepatitis.

The use of cocaine by women during pregnancy is extremely dangerous for the developing fetus. The blood flow to the fetus is restricted, causing a reduction in the supply of oxygen. This can lead to spontaneous abortion or stillbirth. If the child is born alive, there may be physical and neurological damage. The infant is also at risk of being born with a severe dependence on cocaine, which can badly effect its healthy development in the first weeks of life.

Tolerance potential

Some level of tolerance will develop with continued use of cocaine. Regular use of the drug can lead to a point at which the intensity of its effects and their duration become noticeably reduced and the user has to increase the amount of each dose or the frequency of use.

Habituation potential

Very few users become physically dependent on cocaine. The major risk lies in acquiring a psychological dependence upon the drug. This dependence can be deep-seated and difficult to treat. The short duration of effect that is a feature of cocaine encourages the user to keep using. If the user wants to be under the influence of cocaine for the duration of a party or other social event, they will need to take several doses spaced at regular intervals. The adverse effects of withdrawal are thus put off, but as with all such reactions they cannot be put off indefinitely, and the 'crash', when it finally arrives, will be even greater. The feelings of weakness, anxiety and lack of confidence associated with this crash are powerful and can be extremely unpleasant, providing a further impetus to the desire to keep on using the drug.

Withdrawal effects

Following light and irregular use of cocaine, most users can stop using the drug without any great difficulty. Regular and heavy users, particularly if use has been over a prolonged period, may have very real problems in stopping, however. The feelings of anxiety, depression and panic that may result from ceasing to use the drug will be difficult to cope with and result in a severe craving for continued use. Many cases of suicide have resulted from the torment that such withdrawal can bring. No-one who has used cocaine on a regular basis and over a long period of time should attempt to come off the drug without professional help.

Overdose potential

Overdoses can occur with cocaine at relatively low levels. Because of the uncertainty that exists over the strength of any particular sample of street cocaine, it is easy to take too much. The precise level of an overdose for any one person cannot be predicted accurately, and regular users should always be aware of the risks that they run. An overdose of cocaine can lead to the heart rate and body temperature rising to dangerous levels and may result in convulsions and even cardiac or respiratory failure, leading to coma and death.

Street names

Cocaine powder: coke, C, snow, snowflake, Bernice, Charlie, charge, Bolivian marching powder, white lady, white, Percy, toot

Slang associated with use

Snorting – Inhaling through the nose

Line – Line of cocaine on a flat surface ready for snorting

Mixing the gravy – Smoking cocaine mixed with other drugs

Flying – Feeling achieved soon after cocaine use

Speed balling – Mixing cocaine with heroin for smoking

Skin popping – Injecting cocaine just under the skin

Mule – Courier who smuggles cocaine inside their body

Cocaine: benefits and drawbacks

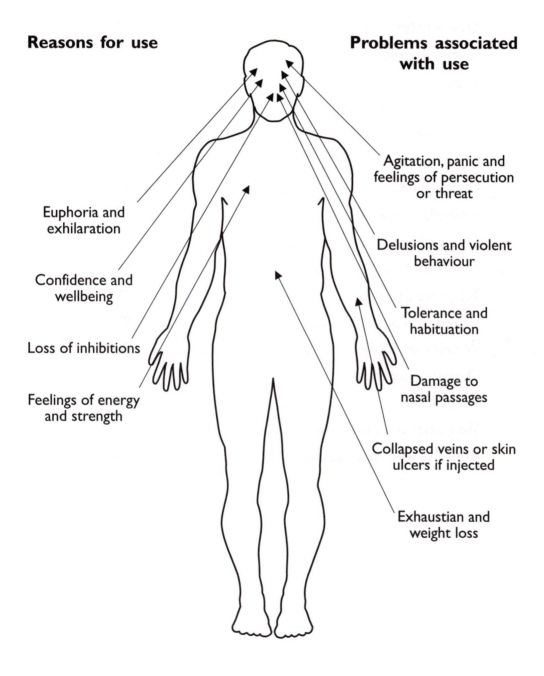

Reasons for use

Euphoria and exhilaration

Confidence and wellbeing

Loss of inhibitions

Feelings of energy and strength

Problems associated with use

Agitation, panic and feelings of persecution or threat

Delusions and violent behaviour

Tolerance and habituation

Damage to nasal passages

Collapsed veins or skin ulcers if injected

Exhaustian and weight loss

Crack and freebase cocaine

Crack and freebase cocaine: quick reference guide

Source

Derived from cocaine hydrochloride by a chemical process.

Forms and appearance

Crack cocaine is seen in crystals of varying sizes and colours that range from a clear yellow or pinkish yellow to a waxy white colour. Freebase is normally seen as a white powder.

Marketing

Freebase and the smaller crystals of crack are normally sold by the gram or fraction of a gram. Larger crystals are often sold singly. There is no established packaging for crack. Smaller crystals commonly are seen in small press-seal bags, while larger crystals often are wrapped separately in clear plastic film or cigarette papers.

Cost

Crystals of crack cocaine are priced according to their size, with prices up to £25 being typical in the UK. Small crystals or pieces broken from larger crystals, and sometimes known as 'clubbing rocks', are priced at around £10.

Legal position

Freebase and crack are forms of cocaine and are classified in the same way. They are class A, schedule 2 controlled substances under the Misuse of Drugs Act 1971.

Methods of use

Freebase and crack are smoked in special pipes or small metal containers or from metal foil. Although very uncommon in the UK, crack crystals are sometimes crushed, dissolved in water and injected.

Effects of use

Extreme elation and euphoria, feelings of power, strength and wellbeing.

Adverse effects

Tiredness, weakness, depression and feelings of being threatened. Heavy use can lead to paranoia and psychosis, with a display of bizarre and often very violent behaviour, especially following withdrawal.

Tolerance potential

Some tolerance develops with continued use.

Habituation potential

Both physical and psychological dependence develop very rapidly with continued use. Babies born to pregnant users may be dependent.

Withdrawal effects

Feelings of aggression, agitation and panic, severe depression and risk of suicide.

Overdose potential

Overdose of freebase or crack can lead to coma and death.

Crack and freebase cocaine: in-depth guide

Source

Crack cocaine is produced by 'freeing' cocaine from its chemical base. The normal form of the drug cocaine is a compound of pure cocaine known as cocaine hydrochloride. Until the mid-1980s, this was the only form of the drug commonly available on the streets. Suppliers of the drug in the USA then began to seek ways of producing it in a form that the human body would accept more readily and would give the user a more intense hit, thus enhancing the effects that normal cocaine provides. Pressure also came from users to develop a form of the drug that could be smoked more efficiently than ordinary cocaine. The normal habit of snorting cocaine had caused nasal problems for so many users that they were seeking a smoking form that would give them all of the effects of snorting without the attendant problems.

The first step in this process was the creation of a form of cocaine called 'freebase'. The production of freebase involves dissolving cocaine hydrochloride with a powerful solvent such as ether and then allowing it to evaporate off. This process is difficult and potentially dangerous. Fires and explosions are commonly the results of such processes. Freebase cocaine produced in this way occasionally is seen on the streets, but most freebase is made by users for their own use.

Another process was then developed that involves dissolving cocaine hydrochloride in an alkaline solution and then gently heating it. This leads to the formation of crystals of freebase cocaine, known on the streets as 'crack'. Freebase and crack are chemically identical, but it is easier and safer to produce crack. Crack can be used for smoking very easily.

Forms and appearance

Freebase cocaine is seen as a white powder. It is less crystalline in appearance than cocaine hydrochloride, but they have the same pure white colour. Freebase can be as much as 95 per cent pure cocaine. It is not generally 'cut' or diluted with anything else. The remaining 5 per cent of the drug will normally be contaminants that remain in the drug after processing.

Crack cocaine is seen in the form of crystals of varying sizes (see Figure 4.3). Many of these crystals will be very small, like granulated sugar, but some can

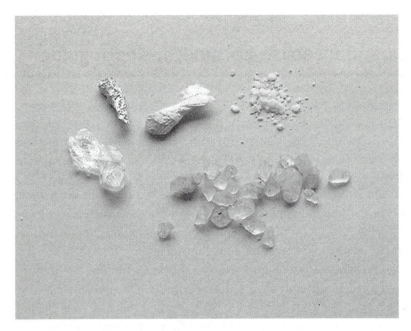

Figure 4.3 Crack crystals and freebase cocaine

measure as much as 1 cm across. Users of crack prefer the larger crystals, and producers will try to make as much of the drug in this form as they can. Purity levels can be very high: 80–100 per cent purity is usual. The colour of the crystals varies a great deal. There is a common belief among users that crack is always a purer type of cocaine because of its crystal form. It is certainly harder to deliberately add adulterants to crack, but many of the contaminants that were present in the original cocaine hydrochloride will be carried over into the crystals during crack manufacture. These additional substances cause the colour variations that are seen. Some crack crystals are transparent and have a yellow or pinkish hue. Others are of a similar colour but are cloudy and translucent. Many crystals have a white or yellow waxy appearance and are opaque.

Marketing

The promotion of freebase and crack cocaine has been a remarkable phenomenon. During the mid-1980s, stories began to emanate from the USA about an amazing new form of cocaine that gave the user an instant hit and had effects that far surpassed those of ordinary cocaine. Despite other stories that described the drug as being able to turn a user into an addict at the first use, there arose an immediate demand for supplies. Details of the production processes quickly began to circulate within the drug-using community, and many users began to produce their own freebase and crack at home. At the same time, small amounts of US-produced freebase and crack began to arrive in the UK. The freebase form of the drug failed to establish itself as a high-demand drug, but the market for crack cocaine grew rapidly. Producers in the UK refined their production processes and began to manufacture the drug in useful quantities and to the same standards as their US counterparts.

Production has now increased to the point where the majority of the crack used in the UK is manufactured in the UK from cocaine hydrochloride imported from elsewhere. Until recently, much of this production was in small quantities from manufacturers only just above the street dealer in the drug-distribution chain. However, in a report published in March 2005, the UK National Criminal Intelligence Service claimed that production of crack in the UK was increasingly being carried out in large quantities at a high level within the drug-distribution chain by organised criminal groups before downward distribution to street level.[2] There are enormous profits to be made from the production and sale of crack, and a great deal of criminal violence occurs where suppliers are involved in 'turf wars' for control of areas in which they can establish a monopoly of supply.

The larger crystals of crack cocaine are often sold separately, with the price being set according to weight. These crystals are normally wrapped in twists of clear plastic film or single cigarette papers. The shape of this form of packaging has led to them being referred to as 'bombs'.

Crack cocaine is used as a means of controlling male and female prostitutes. The drug is first given either free or at a very low price to young males and females who the supplier sees as suitable for involvement in prostitution. Many of these people are in their very early teens and are almost always poor and unemployed or have run away from home or an institution and are living on the streets. The young person quickly acquires a dependence for the drug; being unable to afford the normal street price, they are prepared to do whatever the supplier asks of them. The supplier acts as their pimp, introduces them to clients and takes the majority of their earnings. A steady supply of crack is assured only if the young person continues to obey the pimp.

Crack cocaine has now established itself as an important drug of choice in the UK and is readily available in most large population centres. In some socially deprived areas in major British towns and cities, crack is available from dealers operating on the streets. In other places, it is available from locations such as clubs, cafes and public houses from dealers who are known personally to the users. The drug is

2   UK National Criminal Intelligence Service (2005) *UK Threat Assessment. The threat from serious and organised crime; 2004/2005–2005/2006.* HM Government: London.

also available in smaller towns and villages by special arrangement between the user and a local dealer in other drugs.

Cost

It is only in places where crack is readily available that a market price has become established. In other areas, the price will be agreed between the user and the supplier. Casual and first-time users in such areas seem to be prepared to pay a much higher price in order to experiment with the drug. The larger crystals are sold separately; they are weighed using a small balance and the price is set accordingly. The largest crystals are much sought after by many users; these crystals often attract a premium price that is considerably more than the equivalent weight of smaller crystals.

Legal position

Both freebase and crack cocaine are classified legally as cocaine; as such, both are class A, schedule 2 controlled substances under the Misuse of Drugs Act 1971. Offences involving freebase or crack cocaine attract the following penalties:

- *Possession for personal use*: the possession of any amount of freebase or crack cocaine for personal use is punishable on indictment by a maximum sentence of seven years' imprisonment plus an unlimited fine.

- *Possession with intent to supply*: possession of freebase or crack cocaine with intent to supply by sale or gift to another person is punishable on indictment with a maximum sentence of life imprisonment, plus an unlimited fine, plus seizure of all drug-related assets.

- *Supplying*: as for possession with intent to supply.

- *Importation and manufacture*: as for possession with intent to supply.

Although freebase and crack cocaine are classified within schedule 2 of the Misuse of Drugs Act 1971, this part of the classification refers only to ordinary cocaine. These other two forms of the drug currently have no recognised medical use in the UK.

Methods of use

Both freebase and crack cocaine were designed to be smoked, and it is exceptionally rare for them to be used in any other way. These forms of cocaine are much more able to withstand the high temperatures achieved during smoking compared with the powder form of cocaine. However, if the temperature in the smoking bowl is allowed to reach too high a level, even the crack and freebase forms of cocaine begin to break down, resulting in a loss of effectiveness. Because of this, the user will try to smoke their drug in a way that keeps the temperature as low as possible. It is not necessary to burn the drug in order to smoke it; it is simply necessary for the temperature to reach a point at which the drug vaporises. It is this vapour that is inhaled, and the smoker will try to keep the temperature as close as possible to this vaporisation point to maintain maximum effectiveness.

Many smokers use smaller versions of the bottle pipes used by cannabis smokers (see Figure 4.4). These pipes have a smoking bowl connected to a water-filled container through which the vapour is drawn before reaching the smoker. Most of the crack water pipes used in the UK are home-made, but there is a thriving trade in commercially manufactured water pipes of all descriptions. A large number of websites are devoted to the sale of such paraphernalia.

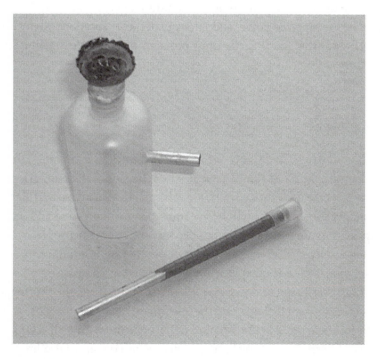

Figure 4.4 Crack pipes

However, it is not necessary to use anything as sophisticated as a water pipe to smoke crack cocaine successfully. Many users simply use a glass or metal tube with a bore wide enough to accommodate the average-sized crack crystal. The user fits the crystal just inside one end of the tube and puts the other end in their mouth. The outer end of the tube is then heated with a match or cigarette lighter until the crystal vaporises and the fumes are inhaled. Other users heat their freebase or crack cocaine on a piece of metal foil or in a metal bottle top or similar and collect the fumes for inhalation with a tube, a matchbox sleeve or simply a cupped hand.

Effects of use

The effects of smoking freebase or crack cocaine occur almost instantly. The drug is absorbed readily through the lungs and passes via the bloodstream to the brain. The users will feel the hit provided by the drug within a matter of seconds of inhaling the vapour. The effects of the drug are extremely short-lived. Depending on the amount smoked at any one time, and the previous experience of the user, the duration of the effects can be as short at 15 minutes and certainly no longer than one hour.

As the hit reaches the brain, the user feels intense sensations of euphoria, great elation, almost superhuman strength, boundless energy and wellbeing. It is hard to exaggerate the reported power and intensity of these sensations. Many users of these forms of cocaine claim that the drug provides the most powerful feelings of any street drug.

Adverse effects

As with most drugs, the higher the freebase or crack user becomes, the lower they sink when the drug has run its course. The intensity of the euphoric feelings provided by freebase and crack cocaine are followed by equally powerful feelings of fatigue and weakness. These will be accompanied by depression and, in many cases, feelings of paranoia and of being under threat from other people.

It takes only a small amount of crack or freebase to produce its effect, and so each individual dose is inexpensive when viewed in comparison with some other drugs. The severity of the down side of the use of this drug, the shortness of the duration of the pleasant feelings, and the low price of an individual dose can encourage users to continue use. A frame of mind of 'just one more time' develops rapidly. The low cost of each dose of freebase or crack is, of course, a false impression. With many users taking repeated doses of the drug over a fairly short period, the monetary cost begins to mount rapidly. It is not uncommon for users to consume many hundreds of pounds' worth of the drug over the course of one heavy session, lasting for only a couple of days.

Heavy or prolonged use of crack or freebase leads in a great number of users to profound psychological problems. Many users develop a deep-seated paranoia and become suspicious of and antagonistic towards other people. These feelings will be focused particularly on those whom they consider to be trying to stop them using the drug, which has become the centre of their lives. This may show itself in violence, often of a very extreme form, towards drug agency workers, police officers, doctors and other officials. Many drug agencies give their workers special instructions on how to work with heavy users of freebase and crack cocaine. Even a relatively short period of continued use can lead to the development of complex psychosis in which very elaborate delusions may be present, which makes it even more difficult to help them.

These psychological conditions can be difficult, if not impossible, to control or cure and may require prolonged periods of inpatient treatment at a psychiatric hospital.

An area causing increasing concern is the use of crack and freebase by pregnant women. Many of these women suffer spontaneous abortions. The baby may die in the womb due to displacement of the placenta or may be stillborn. The chief cause of these problems is the way in which all forms of cocaine restrict the flow of blood along veins and arteries. This significantly reduces the volume of blood flowing through the umbilical cord into the fetus. Together with the consequent decrease in oxygen supply, this often leads to the baby being born physically and/or neurologically damaged; some of this damage can be extreme. No figures are available for the number of such births in the UK.

Tolerance potential

Some degree of tolerance to freebase or crack will develop with continued or regular use, although it is unlikely to be as marked as that seen with other street drugs. These forms of cocaine seem able to maintain the power of their effect without the need to increase dosage levels for much longer than is usual with other drugs.

Habituation potential

Many users of freebase and crack cocaine develop a powerful physical dependence on the drug. They experience severe cravings for it if they try to stop using it or their supplies are not available. This may cause the user to become unstable and lose control. Many of the cases of violence carried out by freebase and crack users have taken place under these conditions.

Along with the development of a physical dependence, a deep-seated psychological dependence on the drug forms. The user feels unable to face the world without it. The unpleasantness of the physical feelings that withdrawal can bring serve only to reinforce the psychological feelings that life is too difficult or stressful to cope with without the drug. Many users report that they are afraid – even terrified – to try to stop using.

Because of the degree of unpleasantness associated with coming down from the drug, many users are now experimenting with a practice called 'mixing the gravies'. This involves mixing heroin powder with freebase or crack and smoking the two together. The heroin is absorbed more slowly by the lungs and the hit that it provides is masked by that of the crack. The effects of heroin are much longer-lasting, however; as the effects of the crack begin to fade, the heroin takes over and acts as a 'parachute drug' to ease the user through the come-down phase. Users who have been bingeing on freebase or crack cocaine by taking it repeatedly often add heroin to their last dose to achieve this parachute effect. The addition of heroin exposes the user to the development of physical dependence on that drug, and so although it eases the user through the come-down from freebase or crack cocaine, it can eventually lead to greater problems.

Withdrawal effects

The speed at which dependence can develop means that any user who has experimented with crack or freebase on more than an occasional basis is liable to suffer some form of withdrawal when use is stopped. Users may experience extreme agitation and feelings of disorientation, combined with a state of panic. They may become very depressed; this, together with the psychological problems that use of the drug often causes, can lead to the user becoming suicidal. This risk is very real, and no-one who has used crack or freebase over a period of time should attempt to withdraw without seeking professional help.

Overdose potential

Heavy doses of freebase or crack cocaine can lead to respiratory and cardiac failure, collapse, coma and death.

Street names

Crack cocaine crystals: rocks, wash, flake, cloud nine, eight ball, gravel, nuggets, Roxanne

Freebase cocaine: base, freebase, baseball

Slang associated with use

Freebasing, basing – Smoking freebase or crack

Washing – Producing crack cocaine from cocaine hydrochloride Powder

Crack head – Crack user

Crack baby – Infant of a crack-using mother

Crack pipe, crack bottle – Pipe used for smoking

Bomb – Single wrapped crystal

Crack and freebase cocaine: benefits and drawbacks

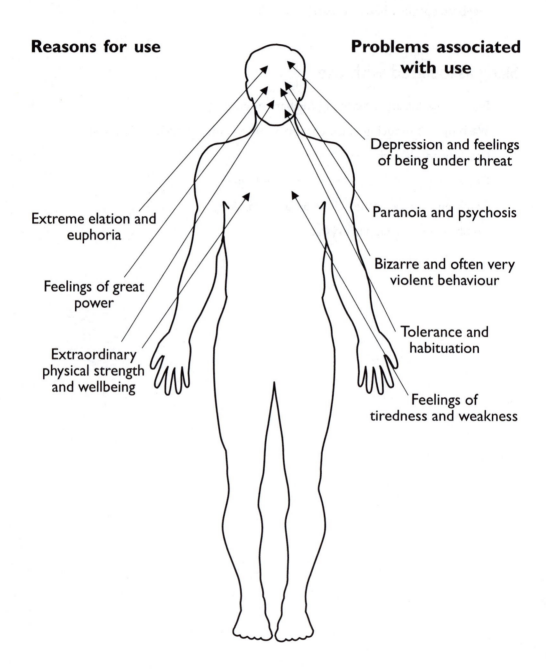

Reasons for use

Problems associated with use

Depression and feelings of being under threat

Extreme elation and euphoria

Paranoia and psychosis

Feelings of great power

Bizarre and often very violent behaviour

Extraordinary physical strength and wellbeing

Tolerance and habituation

Feelings of tiredness and weakness

Chapter 5

Hallucinogens

LSD (lysergic acid diethylamide)

LSD: quick reference guide

Source

Derived by a chemical process from ergot, a naturally occurring fungus of certain cereal grains.

Forms and appearance

Pure LSD occurs in the form of colourless crystals, but it is not seen as such as a street drug. LSD for street use may be impregnated onto small squares of blotting paper, each printed with a picture, and known as 'trips' or 'tabs'. LSD is also supplied on small squares of clear yellow gelatine known as 'windows' and can be found in the form of pinhead-size pills of various colours known as microdots.

Marketing

All forms of LSD are sold by the dose.

Cost

A single dose of LSD costs between £1.50 and £5.

Legal position

LSD is a class A, schedule I controlled substance under the Misuse of Drugs Act 1971.

Methods of use

LSD is normally taken orally by placing the paper square or pill in the mouth or in a drink. The gelatine squares are normally placed under the eyelid so that the blood vessels of the eye absorb the drug; this is known as 'looking through the window'.

Effects of use

Visual, auditory and tactile hallucinations. These can feel very real and may vary from extremely pleasant to extremely unpleasant.

Adverse effects

There is a risk of the user becoming involved in an accident while they are hallucinating. Many users experience a recurrence of the hallucination many weeks or months after using the drug – 'flashbacks'. Use of LSD may bring to the surface a latent psychiatric disorder.

Tolerance potential

Tolerance to LSD develops quickly with repeated use over a period of a few days but will disappear if the user abstains for a week or more.

Habituation potential

LSD is not thought to cause the development of any physical dependence. Regular users may develop psychological dependence on the drug, although this is not common.

Withdrawal effects

LSD produces little in the way of physical effects when use ceases. Regular users may have to cope with feelings of anxiety, but these will be of a low level.

Overdose potential

It is not thought to be possible to overdose on LSD.

LSD: in-depth guide

Source

LSD is produced by the chemical processing of a substance contained in ergot, a naturally occurring fungus that affects many cereal crops. The chief source of the fungus is rye, which is grown in the USA.

LSD was first isolated in 1938 by Albert Hofmann, a Swiss chemist who was investigating the properties of the many compounds that can be derived from ergot. He was seeking compounds that would be of use for medical purposes. Having isolated and then synthesised the drug, he carried out some experiments with it on a range of animals. Because LSD has almost no physical effect on living organisms, he noted no useful reactions and the drug was largely forgotten. In 1943, Hofmann returned to the study of LSD; during the course of an experiment, he accidentally ingested a small quantity of it, probably by licking his fingers after handling it. During the course of the next few hours, he experienced the world's first recorded hallucinogenic LSD 'trip'. Being a scientist, he recorded his impressions of the experience in his diary, which mentions that the shapes of objects and people around him changed and that he saw fantastic images of extraordinary clarity and with intense and changing colouration. The whole hallucinatory period lasted for about two hours. This experience was totally unexpected and so Hofmann set out to replicate it under more controlled conditions. He had no idea what the most effective dose would be, so he decided to take 0.25 milligrams, which he thought would be a very mild dose. Unknown to him, he was in fact taking a dose equivalent to five times the normal strength of the street forms that we see today. He then recorded, as carefully as he could, his impressions as the effects began to take hold. His notes refer to him feeling a little dizzy after about 40 minutes and then beginning to suffer some distortion of his vision. He records that he felt as though he had left his body and was able to observe himself from the outside. He also describes how the sounds in the laboratory were translated in his brain to images, and he was able to 'see' the sounds of people talking and a tap running. Throughout the hallucination, he remained aware that all that was happening to him was only the result of the drug, but still he felt a great fear that he was going out of his mind. After several hours, he fell asleep and woke up later feeling perfectly well.

Over the next few years, supplies of LSD were made available to doctors in the USA and Europe for experimental use in the treatment of certain psychiatric disorders. Many psychiatrists felt that LSD would provide a useful tool in helping patients to vocalise their inner feelings and psychoses. Experiments were also carried out by the US government into the possibly of using LSD as a 'truth drug'. Some doctors working with terminally ill people used LSD as a way of helping their patients approach death with calmness.

These experiments were abandoned within a fairly short time due to the ineffectiveness of the drug as a therapeutic tool and because many of the patients who were given it had begun to experience what we now know as 'flashbacks'.

It is worth noting that during 1995, 50 of the UK patients who were given LSD as part of these experiments were granted permission to sue the participating health authorities for damages due to the problems caused by LSD.

Forms and appearance

Pure LSD is in the form of small colourless crystals, but it is never seen on the streets in this form. The vast majority of pure LSD today is manufactured on the west coast of America. The LSD required to service the demand in Europe is exported from the USA in pure form for preparation into the familiar street forms, most of this work being carried out in Holland and Belgium. This was not always the case: during the early 1970s, extensive production of LSD took place in the UK. The police then mounted an extensive operation to close down this production – 'Operation Julie' – which involved many hundreds of officers over several counties and resulted in the prosecution of 122 people for offences relating to the production and distribution of LSD. At its height, it is thought that the production of LSD in the UK was supplying 95 per cent of the British market and 65 per cent of the US market. Following the success of the British police operation, the market for LSD collapsed. It became very difficult to obtain the drug and the price escalated wildly, causing many users to change to other drugs or cease use altogether.

The dose of LSD needed to produce the desired effect is extremely low, an average dose being in the region of 40–60 micrograms (a microgram is one-millionth of a gram). In order to understand just how small this dose is, a full-stop written on a piece of paper with a ballpoint pen contains around 120 micrograms of ink. Therefore, to dose the drug accurately for use is very difficult.

When it first appeared on the streets in the 1960s, LSD was in the form of a dilute, clear, colourless, odourless liquid that was placed with an eye dropper on to a sugar cube and eaten. This is a very inconvenient method of use, and it soon disappeared. Today, most LSD is seen impregnated on to sheets of absorbent paper, similar to poor-quality blotting paper. The sheets usually are then divided into 5mm squares, although larger sizes are also seen. These squares are called 'trips', 'tabs' and, occasionally, 'blotters'; each is decorated with a small picture or symbol (see

Figure 5.1). Most commonly, a complete picture is printed on each square, but it is not unusual for one larger image to cover multiple squares. There are many hundreds of different designs and new ones appear all the time. The reason for these pictures is unclear. To some users, they indicate quality. If the manufacturer of the drug has produced good-quality images on the squares, then users believe that the drug will also be of high quality. Other users have favourite pictures and believe that they have found the form that suits them best. The constant arrival of new designs also serves as a sort of sell-by date: most users know that LSD deteriorates with time if it is not stored properly and feel that if the picture is new to them, then the drug is also fresh. Some users, particularly very young people, want to try as many of the different designs as possible, in the same way that they might collect pictures of footballers or pop stars.

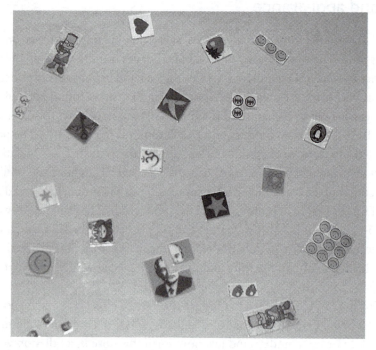

Figure 5.1 LSD 'trips' or 'tabs'

Many of the designs have survived from the earliest appearance of this form of the drug; for example, the strawberry picture and the little figure known as 'sad ant' have been used since the 1960s. Many of the older designs have a quasi-religious significance, such as the Buddha, 'the keys to the heavenly kingdom' and the Hindu 'om' symbol. Important figures from world affairs, such as Saddam Hussein and Mikhail Gorbachev may be used. More recently, LSD tabs have been produced with images that appear to have been designed to attract a very young clientele, with images of Batman, Superman, Sonic the Hedgehog and the Super Mario Brothers being very popular. The dose of LSD contained on these paper squares normally varies between 40 and 60 micrograms, but because of failures in the production system, some squares contain none at all while others have been found that contain several hundred micrograms of the drug.

Sheets of translucent yellow gelatine impregnated with LSD are seen occasionally. The sheets are usually printed with a grid of cutting lines to enable them to be divided easily into 5-mm squares. These gelatine sheets are known as 'windows'.

Small tablets of inert material that have been impregnated with LSD are also available. These tablets are known as 'microdots' or 'dots'. They are very small, most examples being no more than 2 or 3mm in diameter. They are available in a wide variety of colours, the colour being simply the result of vegetable dyes added to the tablet mix.

Special note

At regular intervals over the past 20 years or so, documents have turned up across Britain, the USA and Canada with titles such as 'Drug-laced tattoos and transfers'. These documents are all very similar in wording and usually come to people's attention as a result of being circulated to parents and children by well-meaning schools and community groups.

The documents, of which some examples found in the UK claim to be a Metropolitan Police warning, draw attention to the sale to children of tattoos or transfers that contain LSD. The document goes on to describe the drug-laced tattoos as being called 'Blue Star' or 'Red Pyramid'. It also describes others as having pictures printed on them. The reader is asked at three different points in the document to pass on the information to other parents and children and to 'feel free to reproduce this article and distribute it within your community'.

We have made extensive enquiries but without success, to trace the source of this document. The National Drugs Intelligence Unit (NDIU) at New Scotland Yard in the UK has made its own enquiries and also drawn a blank.

The NDIU makes the point strongly that enquiries within the UK and abroad have failed to turn up any examples of such drug-laced tattoos or transfers or a child affected by one. Common sense would dictate that if they existed, we would have seen an example by now.

The history of the document appears to be as follows. It was first seen in Canada more than 20 years ago. Early examples that we saw some years ago had an American feel to the wording, although this has disappeared in later UK versions. It next came to prominence by being circulated among families of the British Army stationed on the Rhine in Germany. It then seemed to get into the international email system. Many companies run 'notice boards' within their email systems that can be used by employees to advertise articles for sale, local events and other matters of interest. For several years now, this has been the apparent channel through which the document circulates. It is then picked up and printed out by some employees and brought to the notice of a school or community group for further copying and distribution.

This document has become an international electronic chain letter, the circulation of which to parents and children often results in panic and a flood of enquiries to the police and the various drug agencies.

Much of what is said in the document is a mixture of half-truths about LSD and its methods of use but also complete nonsense. Anyone coming across such a warning leaflet or poster is advised to destroy it. A search of the Internet will reveal countless examples of what has now acquired the status of an urban myth.

Marketing

All of the forms of LSD are sold by the dose, with reductions available for buying in bulk.

Cost

The street price of LSD is now at its lowest ever level. Prices for the paper trips vary from £1 to £5; gelatine windows and microdots attract a slightly higher price because of their rarity. This represents an enormous drop in price since the drug was last in vogue during the 1960s. In those days, a single paper square often cost as much as £5, which in today's values would be in excess of £25. This reduction in price is a reflection of the large quantities of LSD currently available on the streets and places the drug well within the reach of even the youngest potential customers.

Legal position

LSD is a class A, schedule 1 controlled substance under the Misuse of Drugs Act 1971. Offences involving it attract the following penalties:

- *Possession for personal use:* the possession of any amount of LSD for personal use is punishable on indictment by a maximum sentence of seven years' imprisonment plus an unlimited fine.

- *Possession with intent to supply*: possession of LSD with intent to supply the drug by sale or gift to another person is punishable on indictment with a maximum sentence of life imprisonment, plus an unlimited fine, plus seizure of all drug-related assets.

- *Supplying*: as for possession with intent to supply.

- *Importation*: as for possession with intent to supply.

The position of LSD within schedule 1 indicates that it has no current medical use.

Methods of use

LSD is normally taken orally by placing the paper square or small pill in the mouth or in a drink. The gelatine squares are normally placed under the eyelid so that the blood vessels of the eye absorb the drug, this practice being known as 'looking through the window'.

Effects of use

The level of dosage has shown a considerable reduction over the years. When LSD first became a popular street drug in the 1960s, it was usual for the paper squares to contain between 120 and 150 micrograms of the drug. This meant that the effects of the drug were very intense and precluded the user from being involved in any other activity. Today's users wish to take the drug while engaging in other social activities, such as raves and parties. As a result, the general dosage level has declined considerably, most doses containing levels of between 40 and 60 micrograms.

The physical effects of taking LSD are very slight. Normally, the pupils of the eyes dilate (widen), blood-sugar levels increase and blood pressure and pulse rate increase slightly.

It is the psychological effects that the user is seeking, however. LSD has a powerful effect on the brain, which becomes apparent about 30–40 minutes after taking the drug. The user will go through a period in which their perception of the world around them begins to become distorted. The colours of objects change, light and sound levels rise and fall, and some tactile sensations occur. This distortion increases steadily over the course of the next 30 minutes or so, until the user reaches the stage at which the full effects are experienced. At this stage, a full state of hallucination or 'tripping' will become established, in which the user is assailed by a range of realistic visions and sensations. Many users see strange creatures or extreme alterations in the forms of people and objects around them; some users experience these changes happening to their own bodies. The colours, shapes and natures of everyday objects may change so dramatically that the 'tripper' feels that they have entered a completely new world. Many but not all users are able to remain aware of their true identities throughout the hallucination and will know that what they are seeing and feeling is only a false drug-induced reality. The nature of the trip may be very pleasant, or it may be neutral, unpleasant or even totally terrifying. It could be the person's worst nightmare brought to life. The degree of alteration to perception that the user experiences will depend on several factors: the dose of the drug taken, their previous experience of the drug, and some personal factors that are, as yet, little understood. The nature of the hallucination will depend largely on the mood of the person when they use it. This mood is known to users as the 'mindset' or simply the 'set'. A person who takes the drug when they are in a good frame of mind and in congenial and relaxed circumstances and environment is more likely to experience a 'good trip'. A person who takes the drug when they are unhappy, under stress, depressed, or in circumstances or environments that are stressful is more likely to have a much more unpleasant experience.

The duration of the hallucinatory effects of LSD is difficult to predict and can vary between 6 and 24 hours. The duration does not seem to be affected by any particular factors and can be quite random.

As the effects begin to fade, the user normally experiences a period of tiredness and disorientation for several hours. A reasonable period of sleep will usually return the user to normal; however, it often takes a considerable length of time to clear any unpleasant images from the mind.

Adverse effects

The physical effects of LSD carry little risk for the user. However, the state of hallucination can be extremely intense and so real that the user puts themselves at risk of becoming involved in a dangerous accident. During a 'bad trip', it is not uncommon for users to try to escape from the frightening apparitions around them by running away, and many have suffered serious injury or death by running across roads or climbing out of windows. Some users lose touch with reality during particularly powerful trips and attempt impossible feats that place them in danger. Many deaths have occurred in users who thought that they could fly and launched themselves off high balconies or out of windows. Other users have believed they could breathe under water and tried to do so with fatal consequences. Others have attempted to physically stop oncoming traffic by standing in the path of motor vehicles.

There is no known antidote to LSD, and anyone dealing with a user who is under the influence of the drug can do little else but keep them from harming themselves and to keep reassuring them that what they are experiencing is not real and only the result of the drug.

Another major problem with LSD use is the likelihood of the user experiencing a rerun of the hallucinatory state long after use. These reruns or flashbacks can occur weeks, months or even years after the person has stopped using the drug. They are generally of a shorter duration than the original trip, but they can be just as intense and are often unpleasant. They may occur at a most inappropriate moment, such as when the person is driving a car, operating machinery, or performing a delicate task that requires great concentration. Imagine the possible results of a surgeon who used LSD in their youth suffering a flashback while operating on a patient. Some recent research suggests that if cannabis is taken after a period of LSD use, then the likelihood of flashbacks is increased dramatically.

In the long term, most LSD users suffer little in the way of permanent harm, but the action of LSD on the brain is little understood and in some cases it has been known to bring latent mental disorders to the surface. In a small number of people, it may even contribute to the onset of psychiatric illness.

Tolerance potential

Tolerance to LSD develops quickly if the drug is used repeatedly over a short period. This tolerance rises to the point where the user gets very little effect from their normal dose, and simply increasing the dose will seldom achieve the required degree of effect. This tolerance fades rapidly if the user abstains from the drug for a week or so. This pattern of use is well-understood by regular users, and they will build periods of rest or abstinence into their LSD use. If they wish to use the drug at a particular time or venue or with particular people, then they will ensure that they have cleared their tolerance so as to achieve the highest level of effect at the right time.

Habituation potential

LSD does not produce any physical dependence. Most users will not experience any psychological dependence either, but a few people may feel unable to enjoy their lives without the added spice of LSD use.

Withdrawal effects

There are no physical withdrawal effects from LSD, even after prolonged use. Most users will not suffer psychological effects either. Some users will need to reorganise their lives in order to avoid situations in which they had become accustomed to taking the drug, so as to avoid the temptation to reuse.

Overdose potential

It is not thought to be possible to overdose fatally on LSD. Even quite heavy doses do not produce dangerous physical reactions.

Street names

LSD: acid

LSD-impregnated paper squares: trips, tabs, blotters; there are hundreds of different printed designs, each with its own name, for example Bart Simpson, smiley faces, Batman, Superman, the Flintstones, 101 Dalmations

LSD-impregnated gelatine squares: windows

Small LSD tablets: microdots, dots, micros

Slang associated with use

Tripping, dropping acid – Using LSD

Looking through the window – Placing a gelatine square impregnated with LSD under the eyelid

Trip – Hallucination

Good trip – Pleasant hallucination

Bad trip – Unpleasant or frightening hallucination

Mindset, set – Mood of the user at the time of use

Acid head, psychonaut – LSD user

Flashback – Rerun of a previous trip without further use of LSD

LSD: benefits and drawbacks

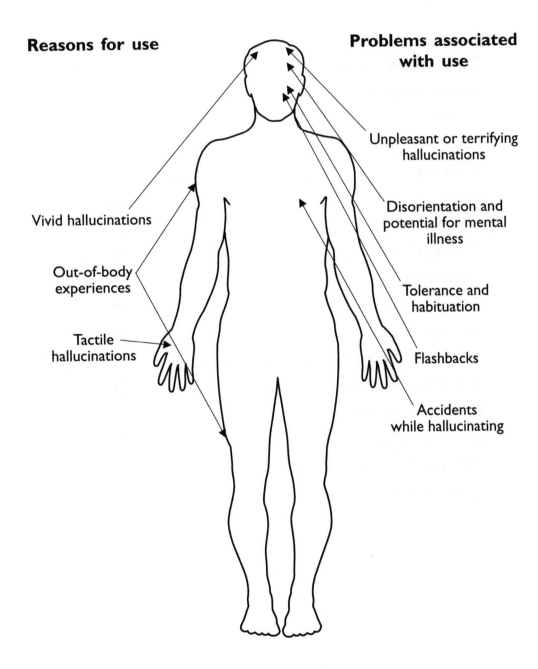

Reasons for use

Vivid hallucinations

Out-of-body experiences

Tactile hallucinations

Problems associated with use

Unpleasant or terrifying hallucinations

Disorientation and potential for mental illness

Tolerance and habituation

Flashbacks

Accidents while hallucinating

Ecstasy (methylenedioxymethamphetamine, MDMA)

Ecstasy: quick reference guide

Source

A totally synthetic product, similar to amphetamine but with hallucinogenic properties.

Forms and appearance

Commonly found in tablets and (much more rarely) capsules in a wide range of colours, sizes and shapes. Very occasionally seen as powders of various colours.

Marketing

The tablets are sold singly. The powder, when available, is sold by the fraction of a gram. Major outlets for sales are the rave and dance club scenes, although it is also commonly available from street dealers.

Cost

Ecstasy can cost between £5 and £10 if bought as single doses, but, as with most other drugs, discounts are available for bulk purchases. Bought in quantity, the price can fall as low as £3 per dose. There is no established price for the powder form due to its rarity.

Legal position

Ecstasy is a class A, schedule 1 controlled substance under the Misuse of Drugs Act 1971.

Methods of use

Ecstasy is taken orally, but recently some users have injected crushed and dissolved tablets.

Effects of use

Feelings of euphoria, sociability, empathy to others, increased sexual arousal, increased energy, changes in perception of surroundings.

Adverse effects

Ecstasy use may cause mood swings and irritability, long-term depression, nausea and vomiting, overheating (hyperthermia), high blood pressure, dehydration, convulsions and sudden death.

Tolerance potential

Tolerance develops with repeated use.

Habituation potential

There is little evidence of any physical habituation to ecstasy, but many users develop a low-level psychological dependence. Other drugs used as adulterants in the manufacture of ecstasy may cause habituation or addiction.

Withdrawal effects

Ecstasy causes no physical problems when use ceases, but some users will suffer anxiety, mood swings, irritability and depression.

Overdose potential

Overdose can lead to coma and death.

Ecstasy: in-depth guide

Source

Ecstasy is a completely synthetic hallucinogenic form of amphetamine. It was first synthesised in Germany in 1910 and patented by a German chemist as an appetite suppressant in 1914. The drug failed to find financial backing and was never marketed commercially. Military authorities in several countries showed an interest in the drug, and a number of experiments were carried out in order to assess its value as a stimulant and mood enhancer for soldiers engaged in physically strenuous and dangerous activities. It was considered as a possible chemical alternative to the traditional tot of rum. These experiments came to little, but for a short time the drug was used in mental hospitals as a treatment for certain psychiatric disorders. The level of side effects proved to be high, and the drug again fell into disuse. It was then forgotten for many years until it next came to light in the USA. During the early 1970s, ecstasy was experimented with as an aid to psychotherapy and to put people into a relaxed frame of mind during counselling sessions. The level of side effects was still too high, and the US health authorities banned its use in medicine.

During this same period, the drug began to appear on the streets of the USA as a drug that seemed to offer the combined effects of amphetamine and LSD. It was at this stage that it acquired the name 'ecstasy', a name that seemed to capture the effects that users were seeking. This name has now become accepted universally, with all other street names used merely to describe the different forms of the drug. It reached the UK during the late 1980s and established itself rapidly as the drug of choice for people involved in the 'acid house' music craze. As this evolved into the 'pay party', rave and dance club scene, the drug moved with it; along with LSD, ecstasy is now connected very firmly with young people who are part of the commercial dance scene. So close is this association that ecstasy is known as a 'dance drug'.

Forms and appearance

Ecstasy in its pure form is seen as a white powder. However, it is impossible to give a definite description of the drug in tablet or capsule form. It is not manufactured commercially anywhere, and the form that it takes on the streets is determined by whoever manufactures it. The colour depends on whether any colouring agents have been added. Vegetable dyes are often added to produce a wide range of colours.

The size and shape of the tablet forms depend on the machines used to produce them; any imprints on the tablets result from the different formers used (see Figure 5.2).

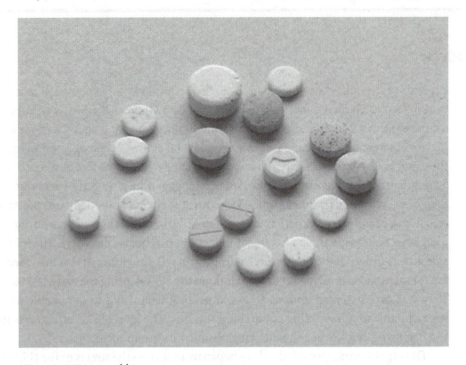

Figure 5.2 Ecstasy tablets

At least 30 different forms of ecstasy tablet are available on the streets and in dance clubs and raves. Some forms are much more popular than others, such as 'Mitsubishis' or 'mitzis', which are small white tablets imprinted with a Mitsubishi car symbol. Another small white form, often containing minute specks of other colours, is known as 'Adam' or 'Eve'. Many forms have images imprinted on the tablet surface. Two popular tablets are imprinted with a rather crude image of a bird, known as a 'dove', 'love dove' or 'rocking robin', and a euro symbol, known simply as a 'euro' or 'dollar'.

Although tablets now appear to be the most common form of ecstasy available, there are also a number of capsule forms. It is fairly easy to obtain empty medicinal capsules as they can be purchased legally or obtained by theft from medical manufacturers. It is possible to purchase empty gelatine capsules from suppliers of alternative medicines in order to make up one's own herbal medicines. Many cases have occurred in which ecstasy has been placed in the capsules of genuine medical preparations from which the original contents have been emptied.

This means that ecstasy can be produced in capsules of all sorts of sizes and colours. In the past, popular forms included a red and black capsule called 'Dennis the menace', named after the red and black tee-shirt worn by the comic-book character; a red and yellow capsule called 'rhubarb and custard'; and red-and-white and blue-and-white capsules called 'United' and 'City', respectively, after certain English football teams.

This variation in form and colour has led to a large trade in what are known on the streets as 'snidey drugs', substances that are sold falsely as particular drugs. A vast range of products are sold to young people as ecstasy, with most snidey drugs being genuine tablets and capsules originally intended for other uses. Various pain-relieving tablets are sold that have been coloured by dipping them in vegetable dye or even by spraying them with car paint. The brown 'disco burger' form of ecstasy is replicated almost perfectly by a brand of dog-worming tablet, and many hundreds of these are sold in dance clubs by dealers who make their escape before the fairly predictable results of taking such a preparation are experienced by their customers. The 'Dennis the menace' capsule is identical to a particular form of powerful antibiotic. Many people are allergic to antibiotics, with reactions that vary from the uncomfortable to the extremely dangerous, and many have discovered that they were sold powerful antibiotics when they thought they were buying ecstasy. Other drugs that have been passed off as ecstasy include hormone replacement therapy (HRT) medication, contraceptive pills, tranquillisers and, in one recent case known to the authors, a pessary for the vaginal condition thrush.

In many cases, the drug in the capsule will be far from pure. Despite the relatively simple process involved in producing ecstasy, it is not uncommon for amphetamine or LSD, or a combination of both, to be added to bulk out the filling. A laboratory test is required before a definitive identification of any tablet or capsule as ecstasy can be made.

Marketing

The major consumers of ecstasy are young people who frequent dance and rave clubs. Many of these establishments make a genuine effort to exclude the drug from their premises, but many cases have occurred in which club staff have been taking a percentage of the profits made by the dealers, whom they allow to operate freely within the club. Even in clubs where care is taken to exclude dealers, customers may simply buy their ecstasy from a dealer operating on the street outside and take it before they enter the club. Ecstasy is also available in a great number of public houses, cafes and other places frequented by young people. Supplies of ecstasy in all its forms can be obtained from a number of websites dedicated to the dance-drug scene.

Cost

Tablets and capsules of ecstasy are usually sold for between £5 and £10. The price depends a great deal on the type of customer. If the clients of a particular venue are well off, then the price may be high; however, if they are poorer, the drug will be cheaper. The production costs of ecstasy are very low, and high profits can be made even when selling the drug at lower prices. Bulk buying could bring the price down to as little as £3 per tablet.

There is no established market for ecstasy in powder form and, therefore, no established price.

Legal position

Ecstasy is a class A, schedule 1 controlled substance under the Misuse of Drugs Act 1971. Offences involving it attract the following penalties:

- *Possession for personal use*: the possession of any amount of ecstasy for personal use is punishable on indictment by a maximum sentence of seven years' imprisonment plus an unlimited fine.

- *Possession with intent to supply*: possession of ecstasy with intent to supply the drug by sale or gift to another person is punishable on indictment with a maximum sentence of life imprisonment, plus an unlimited fine, plus seizure of all drug-related assets.

- *Supplying*: as for possession with intent to supply.

- *Importation*: as for possession with intent to supply.

The position of ecstasy within schedule 1 indicates that it has no medical use.

Methods of use

Ecstasy is most commonly taken orally, the user simply swallowing the tablet or capsule. This gives it a real advantage over most other drugs, as no paraphernalia is needed, thus saving time and effort and meaning that there is no incriminating evidence to be discovered in the possession of the user. There is a reluctance on the part of many people to use drugs in smoking or injecting form; a drug that can simply be swallowed in the form of a tablet or capsule raises no such reluctance.

There have been some examples of users experimenting with ecstasy by injecting it or snorting it up the nose, but these methods are still rare and show little sign of becoming popular with the vast majority of ecstasy users.

Effects of use

For most users, ecstasy provides a feeling of euphoria and of being at peace with the world, together with an increase in confidence and empathy towards other people. At its best, its effects can include a feeling of great warmth and love to those around the user. Ecstasy dilates the pupils, making the user look more attractive to others. Being an amphetamine derivative, ecstasy also provides the user with feelings of energy and freedom from hunger, allowing them to dance for long periods without the need to stop for rest or food. It is the combination of these effects, which may last for between two and six hours, that make the drug so attractive for use within the party and dance club scene.

Ecstasy is mildly hallucinogenic at normal doses. These hallucinations are of a much lower level than those experienced with LSD and comprise mostly subtle changes in the user's perception of their surroundings rather than the powerful visual and auditory effects associated with LSD. The user's senses may also be affected, so that sound, colour and touch seem enhanced. At higher doses, the hallucinogenic effects can rise to a greater level and begin to rival those of LSD.

Adverse effects

Several tragic cases in which ecstasy has led to sudden death have brought the drug into prominence. The fact that some of these cases have involved very young people on the thresholds of their lives has made them even more poignant. Ecstasy is one of the few street drugs that has the power to cause death in such a sudden and often very distressing way. Many other drugs can lead to eventual death or even sudden death when used in overdose, but the use of ecstasy can be very much a case of playing Russian roulette. The causes of death can vary, but none appears to be particularly dose-related. It is just as possible to suffer sudden death after taking what would be considered a 'normal' street dose of the drug as it would be following a much higher dose. This danger is not related to the user's previous experience of the drug; the fact that a person has used ecstasy on several previous occasions without mishap is no protection. A sudden adverse reaction can happen to both experienced and first-time users.

Most of the sudden deaths associated with ecstasy seem to have been caused by two major effects of the drug. The first, and the rarest, is the formation of small clots within the blood system. These clots can migrate around the body until they lodge within the narrowest of the blood vessels. Many of these blood vessels are found in the brain; a clot lodging there can have disastrous results, leading to collapse and death in a very short time.

The reaction that seems to cause the highest number of deaths, however, is the ability of ecstasy to raise the body temperature alarmingly and to limit its ability to dissipate the heat. The exact mechanism of this is little understood, but it would appear that the drug has an effect on the hypothalamus, the part of the brain that controls temperature. Along with this rise in temperature, the user is often involved in a prolonged session of energetic dancing in a crowded and very hot club, so the body temperature rises to such an extent that the user may develop hyperthermia, at which point the user is at risk from potential convulsions and collapse. These can and often do lead to respiratory and cardiac failure and death.

The heat will also cause profuse sweating and the user may become dehydrated in the extreme. Some dance or rave clubs recognise that their clients are likely to use ecstasy and provide cool rooms away from the dance area – 'chill-out rooms' – where clients can rest, rehydrate with cold non-alcoholic drinks and cool down. However, some unscrupulous clubs provide no such rooms and restrict access to water by closing off the taps in the toilets, in an attempt to maximise profits from a vulnerable clientele by making them pay for water. Many unscrupulous club owners will ruthlessly exploit young users by charging re-entry fees to those who are forced to go outside to cool down and then by selling the drinks needed to prevent dehydration at exorbitant prices. It is not uncommon to see tap water sold at several pounds per pint!

Drinking large quantities of water in an attempt to rehydrate carries its own risks. Excessive consumption of water can lead to a condition known as hyponatreamia or 'water intoxication' which, put as its simplest, is the opposite of dehydration. The excessive water intake leads to a significant increase in the volume of blood plasma. This, accompanied by the loss of salts from the bloodstream as a result of sweating, can seriously impair the electrolytic balance of the blood. Symptoms of this condition can include apathy, confusion, nausea and fatigue. If untreated, hyponatreamia can lead to coma and even death. In extreme cases the excess water can be absorbed by the tissues of the brain causing it to swell. Such swelling can lead to a life-threatening condition known as brain herniation, where the swollen brain comes into cantact with the inside of the skull causing an increase in intracranial pressure and displacement of brain tissue.

These dramatic and potentially fatal side effects of ecstasy are not the only problems that the drug can bring. Many users complain of nausea, muscle pain and severe headaches. As the effects of the drug fade, users may experience a feeling of being drained of both energy and emotion.

Prolonged or heavy use of ecstasy can lead to profound changes in the user's personality. They may become depressed, irritable, suspicious and obsessed with the attitude towards them of others; in extreme cases, they may show violence towards other people.

There is some evidence that the effects of prolonged ecstasy use can lead to permanent changes within the workings of the brain. It is thought that the receptors within the brain that receive serotonin, a chemical that we produce naturally when experiencing pleasure, can be changed in such a way that they become incapable of receiving serotonin. This change is thought to be permanent and suggests that prolonged use of ecstasy can lead to a condition in which the user is incapable of feeling naturally happy and must rely on the drug to provide any happiness.

Research has confirmed that long-term regular use of ecstasy can lead to permanent damage to the kidneys, liver, heart and brain.

Tolerance potential

Tolerance to ecstasy develops with repeated use. Users who take the drug on a regular basis soon find that it fails to provide the degree of effect that they once experienced. This inevitably leads to them increasing the dose that they use. As the drug is normally available in tablet or capsule form, it is possible to increase the dose only by increasing the number of tablets or capsules taken. Thus, a user who increases from one to two tablets is doubling their dose in a single step. Such a large increase can have unpredictable consequences.

Habituation potential

There is little evidence of any physical habituation to ecstasy, although it may occur in people who have used the drug heavily over an extended period.

Many users develop a low-level psychological dependence with prolonged use of ecstasy. Some begin to feel that it is not possible to have a good time and that life begins to seem flat without the drug.

Withdrawal effects

Most ecstasy users experience no physical problems as a result of ceasing their use of the drug. Many regular and heavy users go through a period of anxiety and depression, which may be eased if they are given support, care and, in some cases, medication.

Overdose potential

Excessive doses of ecstasy can lead to collapse, coma, permanent brain damage and death.

Street names

Tablet forms: E, love dove, Mercedes, rocking robin, rabbit, crystal splitter, euro, Mitsubishi, mitzi, bean, pill, dollar

Capsule forms: City, Dennis the menace, rhubarb and custard, United

Slang associated with use

Getting cabbaged – Becoming completely intoxicated by use of the drug and energetic dancing

Chilling out – Allowing the body time to cool down and recover from over-heating

Chill-out room – Area in a rave or club set aside to allow users to chill out

Ecstasy: benefits and drawbacks

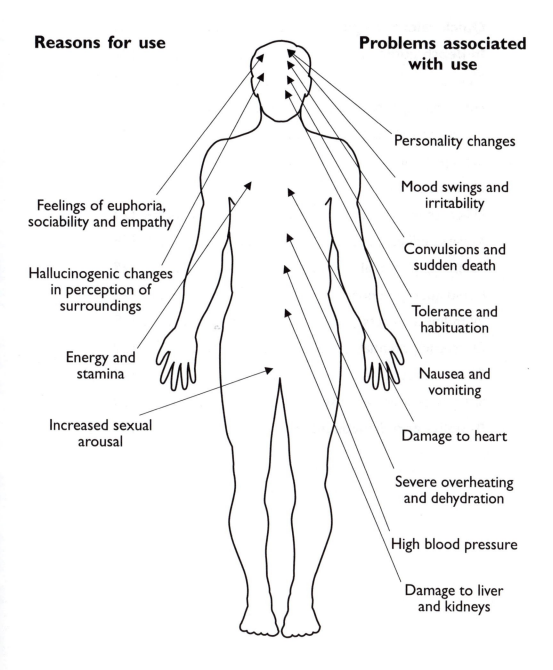

Reasons for use

Feelings of euphoria, sociability and empathy

Hallucinogenic changes in perception of surroundings

Energy and stamina

Increased sexual arousal

Problems associated with use

Personality changes

Mood swings and irritability

Convulsions and sudden death

Tolerance and habituation

Nausea and vomiting

Damage to heart

Severe overheating and dehydration

High blood pressure

Damage to liver and kidneys

Ketamine (ketamine hydrochloride)

Ketamine: quick reference guide

Source

Totally synthetic, rapidly acting, dissociative anaesthetic used in humans (mostly children) and animals. Developed in the 1960s.

Forms and appearance

Has been seen in powder, tablet, capsule, liquid and crystal (after evaporation of liquid form) forms. Medical form seen as vials.

Marketing and cost

Usually sold in the UK in paper wraps of powder for snorting, ranging from £5 to £25 each. Ketamine tablets sell in the UK for around £10 each. Also sold dissolved in plain water or rose water (sometimes imported) for evaporation into crystals or powder.

Legal position

Prescription-only medicine under the Medicines Act 1968, which makes unauthorised supply illegal.

Methods of use

Can be taken orally in tablet or capsule form, or as a powder snorted intranasally. In solution, can be injected intravenously or into the muscle, but this tends to be only when used for medical purposes. Sometimes smoked with other substances.

Effects of use

Can give cocaine-like euphoria. In low doses, acts as a cardiorespiratory stimulant, increasing blood pressure and pulse. Psychological dissociation, hallucinations and near-death and out-of-body experiences may occur.

Adverse effects

Muscle rigidity (catalepsy) may occur, and the user may remain in the same position for some hours. Can cause confusion, slurred speech, distortion to vision, vomiting, loss of muscle coordination, temporary paralysis, memory loss, paranoia and respiratory and cardiac arrest. Flashbacks may occur at a later date.

Tolerance potential

Tolerance develops with continued use.

Habituation potential

Psychological and physical dependence have been noted in chronic users.

Withdrawal effects

None known.

Overdose potential

Like most anaesthetics, excessive administration of the drug can lead to coma and death.

Ketamine: in-depth guide

Source

Ketamine was discovered by Cal Stevens in 1961. It was originally developed for use as a human anaesthetic and was used extensively for this purpose by US forces during the Vietnam War. It is still used today for short-term surgical procedures in humans and animals. In humans, ketamine is used mostly in paediatric practice, as children seem to experience far fewer hallucinations under its influence than adults. Ketamine is manufactured illicitly in facilities worldwide; however, much of the street ketamine seen in the UK is diverted from licit sources supplied to hospitals and veterinary surgeries.

Forms and appearance

As a street drug, ketamine is seen most commonly as a white powder, sometimes crystalline in form, although it has also been known to be offered in tablet and capsule form. For medical use in humans and animals, it is mostly supplied in vials or bottles for injection intravenously or intramuscularly. It has also been found dissolved in rose water that has been imported from Asia for evaporation into its powder/crystal form. As a white-powder street drug, it is easy to mimic and in some cases users may not be acquiring ketamine at all.

Marketing and cost

At present, ketamine does not appear to be used as widely in the UK as other substances linked to the dance and rave scene, but this may change. Like most powder drugs, it can be sold in small paper packages known as 'wraps' or 'deals', usually for snorting. These vary in price greatly and may cost between £5 and £25, depending on the quantity, the purity and where it is being sold. Ketamine in tablet, powder and liquid form can be purchased from a number of websites. A typical website accessed in 2005 offered injectable ketamine in 50ml vials at $20 each, with reductions for bulk orders.

Legal position

In the UK, ketamine is not controlled by the Misuse of Drugs Act 1971; consequently, possession of it is not a criminal offence. It does, however, fall within the scope of the Medicines Act 1968, and as such it is a criminal offence to supply it other than to bona fide medical and veterinary users. Unlawful supply of the drug to another person is punishable by a maximum fine of £5000.

Methods of use

Ketamine powder is most commonly snorted into the nasal cavity (rather like cocaine). A 'normal' dose is considered to be around 60–100mg. As a tablet or capsule, it is usually taken orally; in this form, it may take up to 20 minutes to have any effect. On occasions, ketamine is smoked with tobacco or cannabis. When ketamine is administered by injection in medical or veterinary settings, the effects are seen rapidly, usually in about 30 seconds, but there is little evidence that street users are administering it in this way, especially as they may be affected before the injection is completed.

Effects of use

Ketamine is a 'dissociative anaesthetic'. Under its influence, which can last for three to four hours, users may initially experience a cocaine-like rush and euphoria or mild dream-like feelings with an increase in blood pressure and pulse rate. It has powerful hallucinogenic properties that can affect vision, sense of time and even identity. Many users report out-of-body or even near-death experiences, which for some can be profoundly spiritual. Synaesthesia, in which the user may 'see' sounds and 'hear' colours, may occur. Muscle rigidity (catalepsy) may occur, in which the user feels unable to move from their current position until the drug effect has worn off; as a consequence, the user may be found sitting or lying in one position for the whole duration of the drug experience.

Adverse effects

Ketamine is a powerful anaesthetic. As such, incorrect use can lead to the problems usually associated with such substances, including coma and death through cardiac and respiratory failure. Other lesser conditions can occur, including inadvertent self-injury while under its analgesic (painkilling) effect and interference with speech, vision, attention and ability to learn, even after the drug has been excreted from the body. Paranoia, agitation and aggression have been noted, and flashbacks may occur for 12 months or more following use of ketamine. Effects of very heavy use may not disappear completely for several months or even years. Vomiting and convulsions are not uncommon, so users have to be very careful not to take liquids or solid food before use, as with anaesthetics delivered under medical supervision. Ketamine is also known to have amnesic qualities and therefore has been implicated in some date-rape episodes (see Chapter 11 for more on this subject).

Tolerance potential

As with most drugs, continual use may lead to tolerance, in which the user requires greater amounts of the drug to get the required effect.

Habituation potential

With chronic use of ketamine, a powerful psychological and even physical dependence has been noted in some users.

Withdrawal effects

There are no known withdrawal effects.

Overdose potential

The variable strength of street ketamine makes it very difficult for the user to judge the level of use that could lead to overdose. When taken in excess, ketamine can cause death through cardiac and respiratory failure.

Street names

Special K and vitamin K are common names in the UK. In the USA, ket, jet, super acid, Kit-Kat and cat valium are used widely.

Slang associated with use

Many users report experiencing a 'black hole' or 'K-hole' sensation when using the drug: for some time, they may be in a euphoric or even depressive state while hallucinating, believing that what they are experiencing is real.

Ketamine: benefits and drawbacks

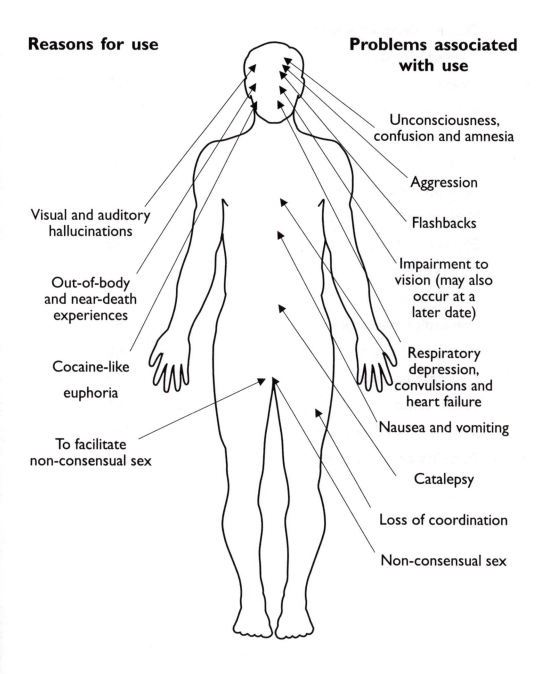

Reasons for use

Visual and auditory hallucinations

Out-of-body and near-death experiences

Cocaine-like euphoria

To facilitate non-consensual sex

Problems associated with use

Unconsciousness, confusion and amnesia

Aggression

Flashbacks

Impairment to vision (may also occur at a later date)

Respiratory depression, convulsions and heart failure

Nausea and vomiting

Catalepsy

Loss of coordination

Non-consensual sex

Hallucinogenic or magic mushrooms

Hallucinogenic or magic mushrooms: quick reference guide

Source

Found growing in woodland, heath and domestic gardens. Most varieties in the UK appear during September and October, the season extending into November if the weather remains mild and frost-free.

Forms and appearance

There are several varieties of hallucinogenic mushroom, all very different in appearance. Identification of them can be very difficult, and mistakes are common. Details of the main varieties are given in the in-depth guide.

Marketing

Many users of hallucinogenic mushrooms pick their own when they are in season. Out of season, they are available in dried or, occasionally, frozen form. The dried forms are normally sold in bags containing between 50 and 60 smaller mushrooms. Availability varies from one area to another and will be affected by the prevailing weather conditions during the previous growing season.

Cost

A bag of 50 or 60 dried hallucinogenic mushrooms sells for around £5.

Legal position

Since the implementation of the Drugs Act 2005, hallucinogenic mushrooms of the genus Psilocybe, whether fresh or prepared, are Class A, Schedule 1, controlled substances under the Misuse of Drugs Act 1971.

Methods of use

Hallucinogenic mushrooms normally are eaten. If obtained fresh, they may be eaten raw or after cooking. Dried varieties are usually infused in boiling water to make a drink. Rarely, users have been known to inject infusions of the mushrooms.

Effects of use

Feelings of euphoria, high spirits and wellbeing, bouts of laughter and giggling, visual and auditory hallucinations.

Adverse effects

Some users suffer bouts of dizziness and nausea. There is the possibility of long-term mental health problems. The major danger lies in consuming a poisonous variety of mushroom by mistake.

Tolerance potential

Tolerance develops rapidly with continued use.

Habituation potential

There is little evidence of any marked physical or psychological dependence developing.

Withdrawal effects

It is very rare for users of hallucinogenic mushrooms to experience any problems on ceasing to use the drug.

Overdose potential

The potential for overdose is low because of the large quantities of mushrooms that the user would need to consume in order to overdose.

Hallucinogenic or magic mushrooms: in-depth guide

Source

Naturally occurring fungi of the genera *Psilocybe* and *Amanita* provide the varieties that are commonly called magic mushrooms. The two most commonly abused are *Psilocybe semilanceata*, known as liberty cap, and *Amanita muscaria*, known as fly agaric.

The liberty cap is found in enormous numbers on open grassland, such as pastures, domestic gardens, parks and roadside verges. It prefers well-watered soil with a high nutrient content. It produces the mushroom that we see above ground during September and October. This fruiting season will extend into November if the weather remains mild and frost-free.

The fly agaric is found growing in woodland, often around the roots of trees such as pine, spruce, birch, hazel and beech. It is capable of growing successfully on very poor and infertile soils. The main fruiting season is September, although it can be found much earlier and later if the weather is wet and mild.

The use of various types of mushroom for hallucinogenic purposes has been known for many thousands of years. Extensive use of the mushroom has occurred worldwide, but there is little evidence of such historical use in the UK. In many other northern European countries, complete cultures grew up around the fungi, which were often thought to be endowed with magical and religious properties. In northern Russia, the fly agaric was found in large numbers growing around the roots of birch trees that abounded in forests. Their presence was thought to be a gift from the gods that were believed to inhabit these trees. The collection of the fungi was a right reserved for priests, and their use was often restricted to the wealthy classes.

The human body transforms the active ingredient of the fungus into another substance, which is excreted in the urine. This substance is also hallucinogenic, and stories exist of the poor people of a village, who were not able to acquire the mushroom itself, waiting near the houses of the rich and offering wooden bowls for them to urinate into, in order to drink it and enjoy the same experiences. It was common practice for reindeer herdsmen to save their own urine after consuming fly agarics that they collected on their travels and then to feed it to their lead reindeer. So accustomed did these animals become to the sensations that the urine gave them that it was only necessary for the herdsman to appear on the snow fields in the morning and urinate on the ground for the lead animals to rush towards them in order to eat the urine-soaked snow and in doing so bring the whole herd together.

Forms and appearance

The liberty cap is the most commonly used magic mushroom in the UK. It is a very small fungus. Its cap is pale creamy yellow or light brown in colour and shaped like a human breast complete with a small 'nipple' in the centre. The cap measures 5–15mm in diameter across. The stalk of the mushroom is very thin and fragile and measures 2–5cm in length. When seen out of the fruiting season, these mushrooms almost always are in dried form. When dried, the mushroom turns a dark brown to black colour and loses much of its shape. It shrivels up and becomes almost indistinguishable from any other small dried mushroom (see Figure 5.3).

Figure 5.3 Dried magic mushrooms

Very rarely, light-brown tablets made from dried and crushed liberty caps have been seen, measuring about 8mm across. These tablets have usually been imported from continental Europe. A number of websites advertise capsules of powdered liberty cap for sale.

The fly agaric is used much less commonly than the liberty cap. It is a larger fungus, the cap growing to 30cm in diameter and the thick stalk measuring 9–40cm in height. The cap has a very distinctive appearance: when young, its surface is a bright red, almost scarlet colour, which fades to reddish yellow as the cap expands to maturity, and is covered in irregular white spots protruding from its surface. The coloured part of the cap is sticky with an exuded substance that is poisonous to insects. Beneath the cap is a large frill of creamy white gills. The fly agaric is often illustrated in cartoons and is used in plaster or concrete form to decorate gardens. When prepared for use outside of the fruiting season, it is usually cut up into pieces measuring about 3cm across before drying. After being dried, the red colour is lost and the fungi is seen as rather hard brown irregular lumps that are indistinguishable from many other varieties of large fungi.

Marketing

Many users of magic mushrooms pick their own during the fruiting season. Some users pick more than they need immediately and dry the surplus for later use. Other collectors harvest in very large quantities and dry them for sale. Small liberty caps are commonly sold in plastic bags containing between 50 and 60 mushrooms.

The fly agaric is available much more rarely, and there is no established market for it. Users who wish to experiment with this fungus will obtain an amount that they think is sufficient and then try out different doses until they achieve the result they want.

The supply of magic mushrooms can be irregular. Following a prolonged warm and damp autumn, there may be a glut of them and ample supplies of the dried forms may be available for months afterwards. If the fruiting season has been affected by cold and dry weather, they may not be available at all. A large number of websites are dedicated to the hallucinogenic mushroom and offer supplies of fresh and preserved mushrooms.

Cost

A bag of 50–60 dried liberty cap mushrooms will cost about £5. There is no established market and no set price for fly agaric mushrooms.

Legal position

In the UK no legal controls are applicable to use of the Fly Agaric mushroom. However, since the implementation of the Drugs Act 2005 the possession of all mushrooms of the genus Psilocybe is now illegal under the Misuse of Drugs Act 1971 as Class A, Schedule 1, controlled substances. The following penalties apply:

- *Possession for personal use:* the possession of any amount of the *Psilocybe* mushrooms for personal use is punishable on indictment by a maximum sentence of seven years' imprisonment plus an unlimited fine.

- *Possession with intent to supply:* possession of *Psilocybe* mushrooms with intent to supply them by sale or gift to another person is punishable on indictment with a maximum sentence of life imprisonment, plus an unlimited fine, plus seizure of all drug-related assets.

- *Supplying:* as for possession with intent to supply.

- *Importation:* as for possession with intent to supply.

It is worth noting that in the UK, the picking of magic mushrooms on land without the land owner's permission could result in a charge under the Theft Act. All wild fungi growing in the UK are protected by conservation legislation, and offences under this legislation may also be committed by the picker.

Methods of use

Magic mushrooms are commonly taken orally. The fresh or dried forms can be eaten raw or cooked in some way. We have known both fresh and dried mushrooms to be added to quiches, omelettes, stews and pancakes and even to be eaten on toast. They may also be infused in boiling water to make a sort of soupy tea, which is then drunk. The tablet forms are also taken orally.

Occasionally, the dried form of the mushroom is mixed with tobacco or cannabis and smoked in hand-rolled cigarettes or pipes. A small number of users have tried liquidising mushrooms in a domestic food processor, straining the resultant liquid and then injecting it.

Effects of use

The effects of magic mushrooms vary a great deal. The exact amount of active ingredient in each mushroom is impossible to determine, except in a laboratory, and so the dosage is difficult to get right. A typical dose is 20–30 small liberty cap mushrooms and $100–150cm^2$ of the much larger fly agaric.

The effects begin some 20 minutes or so after consumption and last for between six and eight hours. Younger users seem to feel the onset of effects more quickly than older users. The mood or 'mindset' of the user before consumption will play a great part in determining what effects are achieved. Most users will experience feelings of euphoria and happiness. Many begin to giggle, often uncontrollably, become excitable and animated, and may be unable to keep still. Users also experience a mild level of visual and auditory hallucination. The 'trips' achieved with magic mushrooms are usually of a lower level than those achieved with LSD, but they are of a similar nature. They may range from mild distortion of the shape and colour of objects and people, to the appearance of strange shapes, objects and creatures. The user may also experience some tactile hallucinations, during which they may feel that insects are crawling all over them or that they are dissolving or changing shape. These hallucinations will be of much shorter duration than those created by LSD. The flashbacks common with LSD are very rare with magic mushrooms.

Adverse effects

Magic mushrooms sometimes cause bouts of nausea and dizziness, particularly in first-time users. This can often lead to the user becoming very concerned that they have eaten a poisonous variety by mistake and will therefore alter their state of mind just as they are entering the hallucinatory phase. This will usually guarantee that they have an unpleasant or even frightening experience.

As with all mind-altering substances, there is always the danger of bringing to the surface latent mental illness within the user. Many cases have occurred in which regular users of magic mushrooms have become depressed or suffered delusions and required inpatient treatment in a psychiatric hospital.

The main danger with the use of magic mushrooms lies in using the wrong variety. This cannot be stressed too strongly. It is difficult enough to be sure of what you are getting when the mushrooms are fresh, let alone when a user is buying them in dried form. It would require careful study by a fungi expert to identify correctly the little brown wisps that are all that is left of the liberty cap after drying. It is not uncommon for bags of so-called magic mushrooms offered for sale to contain many other varieties than those that the user expects. These will have been added either by mistake on the part of the collector or purposefully by the dealer in order to bulk out shortages of the correct fungus. There are many varieties of mushroom that are superficially similar to the hallucinogenic types but that contain very powerful poisons. This is particularly true of the fly agaric, a fungus that has highly poisonous relatives within its genus. Some of the poisons contained within fungi will cause mild discomfort, sickness and diarrhoea, while others can cause respiratory arrest, collapse, coma and death.

Tolerance potential

Tolerance develops very rapidly with continued use of magic mushrooms. The dosage required to achieve the desired effects rises quickly to such a point that it becomes very difficult to achieve anything at all. Users are aware of this and will rest for a week or so following a bout of mushroom use. This restores their tolerance level to normal and they can then make effective use of the drug again. Users of mushrooms develop a cross-tolerance to LSD, and switching to that drug will achieve nothing.

Habituation potential

Because of the rapid development of a high tolerance to mushrooms, to the point where no effects are achieved, it is rare for anyone to keep on taking the drug over an extended period of time. There seems to be little danger of the user developing marked physical or psychological dependence on the drug.

Withdrawal effects

Once a user stops using magic mushrooms, they will experience little in the way of withdrawal effects. Some may find their lives a little flat and will have to devise other ways of getting enjoyment and pleasure, but with a little help and support they should succeed in this.

Overdose potential

The potential for overdose of genuine magic mushrooms is low due to the very large quantities of the fungi that the user would need to obtain and consume. The overdose potential from other varieties of more dangerous fungi is very high. Some of the poisonous varieties require minute amounts to be consumed in order to cause very real problems.

Street names

Hallucinogenic mushrooms: shrooms, mushies, magics

Varieties of mushroom: fly agaric, liberty cap

Slang associated with use

None known.

Hallucinogenic or magic mushrooms: benefits and drawbacks

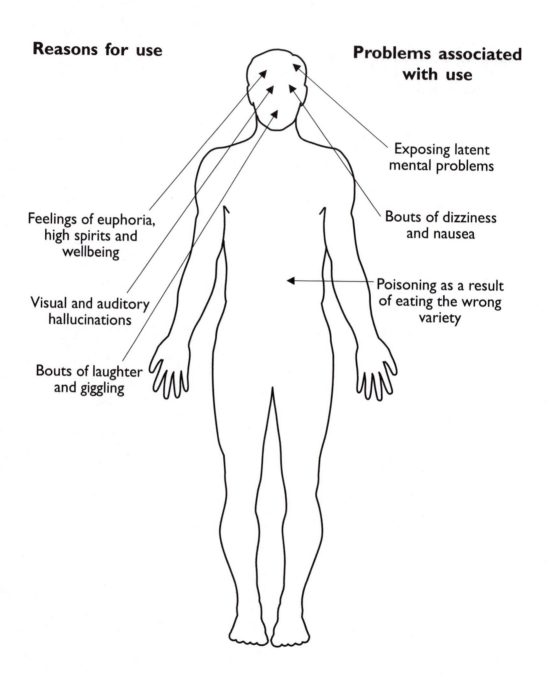

Reasons for use

Feelings of euphoria, high spirits and wellbeing

Visual and auditory hallucinations

Bouts of laughter and giggling

Problems associated with use

Exposing latent mental problems

Bouts of dizziness and nausea

Poisoning as a result of eating the wrong variety

Chapter 6

Opiates

Heroin (diamorphine)

Heroin: quick reference guide

Source

Produced by chemical processes from raw opium collected from the opium poppy.

Forms and appearance

In its pure pharmaceutical form, heroin is a pure-white fine-grained powder. In its street forms, it is coarser and varies in colour from a pinkish cream to dark brown.

Marketing

Heroin is sold by the fraction of a gram, commonly contained in a paper wrap or press-seal plastic bag.

Cost

Price varies according to availability and quality, from £40 to £90 per gram.

Legal position

Heroin is a class A, schedule 2 controlled substance under the Misuse of Drugs Act 1971.

Methods of use

Heroin is most commonly smoked or injected. It can also be sniffed into the nose or taken orally.

Effects of use

Feelings of euphoria, inner peace and freedom from fear, worry, pain, hunger and cold.

Adverse effects

Depressed breathing, severe constipation, nausea and vomiting are common. Also loss of body condition and a lowering of general health, with some effect on the immune system. Injecting can cause vein collapse and ulceration, and there is a risk of serious illness through the use of infected needles.

Tolerance potential

Tolerance to heroin develops rapidly with continued use.

Habituation potential

Continued heroin use can lead to severe physical and psychological dependence.

Overdose potential

Overdose of heroin can lead to coma and death.

Heroin: in-depth guide

Source

Heroin is produced by chemical processing of raw opium. Opium is a natural product obtained from certain varieties of poppy, in particular the oriental opium poppy, *Papaver somniferum*. This is a much larger plant than the familiar UK hedgerow poppy; it produces sizeable flowers, which may be red, white or purple in colour. The plant does not grow well in the UK, as it does not flourish in the climate, preferring higher temperatures and light levels. In particularly warm summers, attempts may be made to cultivate *Papaver somniferum* in the UK, but these produce such small amounts of opium that they play no part in the heroin trade.

The plant is cultivated in vast quantities in two distinct areas of the world. One area is centered on the 'Golden Triangle' countries of Thailand, Laos and Myanmar (formerly Burma), but also includes parts of such countries as China, Afghanistan, Thailand, Pakistan, northern India and Indonesia. The second main area is sometimes called the 'Golden Crescent', which is centred on the eastern Mediterranean and includes Iran, Lebanon, Turkey, Cyprus and Greece. The plant is also cultivated in south-eastern Russia, Central and South America and South Africa, but these are very much smaller players on the international heroin scene.

As the plant matures and the flower is pollinated, a large seedpod begins to swell beneath the fading flower. This pod is green in colour and swells to the size of a small orange. It is segmented internally, with each segment containing many hundreds of minute seeds. The seeds are suspended in milky white, sticky fluid. As the seedpods near maturity, the opium farmer walks along the lines of their poppies and, often using a special knife with three sharp spurs on it, incises a number of cuts in the pod running from top to bottom, with each cut penetrating one of the segments containing the seeds. The pod will then begin to bleed its milky sap through the cuts onto the surface of the pod. The heat of the sun causes the sap to dry to a sticky dark brown material: this is pure raw opium. The plant is revisited at regular intervals and the opium is scraped from the pod into a pouch. The pod is then incised with a number of fresh cuts to different segments and begins to bleed again. This process is repeated until the pod is exhausted of its sap.

The special properties of opium have been recognised for a long time. Archaeological evidence exists in South-East Asia of the use of opium, both in medicine and as a drug for social use, for at least 6000 years. Opium was exported to all the countries of the ancient world.

When used as a painkilling agent in ancient times, opium generally was smoked or dissolved in water or alcohol for drinking. These same methods were also employed by those people who were seeking the many other effects of the substance. Opium is a very powerful drug and induces feelings of peace, euphoria and dreaminess. It drives away emotional and physical pain and hunger, and it makes the user feel at peace with the world. Slowly, the practice of using opium for these effects began to spread out from Asia, and from Roman times onwards its use was an increasingly common phenomenon.

During the first half of the nineteenth century, the active ingredients of raw opium were identified and isolated. Opium contains two very powerful and useful drugs, morphine and codeine, both of which still have their uses in modern medicine. By the end of the nineteenth century, further work with morphine had produced a more powerful version called diamorphine, more commonly known as heroin.

Both morphine and codeine are misused in the UK, but little street trade of these takes place. Heroin has displaced both of these to become the leading opiate street drug.

Forms and appearance

Heroin produced for pharmaceutical use is normally a pure-white fine powder. It is also seen in tablet form and in ampoules of clear injectable liquid. These pharmaceutical forms are occasionally seen on the streets when they have been obtained by theft from doctors' surgeries or pharmacies. This is very rare due to the security precautions that are employed to protect the legally held drugs. The heroin that we see sold as a street drug usually is in the form of a coarse powder, varying in colour from a creamy, almost pinky white, through various shades of brown, to a dark coffee colour (see Figure 6.1). The degree of reddish brown colour depends on the process used to produce the drug. Generally speaking, the lighter the shade of brown, the better the quality of the heroin. Street samples of the drug are usually around 20 per cent pure. The remainder will be made up from impurities resulting from the processing or deliberately added 'cutting' or diluting agents used to increase the bulk of the drug and therefore increase profits. If the user is lucky, these cutting agents can be fairly innocuous substances such as caffeine, glucose or sugar; if the user is not so lucky, they may be curry powder, soup powder or gravy powder; if they are really unlucky, it could well be something such as powdered brick dust.

Occasionally, heroin is seen on the streets in the form of small granules, most of which has been produced in South-East Asia and is intended specifically for smoking.

Figure 6.1 Heroin powder forms

Marketing

Heroin is commonly dealt in fractions of a gram, although the amount varies according to the local market. It can be dealt in as little as a fifteenth of a gram, but more usually it is seen as either a quarter or an eighth of a gram. It is also common for heroin to be sold by value, such as in bags costing £5, £10 or £20 each. The amount of drug per bag will vary according to prevailing prices and quality.

Heroin usually is packaged in paper wraps like other powder drugs, but it has been seen in small press-seal plastic bags, wrapped in plastic film and contained in cooking foil.

Heroin is available in all the UK's major population centres, and its use has spread across all social groupings. In smaller centres, it will be available without difficulty by arrangement with a local street dealer.

Cost

There is a great deal of variation in the price that heroin attracts on the street. It normally varies between £40 and £90 per gram. The variations are the result of the financial situation of the users, the activities of the local police, the amount of the drug that is available, and its quality.

Legal position

Heroin is a class A, schedule 2 controlled substance under the Misuse of Drugs Act 1971. Offences involving heroin attract the following penalties:

- *Possession for personal use*: the possession of any amount of heroin for personal use is punishable on indictment by a maximum sentence of seven years' imprisonment plus an unlimited fine.

- *Possession with intent to supply*: possession of heroin with intent to supply the drug by sale or gift to another person is punishable on indictment with a maximum sentence of life imprisonment, plus an unlimited fine, plus seizure of all drug-related assets.

- *Supplying*: as for possession with intent to supply.

- *Importation*: as for possession with intent to supply.

The position of heroin within schedule 2 recognises that there are some medical uses for the drug, but these are strictly controlled.

Methods of use

Much of the heroin used in the UK is injected (see Figure 6.2). The drug will have been acquired by the user most likely as a powder or very occasionally as a tablet and will have to be prepared into an injectable liquid. If the heroin is in tablet form, the tablets are crushed, usually between two spoons, to as fine a powder as possible. If the heroin is in powder form, the user will need to ensure that it is as fine as possible and free from any obvious contaminants. The required amount of drug is then placed in the bowl of a spoon; a dessert spoon, known as a 'cooking spoon', is usual. The powder must then be dissolved; this is best achieved if the liquid added to it is a little acidic. It is common for users to add water to the heroin powder together with a little lemon juice (citric acid) or vinegar (acetic acid) to give the water the right degree of acidity in order to dissolve the heroin completely. Lemon juice remains a popular acid for use by injectors because of its easy availability and convenient packaging in small plastic bottles. However, lemon juice can contain a fungus that comes from the skin of the fruit. This causes no problems when the juice is used in food, but it can attack the optic nerve if it is injected, causing users to run risks with their sight.

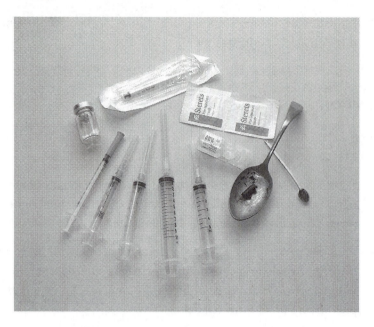

Figure 6.2 Injecting equipment

Because of this, users are advised to use dissolved vitamin C powder (ascorbic acid) instead. Indeed, many drug agencies issue vitamin C powder to their injecting clients.

The heroin and the added liquid are then heated gently from underneath with a match, cigarette lighter or candle to speed up the dissolving; the liquid may be stirred with a match. All of the equipment used in this process should be sterilised to reduce the risk of infection, but many users do not take hygiene very seriously.

Once the powder has been dissolved, a small twist of cotton-wool or a cigarette filter is dropped into the liquid. The injector then impales the cotton-wool or cigarette filter with the end of a hypodermic needle and draws up the liquid into a syringe (see Figure 6.3). The filter helps to remove any undissolved particles, preventing them from blocking the needle or small blood vessels within the user's body.

The syringe is now ready, and the user chooses a site to inject into. Most first-time injectors seek the assistance of an experienced friend to guide them. Many people are given their first few injections by these 'friends', until they feel confident to do it themselves. Some first-time users inject the heroin into muscle tissue under the skin rather than into veins. This is known as 'skin popping' and is a simpler and safer process than intravenous injection. It has the disadvantage for the user that the effect from the heroin is felt more slowly and without the intense hit that most heroin users are seeking.

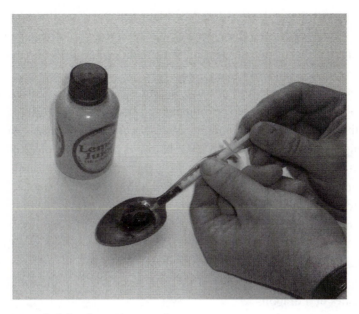

Figure 6.3 Heroin being drawn into a syringe

If the user is going to inject into a vein, then they have a wide choice of suitable locations all over the body. It is very important to make a careful choice and inject into a vein rather than an artery. Arteries carry blood at high pressure from the heart to more distant parts of the body, and attempting to inject into one can cause very rapid and sometimes uncontrollable bleeding that could have serious or fatal results.

The veins of the hands and arms are often chosen. Some users choose the veins of the upper leg or ankle, as it is easier to conceal the marks left by injections at these sites than in the arms. Some people have veins that lie close to the surface of the skin and are easy to see and to reach with a needle; other users have to encourage their veins to stand out by slapping the skin or by using a belt or leather thong as a tourniquet. Most users start by injecting into the smaller veins that lie close to the surface of the skin, but it is not possible to keep injecting into the same site. The area can become inflamed and very painful and may develop ulcerous sores, and the vein may even collapse. Users will then have to seek out the deeper-lying veins of the thighs, neck or stomach. When seeking these deeper and therefore less visible veins, it is much easier to make the mistake of striking an artery or even a nerve with the needle.

Having selected the vein, the user normally inserts the needle and then draws back a little blood into the syringe to check that a good connection has been established. This practice, called 'flushing' or 'backtracking', causes any infection present in the user's blood to contaminate the needle and syringe. The user then depresses the plunger of the needle to inject the heroin into the vein, where it will be carried to the brain within a few seconds to create the hit that is being sought.

Because of the problems caused by blunt and dirty needles, and the very real risks that users run if they share needles and syringes with others, most UK health authorities have set up needle-distribution schemes where injecting users can obtain what are called 'clean works'.

Another popular method of using heroin is by smoking. This can be done by adding the powder to tobacco or cannabis and smoking it in a hand-rolled cigarette or a pipe, but this is not common. Most heroin smokers use a method called 'skagging' or 'chasing the dragon'. The heroin is placed on a piece of cooking foil and heated from underneath with a match, cigarette lighter or candle until it turns into beads of liquid that begin to spit and emit thin tendrils of smoke. This smoke is collected and inhaled with the use of a tube made from a rolled piece of foil or paper, glass or metal or the sleeve of a matchbox. The origins of the expression 'chasing the dragon' are unclear. Some suggest that it is the drug's connection with China and Chinese dragons; others claim that the smoke looks like the tail of a dragon as it floats in the air; and others suggest that the deposit left on the foil looks like the shiny scales of a dragon.

The hit achieved by smoking heroin is very quick to occur and is second only to injecting in its speed of onset.

It is possible to use heroin orally by dabbing it on a wet finger into the mouth, but this is very rare. A little more common, but still rare, is to sniff or 'snort' heroin into the nose, using the membranes of the nose to absorb the drug into the bloodstream. This is a fairly slow way of achieving the hit, but it does avoid the problems that injecting can bring.

Effects of use

Most users of heroin, especially if the drug is injected, experience a distinct hit when the drug reaches their brain. They feel overpowering euphoria and a deep inner peace that then leads to a dreamy and in some cases trance-like state. In this state, feelings of stress, anxiety and fear disappear, and the user feels at total peace with the world. Heroin is a powerful analgesic and removes traces of pain, cold and hunger. It is this dream-like state, which can last for between two and six hours, that makes heroin so attractive to its users.

Adverse effects

Heroin is a very powerful drug, the exact strength of which is impossible to determine on the streets. This means that the dose a user administers can vary considerably. Current average street strengths of around 20 per cent are common, but they can vary from less than 10 per cent to over 60 per cent. This presents obvious problems to the user and increases the risk of overdosing. Many first-time users experience feelings of nausea and may suffer bouts of vomiting. A high dose of heroin may depress the breathing rate and consciousness level of the user; if vomiting takes place in this state, there is the risk of the user inhaling vomit, leading to sudden death.

Heroin use can quickly become the central activity in a person's life, to the point that they fail to take any care of themselves. They may not eat properly or keep themselves clean, and their general body condition can decline rapidly. There is some evidence to suggest that the efficiency of the natural immune system will be reduced, leaving the user more prone to developing infections and other illnesses.

Tolerance potential

Tolerance to heroin develops very quickly with continued use. The body soon learns to cope with heroin, and the same dose of the drug produces weaker and weaker effects as time passes. At the same time, the general state of health of the user is likely to be in decline and the user may feel unwell. A point is soon reached where the drug is being used merely to mask or drive away these unpleasant feelings and return the user to a more normal state. In order to achieve a measure of the original uplifting effects of the drug, the user has to increase the dose or its frequency of use. The process of developing tolerance continues until even this increased amount of the drug will do nothing more than drive away the bad feelings.

Habituation potential

Most heroin users develop very rapidly physical and psychological dependence on the drug. The body chemistry of the user changes until it becomes vital to keep on taking the drug just to feel normal. No heroin addict starts their use of the drug with the intention of becoming habituated to it. Most users feel that they can keep control of their use and stay in control. This is very rarely true, and the 'power of the powder' soon defeats them until they become totally dependent on it. The heroin user's physical habituation can be immensely powerful and the cravings for the drug so strong that the user's life becomes a journey of obtaining the means to pay for the drug, buying supplies and using and experiencing its effects, until the craving drives them to repeat the whole process again and again.

The average heroin habit in the UK is estimated to cost the user some £40 per day – that is £280 each week or £14,560 each year. Dependent users will employ any method to raise this level of money. Most turn to crime of one sort or another, including theft of property by burglary, theft from motor cars and street robbery. Some users become drug dealers themselves, buying heroin in the largest quantities that they can afford and then reselling it at sufficient profit to sustain their own habits. Others turn to prostitution as a way of raising sufficient cash. Prostitution exposes the user to all sorts of health risks; in desperation for cash for their drug, some users agree to have unprotected sex with clients and run the risk of becoming infected with HIV and hepatitis virus, which they can then spread to other users through the sharing of needles, syringes, cooking spoons and other injecting paraphernalia.

As well as physical dependence, most users also develop a powerful psychological dependence on the drug. They begin to rely on the buffer effects that the drug can give them to defend them from the pressures and problems of the real world.

Withdrawal effects

Sudden withdrawal from repeated use of heroin without medical assistance often leads to the user experiencing all of the symptoms of a severe bout of 'flu, such as aching muscles, severe cramps and stiff joints. They will sweat profusely and their body and skin temperature will fluctuate wildly. This may be accompanied by a runny nose, sore eyes, diarrhoea, stomach cramps, sore throat and headache. Withdrawal from heroin in this way is called 'going cold turkey', because of the similarity in appearance between the cold and clammy skin of the user and that of a dead turkey.

In addition to these physical problems, the user will feel a psychological craving to continue using the drug. They know that just one more use of the drug will remove all of their physical problems and reintroduce them to the dream-like state that they have found so comfortable.

So powerful are these urges that relapses in people attempting to give up heroin are the norm. It is not advisable for regular users of heroin to attempt to give up the drug without professional assistance. Users can be helped through their physical withdrawal symptoms with prescribed drugs and can be offered support and counselling for their psychological cravings. However, even with all the best help and support available, it is a very difficult process to withdraw totally from heroin once use has become regular or heavy. It is a very difficult road back to full health, and few users will ever achieve it fully.

Overdose potential

Heroin use carries risks of overdose. Street samples of the drug are of uncertain strength, and it is easy to use too much. Some users get into such a state that they are not capable of thinking clearly and will make grave mistakes in the amount that they use. Overdose with heroin can lead quickly to severe respiratory depression and coma. Unless medical help is obtained rapdily, the breathing rate continues to fall until it ceases altogether and death is inevitable.

Street names

H, horse, skag, smack, stuff, shit, Harry, brown, gravy

Slang associated with use

Cooking – Preparing heroin for injection

Cooking spoon – Spoon used to prepare heroin for injection

Shooting up, fixing – Injecting

Backtracking, flushing – Drawing blood back into the syringe before and during injecting

Works, gun, spike, pistol, barrel – Needle and syringe

Track marks – Scars caused by injecting

Skagging, chasing the dragon, chasing – Smoking heroin

Heroin: benefits and drawbacks

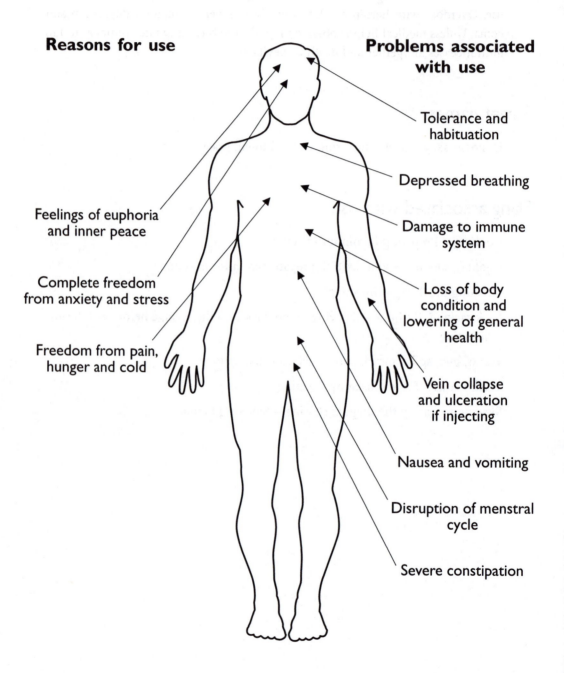

Reasons for use

Feelings of euphoria
and inner peace

Complete freedom
from anxiety and stress

Freedom from pain,
hunger and cold

**Problems associated
with use**

Tolerance and
habituation

Depressed breathing

Damage to immune
system

Loss of body
condition and
lowering of general
health

Vein collapse
and ulceration
if injecting

Nausea and vomiting

Disruption of menstral
cycle

Severe constipation

Methadone (methadone hydrochloride)

Methadone: quick reference guide

Source

Synthetic product.

Forms and appearance

In its pure state, methadone is a white powder. It is more commonly seen in the form of small white tablets, clear injectable ampoules, and as a brown, orange or green linctus and mixture.

Marketing

Methadone is prescribed occasionally as a painkiller and as a treatment for chronic painful coughs. It is frequently prescribed in the treatment of heroin addiction to control withdrawal symptoms. It is also seen as a street drug, where it appears in all its forms except its pure state. There is no established packaging for methadone. Almost all methadone will have originated from prescriptions and is sold in its pharmaceutical packaging or other containers.

Cost

There is no established price for street methadone due to the irregularity of supplies.

Legal position

Methadone is a class A, schedule 2 controlled substance within the Misuse of Drugs Act 1971.

Methods of use

Methadone can be used orally and by injection.

Effects of use

Feelings of relaxation, bodily warmth, freedom from pain and worry, suppression of the withdrawal effects of heroin addiction.

Adverse effects

Some users experience bouts of sweating, disruption of the menstrual cycle, constipation, nausea, itching and tiredness.

Tolerance potential

Tolerance to methadone will develop slowly with continued use. A previously acquired tolerance to heroin can be transferred to methadone.

Habituation potential

Powerful physical and psychological dependence develops with continued use.

Withdrawal effects

Fever, 'flu-like symptoms, diarrhoea, restlessness, anxiety and irritability.

Overdose potential

Overdose can cause respiratory depression, collapse, coma and death.

Methadone: in-depth guide

Source

Methadone is a synthetic product that is similar in chemical composition to naturally occurring opiates such as morphine and heroin. It was first developed during the Second World War by German scientists searching for a powerful painkiller that would replace the natural opiates whose source they were largely cut off from.

Forms and appearance

Pure methadone hydrochloride is a white powder. However, it is almost never seen in this form as it has no medical use. The forms that are seen on the streets are those produced by pharmaceutical companies for therapeutic use.

Methodone is produced under a number of trade names, including Physeptone, Methex, Metharose, Methadose and Synastone. It is produced in the form of small white tablets, as a colourless injectable liquid contained in glass ampoules or as a liquid mixture which may vary in colour from brown or orange to blue or bright green, according to the colouring agents that have been added (see Figure 6.4).

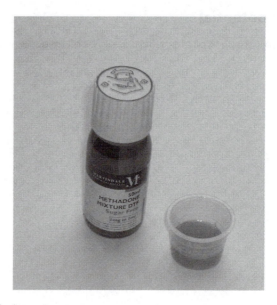

Figure 6.4 Methadone mixture

Marketing

Methadone is sometimes prescribed to patients suffering from extreme pain. It is also prescribed for painful chronic coughing. Both of these conditions are usually associated with a terminal illness, such as lung cancer. The drug is commonly prescribed in its tablet or injectable form for pain relief, while the linctus is usually prescribed for the alleviation of chronic coughing.

Methadone is also available as a mixture that is about two and half times as strong as the linctus form. Here the picture can become very confusing, because many methadone users and some health professionals refer to the mixture as linctus. Methadone mixture is commonly prescribed for people who are addicted physically and psychologically to heroin or other opiates. The other forms of methadone also are prescribed sometimes for this purpose. Methadone is prescribed to alleviate the symptoms that arise as a result of withdrawing from heroin use, often with the intention of slowly reducing the dose of methadone prescribed in order to wean the user away from opiate use altogether. In the UK, some users are prescribed methadone by their own general practitioners, but most users are issued with prescriptions by specialist doctors attached to drug-treatment services. Practices vary, but most UK drug services prescribe methadone in its mixture form to be taken orally. In order to control the amount of methadone that the user takes, many services issue prescriptions on a daily basis providing enough of the drug only for that day. Other services issue prescriptions for a week's supply and in certain circumstances will issue for longer periods. It is also possible for the user to obtain permission to take over 500mg, or more than 15 days' supply, of methadone out of the country with them while on business or holiday, and some services provide prescriptions and authorisation letters to cover this. Some UK drug services dispense their own methadone, but more commonly it is obtained from local pharmacies. Those services that operate a policy of keeping very tight control on the issue of methadone to prevent it reaching the streets usually prescribe the drug only in its mixture form. They then request that the pharmacist issues the drug in an open receptacle so that the user has to drink it there in the presence of the pharmacist. The pharmacist then asks the user to speak to ensure that they have swallowed the methadone and cannot spit it back into a bottle for sale on the streets.

Despite the best efforts of doctors, pharmacists and drug services, a great deal of methadone in its various forms reaches the illegal street trade. The drug can be attractive to heroin users who are unable to afford the generally higher prices asked for heroin, unable to obtain supplies of their preferred drug during times of shortage, or unwilling to engage with drug services.

There is no established trade in illegally produced methadone. All of the methadone available on the streets will have originated from legally prescribed methadone or by theft from dispensaries that hold supplies of the drug.

When sold on the streets, methadone usually will be in its original pharmaceutical packaging, as this will reassure the buyer that they are getting the genuine article. However, many sellers of street methadone may dilute it by adding water, therefore maximising their profits.

Cost

Methadone mixture bought on the streets may be priced as low as £1 for 10mg. Prices vary according to availability.

Legal position

Methadone is a class A, schedule 2 controlled substance within the Misuse of Drugs Act 1971. The possession of methadone is lawful only if the person in possession of it has obtained it by means of a doctor's prescription. This methadone is lawful for their use only. Offences involving methadone attract the following penalties:

- *Possession for personal use*: the illegal possession of any amount of methadone for personal use is punishable on indictment by a maximum sentence of seven years' imprisonment plus an unlimited fine.

- *Possession with intent to supply*: possession of methadone with intent to supply the drug illegally by sale or gift to another person is punishable on indictment with a maximum sentence of life imprisonment, plus an unlimited fine, plus seizure of all drug-related assets.

- *Supplying*: as for possession with intent to supply.

- *Importation*: as for possession with intent to supply.

Methods of use

The tablets, linctus and mixture forms of methadone are designed to be taken by mouth; the ampoules are for injection. When misused, the tablet form may be crushed and dissolved in water, usually with a mild acid added, and then injected. (See the in-depth guide to heroin for further information on injecting methods.)

The mixture and linctus are injected sometimes, although this is rare due to the volume that would have to be injected for the desired effects and the thick syrupy nature of the liquid, which can lead to severe pain.

Effects of use

The effects of methadone use can vary a great deal from one person to another, and the drug is not suitable for everyone. In most users, the effects of methadone are similar to those of heroin. The drug does not produce the intense hit that heroin use achieves. The effects are slower to build up but generally last much longer, perhaps for as long as 24 hours or more. The user will experience relief from physical pain together with feelings of relaxation and freedom from worry, anxiety and stress. There will be a levelling off of the user's emotions, so that no extremes are felt. The majority of users experience a comfortable feeling of bodily warmth and wellbeing. Because of the similarity of the effects of methadone and heroin, methadone is purchased on the streets as a substitute when heroin is not available or is beyond the financial means of the user.

Most people who use methadone are doing so to assist them in coming off heroin. Methadone will largely prevent the worst of the physical effects of withdrawing from heroin and provide support in dealing with the psychological and emotional effects. Once the person is stabilised on methadone, efforts are normally made to reduce the dosage in order to slowly and carefully wean the user away from opiate use altogether.

Adverse effects

The potentially adverse effects of methadone vary greatly from user to user. Some people experience nothing adverse at all, while a small number find the drug completely unacceptable to them. Most users of methadone experience excess sweating and itchiness of the skin. They may become flushed, with a noticeable reddening of the face and neck. Some users find that the drug causes drowsiness in varying degrees. At its least this may result in the user simply feeling tired, but at its most pronounced it may cause the user to fall asleep 'at the drop of a hat'.

As with all opiates and their substitutes, methadone can cause nausea, vomiting, severe constipation and retention of urine; the latter two can lead to stomach and back pain.

Some female users report that methadone causes disruption and loss of regularity of their menstrual cycle. Some users experience a loss of sexual drive.

Tolerance potential

Tolerance to methadone will develop with continued use, but much more slowly than with heroin. This is complicated, however, by the chemical similarity between heroin and methadone. In tolerance terms, the body does not make a great distinction between them: if a user has developed a marked tolerance to heroin before using methadone, then that tolerance will also apply to methadone. If the heroin user has developed a tolerance to only certain effects of heroin, then that pattern of tolerance will transfer to the methadone.

Tolerance to methadone is lost very quickly if the user has a week or so free from taking all opiate drugs. This presents a great danger for the user if they lapse and return to methadone or heroin use. With their tolerance now lowered almost to zero, they may inadvertently take what appears to them to be a normal dose when in fact they are placing themselves in grave danger of overdosing.

Habituation potential

Regular use of methadone produces in almost all users a powerful physical and psychological dependence. There is much debate as to whether the dependence produced by methadone is stronger or weaker than that produced by heroin; the dependence varies from user to user, and may be stronger or weaker in different people.

Withdrawal effects

The withdrawal effects after ceasing to use methadone can be every bit as severe as those of heroin. In some users the effects can be more severe, and in most users they will certainly take longer to pass. No regular methadone user should attempt to make a sudden and unsupervised withdrawal from its use, otherwise they will experience many of the symptoms of severe fever or 'flu. Their body temperature will be high but they will feel very cold. They may have a sore throat and runny nose and suffer bouts of sneezing. Many users become tremulous, restless and anxious and display irritability to people around them. The constipation that use of the drug has caused them previously will be replaced by severe and debilitating diarrhoea. Their appetite may be lost and they may suffer long periods of insomnia. All of these will lower their general body condition and leave them feeling extremely unwell. This period of withdrawal can last for several weeks or even months, gradually getting less severe as time passes.

None of these symptoms is dangerous in the long term, but they are very unpleasant to live through.

Overdose potential

Methadone is a powerful and potentially dangerous drug. Many cases of overdose have occurred in the children of users who have left the attractively coloured liquid forms within easy reach at home. Overdoses in established users are rare due to the control exercised by the prescribing services over their methadone use. Problems may occur if an inexperienced user tries the drug and takes too much, if a previous user returns to the drug after a period of abstinence and fails to adjust the dose downwards in order to take account of their body's loss of tolerance, or if methadone is used along with other depressant drugs, such as heroin, alcohol, tranquillisers or sleeping pills. Overdose of methadone will result in severe depression of breathing and heart rate, which may decline to the point at which consciousness is lost, with death following shortly afterwards.

Street names

Methadone: doll, dolly, red rock, tootsie roll

Ampoules of methadone: phy-amps, phy

Slang associated with use

Script, paper, reader – Prescription for methadone

Scripted, on a script, on maintenance – In receipt of a prescription for methadone from a doctor

Methadone: benefits and drawbacks

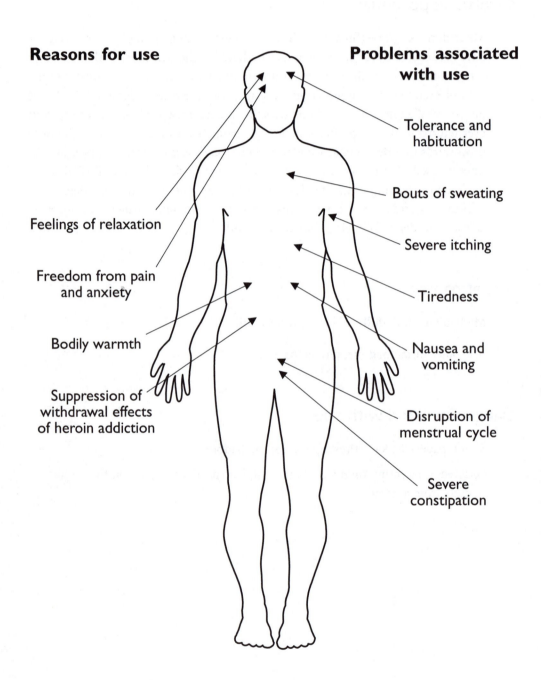

Reasons for use

Feelings of relaxation

Freedom from pain
and anxiety

Bodily warmth

Suppression of
withdrawal effects
of heroin addiction

**Problems associated
with use**

Tolerance and
habituation

Bouts of sweating

Severe itching

Tiredness

Nausea and
vomiting

Disruption of
menstrual cycle

Severe
constipation

Chapter 7

Volatile Substance Abuse: 'Sniffing'

Solvents

Solvents: quick reference guide

Source

Wide range of domestic and commercial products.

Forms and appearance

The range of products that can be abused is immense, and some are present in every home. They fall into three main groups:

- *Liquid petroleum gases (LPGs)*, contained in aerosols, camping-gas cylinders and lighter-gas refills.

- *Liquid solvents*, such as fire-extinguisher fluid, document-correction fluid and thinner, certain types of paint, paint remover, nail polish, nail-polish remover, antifreeze and petrol.

- *Solvent-based glues*, such as impact adhesives used in the application of laminate surfaces, vinyl floor tiles, wood and plastic.

Marketing

Solvents in one form or another are sold in many shops and garages.

Cost

Prices for solvents vary according to the product but generally are low; for example, in the UK, a single gas-filled cigarette lighter can cost less than £1 while 100ml of liquid lighter fluid costs about £1.20.

Legal position

The possession and use of solvents is not controlled. The sale and supply of solvents to young people under the age of 18 can be an offence in certain circumstances. Since 1999, it has been an offence in the UK to supply butane lighter-refill canisters to anyone under the age of 18.

Methods of use

LPGs are usually sprayed directly into the mouth and inhaled deeply. Liquid solvents and solvent glues commonly are inhaled from a plastic bag, a rag or handkerchief, a shirt collar or cuff or a drinks can or other such container.

Effects of use

Intense intoxication, excitability and auditory and visual hallucinations.

Adverse effects

Danger of sudden death caused by overstimulation of the heart or asphyxiation caused by swelling of the throat tissues or inhalation of vomit. Users often expose themselves to the danger of accidents while they are intoxicated or hallucinating. Loss of short-term memory and cognitive skills may be experienced, together with problems with speech and balance. Personality changes may occur.

Tolerance potential

Tolerance can develop with continued use.

Habituation potential

There is little evidence of any physical dependence developing, but a powerful psychological dependence can develop with repeated use.

Overdose potential

Overdose can lead to collapse, coma and death.

Withdrawal effects

No physical problems, but the user may experience bouts of anxiety and mood swings when use ceasesSolvents: in-depth guide

Source

The deliberate inhalation of solvents for intoxication purposes is known as volatile substance abuse (VSA). It is a practice with a long history that may go back several thousands of years. Stories abound of priests and priestesses who inhaled the fumes escaping from cracks in certain volcanic mountains around the Mediterranean Sea and then predicted the future from the visions that they saw. It may well be that the fumes they were inhaling were hydrocarbon gases similar to many of today's solvent products.

The discovery of ether and chloroform in the nineteenth century led to the development of anaesthetics, but it also provided two very powerful solvents that could be inhaled easily. Ether parties were once popular with medical staff, who would get together and use ether to get extremely intoxicated. Cases of similar behaviour among medical students still come to light occasionally.

The next phase in the story took place in the USA in the years immediately after the Second World War. Many thousands of unwanted military vehicles were shipped back to America for disposal. While the military authorities were deciding what to do with the vehicles, they were stored in vast compounds with very little security. Local children took to exploring the vehicles and discovered that many of them were fitted with fire extinguishers containing solvent fluid. These children soon discovered that they could achieve a powerful level of intoxication by inhaling this fluid, and several deaths occurred before security was tightened and the extinguishers removed.

The practice of inhaling solvents was first noted in the UK in the late 1950s, when Glasgow and Portsmouth reported problems with young people inhaling the fumes of impact adhesives from milk bottles. After putting the glue in the bottle, the user placed their nose into the opening of the bottle while inhaling deeply. It is this practice that gave birth to the expression 'glue-sniffing'. From these beginnings, the practice spread throughout the UK. At the same time, the range of products being used and the methods of use changed and evolved, with each locality having its own favourite substance.

An enormous range of ordinary products are used for inhalation, including household products and substances used in offices and workshops. It has been estimated that there are around 30 solvent products in the average house, all of which can be, and often are, used for the purposes of intoxication.

Forms and appearance

The solvent products that are commonly used for intoxication in the UK can be divided into three main groups. Liquid petroleum gases (LPGs) such as butane and propane are the most popular solvents used for intoxication. These gases are now used as propellants in most aerosols, since manufacturers stopped using chlorinated fluorocarbons (CFCs) as propellants because they were implicated in damage to the Earth's ozone layer. LPG is found in gas cylinders for camping stoves, portable lamps and blowtorches, and in gas-powered vehicles. It is also available in aerosol-type canisters for refilling cigarette lighters, cooking-stove lighters and some portable heated hair rollers. This aerosol form of LPG is the most popular with young people who use solvents for intoxication; it is also the most dangerous.

Powerful solvents such as benzene, amyl acetate, hexane, acetone and carbon tetrachloride are available in liquid form in a wide range of everyday products, including nail polish and its remover, document-correction fluid and its thinner, dry-cleaning fluid, suede cleaner and adhesive plaster remover. The range of products is vast, and the list above is given merely to illustrate some of the more popular types.

Another liquid solvent that caused a lot of problems until recently is halon. This solvent is contained in the green-bodied fire extinguishers that are still found in some commercial premises, vehicles and homes. Halon is a superb fire-retarding fluid that can be used with safety in contact with electricity, but it is also very damaging to the ozone layer and its use is now highly controlled. Following the Montreal Protocol, a regulation enacted by the European Parliament in 2000 banned the sale of all halon fire extinguishers and required those in use to be decommissioned by the end of 2003. Since that date, it has been an offence to use a halon extinguisher within the European Union, although the possession of such an extinguisher is not itself an offence. Following such legislation, we can expect the number of halon extinguishers available for abuse to decline sharply.

Liquid solvents also includes petrol, which can be found not only in cars but also in lawnmowers, boat engines and so on.

The final group of products used for intoxication are the solvent-based glues. These include impact adhesives, which contain substances such as toluene and hexane and are commonly used to fix laminate surfaces to desks, kitchen tops and tables and to glue tiles to floors and ceilings. This group of products also includes modelling glues used in the construction of plastic models.

Various household solvents are shown in Figure 7.1.

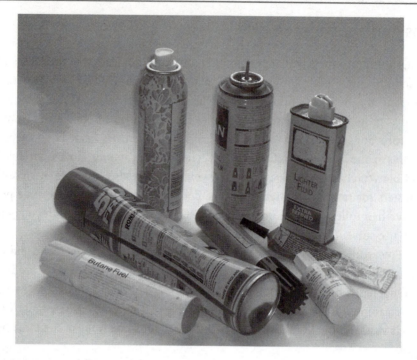

Figure 7.1 Household solvents

Marketing

All of the solvent products described here can be purchased from shops all over the UK. Most young people have their first experience of inhaling a solvent by being offered a share in a product being used by another young person. These may be friends or older siblings. Until about ten years ago, in the UK the abuse of solvents was dominated heavily by males. This has now changed, and in many areas the practice is as common among females as males.

We have had considerable experience in dealing with young people who have become involved in VSA. Based on this experience, we believe that although the problem can be found among young people from all walks of life, solvent abusers can in general be divided into three basic groups:

- *Experimenters, followers of fashion and thrill-seekers*: young people who will try any new craze or fashion and are often talked into trying by their friends. They will experiment a few times and will almost always then stop using.

- *People seeking to change their self-image*: young people who perceive something to be lacking in their personality or the image they have of themselves. They will use solvents to change and enhance certain aspects of their personality. However, solvents can never achieve the change that they seek, and they often move on to other, stronger and more dangerous substances.

- *Escape-seekers*: this is the saddest group of all. They simply want to escape from a life that they find frightening, boring, stressful or empty into a solvent-induced world where their problems don't exist. Unfortunately, however long they remain in that false reality, eventually they will have to return to normality, and their problems will still exist.

Cost

The prices of solvent-based products vary tremendously, but most are well within the reach of young people's finances. One of the most popular products used for intoxication are the canisters of LPG used for refilling cigarette lighters. A standard-size canister costing less than £2 will be sufficient to achieve a very high level of intoxication for several hours.

Legal position

In the UK, the possession and use of solvents for intoxication is not controlled under any legislation. The sale and supply of solvents is regulated by the Intoxicating Substance Supply Act 1985. This makes it an offence for anyone to sell or supply a solvent-based product to a person apparently under the age of 18 or a person who is suspected of acting on behalf of a person under the age of 18, if the supplier has reason to believe that the product is going to be used for the purposes of intoxication.

This legislation, usually applied to retailers, is often misunderstood. It is not illegal to sell solvent-based products to people under 18, and many young people have a legitimate need for these products. The act simply requires the retailer to exercise care as to the use that they think the buyer is going to put the product to. The act also covers the situation in which a person shares some solvent with another young person. No purchase needs to take place, simply supply: a young person giving some solvent to a friend could be guilty of an offence under this act. Offences under this legislation carry a maximum penalty of six months' imprisonment and a £5000 fine.

In 1999, in the UK the law relating to the supply of gas-lighter refill canisters was tightened. The Cigarette Lighter Refill (Safety) Regulations made it an offence to supply any person under the age of 18 with such a product. It is worth noting that this is an absolute ban and applies even when the young person has a legitimate purpose for the refill canister. The penalties under this regulation include a maximum fine of £5000 and the possibility of six months' imprisonment.

Methods of use

LPGs are normally used by the user spraying them directly into his or her mouth (see Figure 7.2). The favourite form of LPG are canister refills of lighter fuel. These are designed with an upright spigot valve at the top that is inserted into a ball valve at the base of the gas reservoir being refilled. The spigot valve is depressed by pushing it into the ball valve, and the liquid gas is transferred into the reservoir. The solvent abuser grips the spigot valve between their teeth and pushes the body of the canister inwards. This releases a stream of liquid gas directly on to the back of the throat. The user inhales air sharply at the same time, and thus draws the gas into the lungs. With other types of LPG cylinders, the user releases the gas through whatever form of valve is fitted to it, and again draws the gas deeply into the lungs.

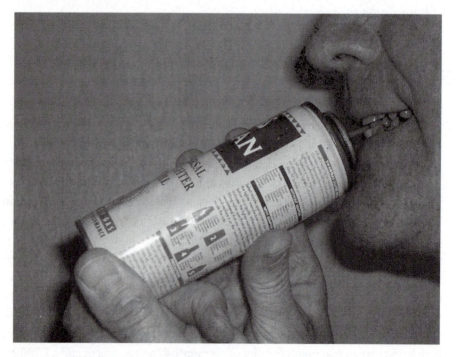

Figure 7.2 Lighter gas being sprayed into the mouth

Domestic aerosols have been the subject of VSA for many years. Until the late 1980s, the propellants used were mostly CFCs, a range of powerful solvent gases that gave users the effects that they were seeking. With the advent of international concern over the depletion of the Earth's ozone layer, CFCs have been removed from aerosols and replaced with LPG. This has made the aerosol more ozone-friendly but more deadly for the solvent user. If the product itself is also solvent-based, then this will increase the effects that are achieved. Provided the product is not too unpleasant-tasting, the user will spray the aerosol directly into the mouth, sucking in air as they do so. Most solvent users are prepared to spray products such as deodorant, air freshener and furniture polish directly into their mouths. If the product tastes too unpleasant, the user will devise methods of taking in the LPG without taking in the product. Shaving-foam aerosols are often inhaled; the user covers their mouth with a handkerchief or a surgical mask and then sprays the foam onto the fabric at very close range. The foam is trapped by the fabric while the gas passes into the user's mouth. Products such as aerosol paint canisters are used by spraying the product onto the surface of a bowl of warm water while the user holds their face close to the water under a towel covering their head and the bowl. This is similar to the method used to inhale various medications. The paint is trapped on the surface of the water and the gas is freed for the user to inhale. The warm water also evaporates any solvent used in the formulation of the paint and makes that available to the user. Solvent users are very adept at finding ways in which they can inhale the gas propellant from almost any aerosol.

Many liquid solvents are commonly used for VSA. They can be sniffed directly from the container that they are supplied in, but this limits the amount of solvent vapour that is available to the user and the practice is rare. Most users pour a quantity of solvent, such as document-correction fluid or dry-cleaning fluid, into a plastic bag, such as a crisps packet or a plastic carrier bag. The bag is opened out to get as much air into it as possible and then the top is gathered together and held over the mouth and nose. The body of the bag is pumped with the hand to drive the vapour-laden air into the user's mouth. The bag is then opened out again and the process is repeated until the solvent has evaporated away. Some users place the solvent into a very large bag and put it completely over their head. This is known as 'space-helmeting' and carries the obvious dangers of asphyxiation if the user loses consciousness. If the user is unable to obtain a plastic bag, they may pour the solvent into a cardboard box or another container and use that in a similar manner.

Liquid solvents can be poured onto a handkerchief or piece of rag, which is then held over the mouth while the vapours are inhaled. These liquids are sometimes sprinkled onto shirt collars or cuffs so that users can sniff directly from the fabric without it being evident exactly what they are doing. This is sometimes done in class at school, although the obvious smell of solvents usually gives them away. This type of liquid solvent can also be poured into an empty drinks can. The user holds the can in their hands until their body heat begins to evaporate the solvent. The user then holds the ring-pull opening to their mouth and deeply inhales the vapours being given off. This method also has the advantage of not being obvious: to the casual observer, the user appears to be drinking.

Solvent-based glues can be sniffed directly from their containers, but commonly they are used from plastic bags in the same way as liquid solvents. In confined spaces such as a garden shed, some users spread the glue thickly onto any handy surface and then breathe the fume-laden air.

Effects of use

The deep inhalation of solvent fumes will bring about a state of intense intoxication within a very short time. If the user is fairly new to the practice, they will become extremely intoxicated, usually within a matter of seconds and certainly within less than half a minute. This state of intoxication will be obvious to any sober observer. The user becomes flushed of face, their speech becomes slurred and they have difficulty in standing or keeping their balance. They may become very excitable and laugh uncontrollably, or they may become morose and burst into tears. In their intoxicated state, the user may fall over repeatedly and become unconscious. If the user carries on inhaling, they may experience the onset of auditory and visual hallucinations. Some users report hearing voices. A 14-year-old boy known to us reported that he had conversations with birds in trees. Others report that the shapes and colours of objects around them change dramatically and that they see creatures and objects that are not really there. One 16-year-old user told us that he was frequently chased along the road by a six-foot gold tooth. If he stopped and looked round, the tooth stopped as well and 'just looked at [him]'. He was so frightened that he often ran blindly for several miles; sometimes he had no idea where he was when the effects of the solvent wore off.

The duration of the effects from VSA can be very short-lived. If the user inhales only until they are intoxicated and then stops, the effects normally wear off within 30 minutes or so. If they keep inhaling to the point at which hallucinations occur, it may take two or three hours before they recover.

Adverse effects

It is very difficult to quote accurate figures for the number of young people who die as a result of the deliberate inhalation of solvent fumes. St George's Hospital Medical School, London, reported 63 UK deaths in 2002 from a variety of causes associated with VSA; this figure was the same as that for 2001. Of the 63 deaths in 2002, 37 were associated with use of butane gas. These figures represent a minimum, as there is no mechanism for recording deaths centrally, and the hospital has to rely on its own enquiries. Whatever the true figures, it is clear that by becoming involved in this practice, young people place their lives at risk. A disturbing fact emerges from the enquiries at St George's Hospital: VSA mortality figures for 1996 indicated that some 38 per cent (29 cases) of those who died had no previous history of solvent use. It must be stated very clearly that there is no room to experiment with solvents. They may, and often do, kill on the first time.

Most sudden solvent deaths are the result of one of two causes. First, the inhalation of LPG can cause the body to overproduce the hormone adrenaline. This is sometimes known as our 'fight or flight' hormone, as it is produced naturally by the body when we are startled, frightened or excited. The reflex action that triggers the production of adrenaline is ancient, possibly dating from primitive times when our survival depended very much on being able to fight or to run away from danger. Adrenaline closes down the small blood vessels close to the surface of the skin, in order to prevent excessive bleeding in the case of injury. It also stimulates the heart to beat faster and to pump oxygen-carrying blood around the body at a faster speed, in order to provide our muscles with the fuel needed to exert ourselves strenuously. LPG can cause this production of adrenaline to become excessive, resulting in over-stimulation of the heart and causing major disturbance to its rhythm. The normal rhythm may become irregular, and there is a danger that it may stop, which will lead quickly to death unless help is immediately at hand. Even if full arrest does not occur, such heart problems can lead to the user vomiting, with the subsequent danger that in their intoxicated state they may inhale the vomit and choke to death.

The second major cause of death is associated with the method of use of LPG and aerosols. When any pressurised gas or liquid is decompressed, its temperature drops dramatically. LPG and aerosol users often spray the contents directly against the back of the throat. This causes the tissues of the throat and the larynx to become deeply chilled and to swell. This swelling can be of such a degree that the passage of air through the throat becomes severely restricted or even cut off altogether. This can lead quickly to asphyxiation, with death following closely if expert help is not obtained very quickly.

The intoxication from solvent use can be very intense, which, together with the powerful hallucinations, often leads solvent users into situations of grave danger. They may become reckless with regard to their own safety, and many deaths and serious injuries have occurred when users have wandered out into a road or on to a railway line or fallen into deep water. Most solvents are highly flammable, and many horrific fires have resulted from their careless use in confined spaces.

Prolonged and repeated use of solvents can lead to profound changes in the user's personality. The user may exhibit wide mood swings, often being in a state of ecstatic happiness one minute and seeming to change to an aggressive and sometimes violent character shortly afterwards. It is often as a result of such mood swings that parents begin to suspect their child's involvement with solvents.

Some heavy users may also begin to experience a loss of short-term memory and have difficulty concentrating on any task that they are engaged in. This often begins to show itself at school as a marked reduction in the quality of their work and should lead teachers to investigate the possibility of VSA.

Extensive use of solvents over a long period can lead to problems with the user's speech and balance. Although they may not have used for some time and therefore are sober, they may exhibit slurred speech and difficulty in finding the right words and show signs of staggering and unsteadiness on their feet. In some users, these problems do not clear up when solvent use ceases and may become permanent.

It is worth noting that there are a number of notifiable industrial diseases that affect workers within the solvents industry who may be exposed to low levels of solvent fumes over an extended period.

Tolerance potential

Tolerance to solvents builds up fairly quickly with repeated use. The user finds that they need longer exposure to the substance to achieve the same effects. Some users also learn how to control their intake of fumes so as to maintain themselves at the level of intoxication that they desire.

Habituation potential

There is little evidence of the development of physical habituation from continued solvent use, but many long-term users do develop a powerful psychological habituation to the practice. They come to rely on it to cope with everyday life or to add the degree of excitement that they require into their lives, which they consider dull or empty. Some chronic users also feel that they need the escapism of solvents and are frightened to face the world without them.

Some chronic users of solvents may go on to become heavy alcohol or drug users in later life.

Withdrawal effects

No physical problems occur when withdrawing from solvent use. The user may feel anxious and unsure and will require the help and support of those around them.

Overdose potential

The risk of sudden death is not related to the amount of solvents inhaled. Death can and does occur at very low solvent levels.

Street names

Glue: impact adhesives

Gas: LPG

Can: canister of LPG

Cog: can of gas

Slang associated with use

Glue-sniffing, sniffing, sucking, huffing, cogging – Inhaling solvents for intoxication

Cogger, gasboy – LPG user

Bagging – Inhaling solvents from a bag

Space-helmeting – Placing a large bag completely over the head

Solvents: benefits and drawbacks

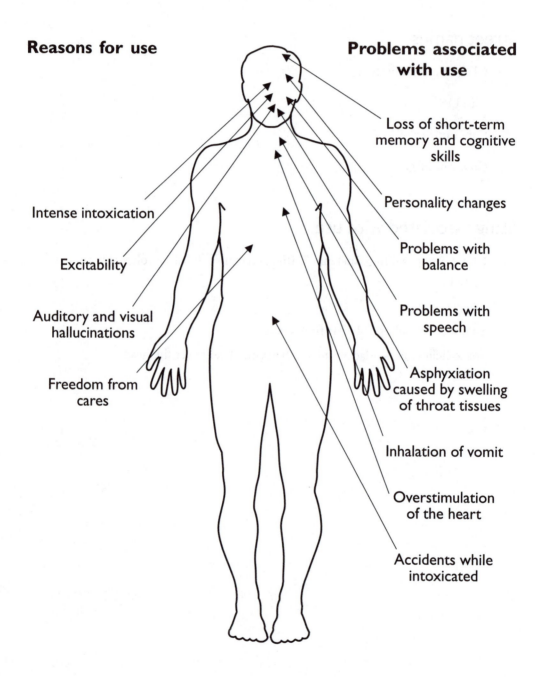

Reasons for use

Intense intoxication

Excitability

Auditory and visual
hallucinations

Freedom from
cares

**Problems associated
with use**

Loss of short-term
memory and cognitive
skills

Personality changes

Problems with
balance

Problems with
speech

Asphyxiation
caused by swelling
of throat tissues

Inhalation of vomit

Overstimulation
of the heart

Accidents while
intoxicated

Nitrites

Nitrites: quick reference guide

Source

Range of synthetic volatile chemicals from the alkyl nitrites group.

Forms and appearance

Sold in small glass bottles under trade names that include Rush, Liquid Gold, Locker Room, Ram, Thrust and Rock Hard.

Marketing

Sold openly in sex shops and other establishments, from street markets and through mail order.

Cost

In the UK between £2 and £6 for a small bottle.

Legal position

Amyl nitrite is a controlled substance under the Medicines Act 1968 and as such can be supplied only via a doctor's prescription. Butyl nitrite and isobutyl nitrite are not controlled directly, although in certain circumstance the Intoxicating Substance Supply Act 1985 could apply.

Methods of use

Nitrites are used by inhaling their fumes.

Effects of use

Feelings of excitement and exhilaration may be experienced, along with sexual arousal and increased sensitivity of the sexual organs. It is also claimed that use enlarges the penis in some users and relaxes smooth-walled muscles, allowing easier anal intercourse.

Adverse effects

Inhaling nitrites can cause nausea, vomiting, headache and dizziness. Nitrites are poisonous if swallowed and can damage vision if they come into contact with the eyes. Skin problems are also seen in some users.

Tolerance potential

Tolerance develops quickly with repeated use.

Habituation potential

No marked physical or psychological dependence develops with use.

Withdrawal effects

No marked effects.

Overdose potential

Little risk of serious overdose unless swallowed.

Nitrites: in-depth guide

Source

A range of synthetically produced alkyl nitrites, designed to be inhaled, have been freely available in the UK for many years. Until the advent in recent years of a range of specific drugs for heart disorders, nitrites were sold in pharmacies as a treatment for heart problems such as angina. A small quantity of the liquid was contained in small glass capsules called vitrellae, which the sufferer carried with them at all times in a special case. When chest pains were felt, the sufferer placed the glass capsule inside a handkerchief and crushed it with the pressure of the fingers. The 'popping' of the capsule in this way gave rise to the common name – poppers – now used universally for this type of substance. The fumes released were inhaled from the handkerchief and had the effect of dilating the blood vessels supplying blood to the heart muscle. This increased the blood flow and eased the pain. Little medical use is now made of these products to treat heart problems, although amyl nitrite is still used to counteract cyanide poisoning.

Forms and appearance

Poppers are sold in small glass bottles under various brand names (see Figure 7.3). The bottles are usually between 5 and 7cm high and made of brown glass, and have very bright, often fluorescent labels. The brand names used are intended to indicate the sort of uses that they might be put to: they include Ram, Stud, Locker Room, Liquid Gold, Liquid Incense, TNT, Thrust and Rock Hard.

Marketing

Poppers in small bottles can be seen on open sale in sex shops, on market stalls and in establishments that specialise in soft pornographic magazines. They are also sold in some dance and night clubs. Certain magazines carry advertisements for supplies of poppers that can be bought by mail order. They are also widely available over the Internet.

Figure 7.3 Liquid Gold poppers

Cost

A bottle of poppers in the UK will cost between £2 and £6. This will be enough for several doses for one person or for a number of people to use.

Legal position

Amyl nitrite is a medicine under the terms of the Medicines Act 1968. As such, in the UK it is an offence to supply it to anyone without a doctor's prescription. Such a restriction does not apply to butyl or isobutyl nitrite unless they are deliberately marketed as a sexual dysfunction therapy. Such a claim could potentially lead to them being considered as 'medicines' and thus to them falling under the Medicines Act 1968. To avoid this problem, most suppliers deal only with butyl nitrite or isobutyl nitrite and market them as room deodorisers or air fresheners. In our view, butyl nitrite and isobutyl nitrite could come within the scope of the Intoxicating Substance Supply Act 1985. This makes it an offence for anyone to sell or supply a solvent-based product to a person apparently under the age of 18 if the supplier has reason to believe that the product is going to be used for the purposes of intoxication. It can be argued that the range of nitrites sold under the title of poppers are solvents within the meaning of the act, and that the effects of nitrites can be called 'intoxication'.

This piece of legislation is usually applied to retailers and is often misunderstood. It is not illegal to sell nitrite-based products to people under 18. The act simply requires the retailer to be satisfied that the nitrite is not going to be used to induce intoxication. The retailer or supplier might put forward the defence that the product was supplied as a room deodoriser or air freshener, but the circumstances of each case would need to be considered in detail. This act also covers the situation in which somebody shares nitrite with a young person. No purchase needs to take place, simply supply, and a young person giving some nitrite to a friend could be guilty of an offence under the act.

Methods of use

Instructions for the use of these products are usually given on the side of the bottle. The instructions tell the user to remove the cap and leave the bottle in a room so that the aroma can develop as the liquid evaporates. The instructions go on to tell the user never to inhale the product directly. This is a complete sham, as the majority of users of poppers have no interest in creating a background odour. They purchase them with the intention of doing nothing else but inhaling directly.

Most users will inhale either directly from the bottle or from a handkerchief, tissue, piece of fabric or the end of an unlit cigarette that has been dipped into the bottle. Very small quantities of the liquid are needed to achieve the effects. It evaporates very quickly leaving a chemical solvent smell if used in a room.

Effects of use

The original use of poppers as a vasodilator for angina gives a clue as to the effects that today's users are seeking. The fumes dilate the blood vessels in the body, leading to an increase in the flow of blood to the brain. The user will therefore feel a head rush as the brain receives the increased oxygen supply. This will be followed by short-lived feelings of excitement and some exhilaration. The heart rate will increase and there may be pleasant feelings of dizziness and disorientation. The blood supply to the sexual organs will also be increased, which may lead to sexual arousal and erection in males. Some users claim that the increased blood flow causes an increase in penis size and enhances their ability to maintain the erection for longer periods. Some users claim that poppers relax the smooth-walled muscles of the anus and therefore facilitate anal intercourse.

Adverse effects

The dilation of the blood vessels leads to a dramatic drop in blood pressure. The heart rate rises in an attempt to maintain adequate blood pressure, but severe dizziness and blackouts are common. There may also be nausea and vomiting. These factors increase the risk of a user inhaling their own vomit and choking to death. There have been reports of stroke and heart attack following extensive use of poppers in people who may have had some underlying defect of the cardiovascular system. We have spoken to a number of users of poppers who have combined their use with Viagra™, a male impotence medication, in the belief that the two substances will have an additive effect on their sexual performance. The combining of these two substances carries very high risks. Indeed, Pfizer, the manufacturer of Viagra, states in its patient information summary: 'If you take VIAGRA with any nitrate medicine or recreational drug containing nitrates, your blood pressure could suddenly drop to an unsafe level. You could get dizzy, faint, or even have a heart attack or stroke.' Pfizer then goes on to state that poppers, which are all nitrites, are included in that advice.

Some users report that their use of poppers leaves them with a severe headache and sore eyes. Poppers can cause a variety of skin problems, including burning and dermatitis, if they come into contact with the skin. Users who place the chemical on a handkerchief or rag to inhale it run the risk of the chemical coming into contact with their hands and face.

Poppers can cause damage to the eyes if they come into contact with them. There have been a number of cases where the liquid has been splashed into a user's eyes and a loss of sight in one or both eyes has resulted.

It is not unknown for inexperienced users to attempt to drink the liquid instead of inhaling the fumes. This may arise as a result of confusing poppers with gamma-hydroxybutyrate (GHB), another liquid drug used in the dance club scene. GHB is also sold in small brightly coloured bottles, but unlike poppers it is designed to be taken orally.

All of the nitrites sold as poppers are poisonous and present a very real danger to health and even life if swallowed; medical help may have to be obtained very quickly if a tragedy is to be avoided.

Tolerance potential

Regular users of poppers soon develop a tolerance. The effects achieved become less and less, until continued use becomes a waste of time. This tolerance soon fades once use is stopped, and within a week or so will have returned to normal levels.

Most regular users manage their use so that tolerance does not develop to any great degree and they are always able to achieve the effects they desire.

Habituation potential

There appears to be no physical habituation to these chemicals, and very few users ever develop any psychological dependence. For the vast majority of users, it is simply one substance among many others that they will experiment with and then leave alone. Even for those who use poppers regularly, it becomes simply an important but not essential part of their lifestyle.

Withdrawal effects

There are no known withdrawal effects associated with cessation of the use of poppers.

Overdose potential

It is not generally thought possible to overdose on poppers, unless they are taken orally. The problems that they can cause do not appear to be particularly dose-related.

Street names

Range of inhaled nitrites: poppers, nitro, nitrite

Brand names: Ram, Stud, Locker Room, Liquid Gold, Liquid Incense, TNT, Thrust, Rock Hard

Slang associated with use

Popping – Inhaling nitrites

Nitrites: benefits and drawbacks

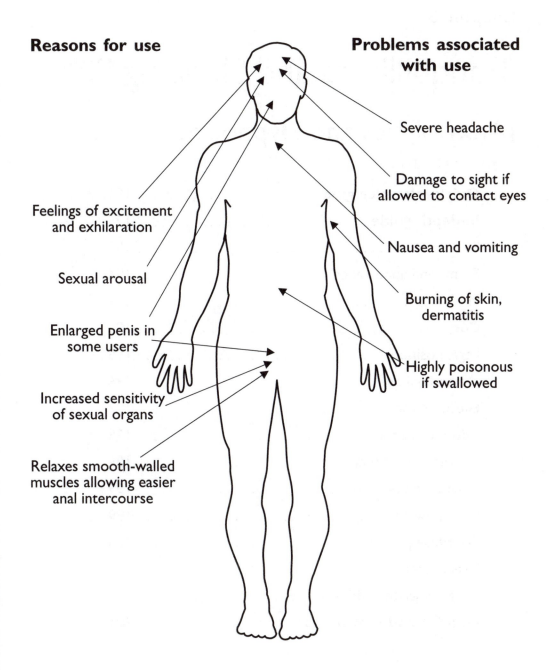

Reasons for use

Feelings of excitement
and exhilaration

Sexual arousal

Enlarged penis in
some users

Increased sensitivity
of sexual organs

Relaxes smooth-walled
muscles allowing easier
anal intercourse

**Problems associated
with use**

Severe headache

Damage to sight if
allowed to contact eyes

Nausea and vomiting

Burning of skin,
dermatitis

Highly poisonous
if swallowed

Chapter 8

Tranquillisers and Sleeping Pills

(Anxiolytics and Hypnotics)

Tranquillisers and sleeping pills: quick reference guide

Source

Wide range of synthetically produced drugs manufactured by the pharmaceutical industry to treat patients with problems of anxiety, depression and insomnia.

Forms and appearance

Many tranquillisers are based on either benzodiazepine or, more rarely, barbiturate. They are seen in tablet and capsule form in a wide variety of shapes, sizes and colours. Some are dispensed in an oral liquid form for ease of swallowing.

Marketing

Tranquillisers and sleeping pills remain the most commonly prescribed mind-altering drugs in the UK. Many of these drugs reach the street market from people who have been prescribed them and as a result of thefts from pharmacies and manufacturers.

Cost

There is no firmly established price for these drugs, except in areas where use is common. In areas where supplies are irregular, the vendor will set the price to suit the prevailing market. Prices can vary from as little as three tablets for £1 to £2 per tablet or capsule.

Legal position

Benzodiazepine-based tranquillisers and sleeping pills are classified as class C controlled substances within the Misuse of Drugs Act 1971. Possession for personal use is not illegal, but supplying them to a person other than as a result of a doctor's prescription is illegal.

Barbiturate-based variants are classified as class B controlled substances under the same act.

Methods of use

Tablets, liquids and capsules are usually taken orally, but they can be prepared for injection. There is evidence of a considerable rise in the use of these drugs by injection following crushing and dissolving the tablets into a solution. Other liquid forms are marketed for use by injection only.

Effects of use

When used as prescribed, the user will experience some relief from their symptoms of anxiety, depression and insomnia. When used in higher doses, the user will experience feelings of euphoria, dreaminess and elimination of worry, fear, hunger and cold.

Adverse effects

When used in high doses, the user may experience violent mood swings, aggression, bizarre sexual behaviour, deep depression, lethargy, tiredness, physical weakness and disorientation.

Tolerance potential

Tolerance develops very quickly with continued use.

Habituation potential

A powerful physical and psychological dependence on tranquillisers can develop quickly with continued use.

Withdrawal effects

Withdrawing from regular tranquilliser use can lead to confusion, nausea, insomnia, violent headaches, bizarre behaviour and depression. Sudden withdrawal from heavy use can lead to convulsions and even sudden death.

Overdose potential

Overdose can lead to convulsions, respiratory depression, coma and death; this is far more common with barbiturate-based products. The potential for overdose for both benzodiazepine and barbiturate drugs is increased significantly if their use is combined with alcohol consumption or use of other depressant substances.

Tranquillisers and sleeping pills: in-depth guide

Source

Tranquillisers and sleeping pills are based on synthetically produced substances and are manufactured by the million in a variety of forms by the pharmaceutical industry. They are designed mainly for short-term use in the treatment of a wide range of problems, most of which are of a psychological nature, including anxiety, stress, panic attacks, general restlessness, depression and insomnia. They are also used in the treatment of epilepsy, and some can be used as muscle relaxants.

Most commercially produced tranquillisers fall into two groups. The oldest group, now little used, are the tranquillisers based on barbiturate. Barbiturate was first isolated at the end of the nineteenth century, and it rapidly became popular in the treatment of a wide range of nervous disorders and to induce sleep. It became a prescription-only drug early in the twentieth century and was prescribed in vast quantities by doctors, who saw it as an effective and safe treatment. During the 1950s and 1960s, it became clear that use of barbiturates was not without its problems. Many thousands of users were prescribed barbiturates over a long period and became totally dependent on them. Overdoses were common, both accidental and deliberate. Barbiturates can be very dangerous if used at the same time as alcohol, and in the 1970s barbiturate overdose accounted for almost 50 per cent of all suicides recorded in the UK.

Chemists began to search for a safer drug that could offer the benefits of barbiturate but without the serious problems that it was causing. During the 1950s, a group of Swiss chemists isolated the active ingredient of the plant *Rauwolfia serpentina*, a bush that grows in Asia and Africa and that has been used as a herbal medicine for hundreds of years. Shortly after this first breakthrough, they managed to produce a synthetic form of the same substance, and an enormous industry was built up around the production of a whole range of benzodiazepine-based tranquillisers and sleeping pills.

Benzodiazepine tranquillisers offer all of the advantages of the earlier barbiturate-based products without some of the more dangerous side effects. As a result, their use has grown very rapidly, and they now represent the biggest group of mind-altering substances prescribed by doctors. They are not without their own problems, for tolerance to them can build up quickly and it is necessary to take larger doses as time goes on to achieve the beneficial effects. Continued use can lead to profound dependence, and withdrawal can be very difficult. These problems occur even in people who are taking tranquillisers on doctors' advice and who are adhering to the recommended dosage. The problems that occur in street users are far worse and are covered later in this chapter.

Forms and appearance

Tranquillisers and sleeping pills are produced by the pharmaceutical industry in both tablet and capsule form in a bewildering array of different shapes, sizes and colours. Some varieties are also produced as oral liquids and ampoules for injection. It is impossible to list all of the brand and generic names that describe the range of tranquillisers currently available, but it is worth mentioning a few that are well known in the UK and that have become popular with street users.

Diazepam, known commonly under its tradename of Valium, is a benzodiazepine-based tranquilliser manufactured as small tablets that may be white, pale yellow or blue in colour; the white type are the lowest strength and the blue the highest. Veterinary forms of diazepam are seen occasionally on the streets in the form of small white tablets. Diazepam is sometimes seen as an oral solution or in ampoules of injectable liquid.

Tuinal, Amytal and Soneryl are barbiturate products. They may be seen as blue-and-orange capsules or pink tablets.

Temazepam is a benzodiazepine-based hypnotic prescribed to overcome insomnia. It used to be produced in the form of gel-filled capsules in a variety of colours, the two most common being bright yellow and dark green. The capsules were available in a variety of sizes; the larger the capsule, the higher the strength. Because of the problems that have occurred with the misuse of the gel-filled capsules (see later in this chapter), dispensing in this form has been phased out and replaced with tablet forms in the UK. Temazepam is also seen as an oral solution.

Flunitrazepam (Rohypnol) is discussed in Chapter 11.

Marketing

Many millions of tranquillisers and sleeping pills are prescribed every year in the UK. The vast majority of these are used in a perfectly proper and responsible fashion and do not find their way on to the streets. However, a small percentage of prescriptions are written for patients who are only too willing to sell on their tranquillisers to others. Some users will visit a number of different doctors in order to obtain multiple prescriptions to feed their habit and to sell on. In order to increase the amount of tranquillisers that they have available for sale, some will attempt to increase the amount of the drug that has been prescribed by altering the prescriptions or by demanding higher doses. This is becoming much more difficult to do now that the majority of general practitioners use computer-generated prescriptions and are aware of the abuse potential of tranquillisers. The money raised by patients selling their tranquillisers is often used to buy other street drugs. This source accounts for the majority of street tranquillisers and sleeping pills; the rest arrive on the street scene from a variety of sources. Prescription pads may be stolen from doctors' surgeries, cars and bags and then filled out in imitation of that doctor's handwriting to obtain drug supplies for sale. Other supplies are obtained by burglary of pharmacies, hospitals and manufacturers' premises. Some employees of pharmaceutical companies have also been known to steal medication for sale on the streets.

Tranquillisers and sleeping pills are available in most urban population centres. Some areas have an established use among the street-drug-using population; this has been particularly true of temazepam in the urban centres of Scotland in past years. It is still true to say that illicit tranquilliser and sleeping pill use is patchy, and there may be areas where its use is still rare, but this is a rapidly changing scene. It is clear that the regular use and availability of street tranquillisers and sleeping pills has spread all over the UK.

Cost

Prices can vary widely. In areas where there is established use, the price will have settled to a recognised level. In areas where the use is relatively new and supplies are more irregular, the price will be set by the supplier, reflecting the amount available and the financial means of the buyers. A typical price range for tablets and capsules is between 50p and £2 each, with higher prices applying to any supplies of the drugs in injectable form. As with other street drugs, there are discounts available for bulk purchases.

Legal position

The legal position of these drugs is somewhat confused. Products based on barbiturates are class B, schedule 3 controlled substances within the Misuse of Drugs Act 1971. As the inclusion in schedule 3 would indicate, possession is permissible only when the drug has been obtained as a result of a doctor's prescription; otherwise, the following penalties apply:

- *Possession for personal use*: the possession of any amount of barbiturate for personal use is punishable on indictment by a maximum sentence of five years' imprisonment plus an unlimited fine.

- *Possession with intent to supply*: possession of barbiturate with intent to supply the drug by sale or gift to another person is punishable on indictment with a maximum sentence of 14 years' imprisonment plus an unlimited fine, plus seizure of all drug-related assets.

- *Supplying*: as for possession with intent to supply.

- *Importation*: as for possession with intent to supply.

The position of benzodiazepine products is less clear. Some of them are controlled only by the Medicines Act 1968, which allows unauthorised possession but forbids the supply by unlicensed people. Other forms are controlled substances under class C, schedule 4 of the Misuse of Drugs Act 1971. As schedule 4 substances, it is not an offence to possess them, even without a prescription, providing that the tranquilliser is still in its original form. If it has been altered in any way, e.g. by crushing tablets to prepare them for injection, then class C penalties apply:

- *Possession for personal use*: possessing benzodiazepine that has been altered in any way so that it is not in its original medicinal form is punishable on indictment by a maximum penalty of two years' imprisonment and an unlimited fine.

- *Possession with intent to supply*: possessing benzodiazepines in any form with intent to supply them by gift or sale to another person is punishable on indictment by a maximum penalty of five years' imprisonment, plus an unlimited fine, plus seizure of all drug-related assets.

- *Supplying*: as with possession with intent to supply.

- *Importation*: importing benzodiazepines is not an offence provided that they are in their original medicinal form.

Methods of use

The tablet, capsule and oral suspension forms are usually taken by mouth, but an increasing amount are being prepared for injection. The tablets can simply be crushed between two spoons into as fine a powder as the user can achieve, which is then dissolved in water. It is less common with tranquilliser use to add acidic substances, such as lemon juice, than when preparing other drugs, such as heroin, since most tranquilliser preparations will dissolve easily in water. The resultant mix is drawn up into a hypodermic needle and syringe through a filter of some sort to remove any undissolved particles. A portion of a cigarette filter or a twist of cotton-wool is commonly used for this purpose. The drug is then injected into a vein. Even if the user is an experienced injector and takes a great deal of care, it is common for small undissolved particles of the drug to get into the syringe and then into the bloodstream. These particles can lodge within the veins or tissues around them, and cause ulceration, infection and gangrene. We once dealt with the suicide of a Valium injector, whose veins of choice were in the back of his hands. He developed an infection at one injection site that developed into gangrene, resulting in him having the hand amputated above the wrist. He carried on injecting into the stump until he took his own life a year or so later.

Recently, there was a dramatic increase in the injection of temazepam. Temazepam was commonly found in the form of a range of brightly coloured oval capsules that contained the drug in the form of a gel. These were known on the streets as 'eggs', 'jellies' or 'jelly beans' because of their appearance. It was thought at first that this would make it much more difficult to inject the drug, but the ingenuity of determined users was up to the task and the problem soon solved. Users found that if the capsules were heated, e.g. in a microwave oven for a very short time, the gel would liquidise and could be drawn out of the gelatine case of the capsule with a needle and syringe. The capsules were emptied to provide the user with their chosen dose, and the liquid was then injected while still warm and in concentrated form. If the liquid was diluted with water, there was a tendency for the gel to reform, making injection more difficult. This also happens if the liquid is allowed to cool too much. It was not uncommon for the gel to reform once inside the veins of the user and cause, in some cases, a total blockage. Because of the problems with temazepam in gel form being used for injection, it was decided to phase out these capsules. Temazepam is now available only in tablet form in the UK. This does not prevent the product being injected, but it does remove some of the problems for injectors of the gel form.

Effects of use

Tranquillisers and sleeping pills can bring great relief when prescribed by doctors to people suffering from conditions that respond to these drugs. It is not this use that we are concerned with here. It is the misuse of these drugs that has grown to problem proportions in recent years.

Many street users of these drugs take them in doses that are higher than the recommended maxima to achieve feelings of euphoria and dreaminess. The user drifts off into a drug-induced state of mind, where all anxiety, stress and fear disappear, and they will exist in a twilight world of intoxicated peace, congeniality and sociability, which can last for several hours. Users often combine the use of tranquillisers with alcohol, which exaggerates the effects of the tranquillisers. People whose living circumstances are poor may use the drugs to help them escape feelings of hunger and cold.

Other users take tranquilliseres to alleviate the withdrawal problems associated with other drug use. Opiate users often inject tranquillisers to obtain relief from the withdrawal symptoms of dependence when supplies of their usual drug are not available. Some opiate users will self-medicate with high levels of tranquillisers when attempting to detox from opiate use without medical help.

Because of the calming effects of tranquillisers, many users of stimulants such as amphetamine, cocaine and ecstasy take tranquillisers towards the end of a prolonged spree of stimulant use to act as a 'parachute drug' and ease the unpleasant effects that result when stimulant use ceases, such as insomnia.

The injection of tranquillisers increases the speed of onset of their effects and their intensity.

Adverse effects

It is very common for street users of tranquillisers and sleeping pills to take very high doses – many times the normal medicinal dose is not unusual. This can be exacerbated further by heavy alcohol use and the use of other drugs. The combined effects of such use can be extremely unpredictable and often very unpleasant.

Users may experience extreme changes of mood, with feelings that swing from euphoria and peace to extreme agitation, irritability and aggression. This can be coupled with paranoid feelings that everyone is against them and may even result in acts of violence. Other users display bizarre behaviour, often acting in a totally inappropriate way in relation to the circumstances they find themselves in; such behaviours are often sexual in nature.

Long-term users often become depressed and withdraw from the world completely. They may experience extreme tiredness and loss of strength and have no energy to do anything. This includes keeping themselves clean and eating adequately, and as a result their general body condition often declines alarmingly.

Injecting tranquillisers carries with it all of the risks associated with injecting any drug. Ulceration and infection of injection sites is common, with the added potential for the infection to become gangrenous, often requiring the amputation of a limb to prevent its spread. The sharing of injection equipment with other users carries the risk of passing infections from one person to another, and such users run very real risks of contracting HIV or hepatitis or of developing septicaemia.

Tolerance potential

All tranquillisers have the potential to lead rapidly to tolerance. The body learns quickly to adapt to the drugs and their effects begin to decrease. It is then necessary for the user to increase the amount of drug or the frequency of use. Another way of overcoming tolerance is to increase the amount of alcohol that is used at the same time, so that the tranquilliser's effects are strengthened. Little is gained by changing to another form of tranquilliser, as tolerance developed to one form is almost always carried over to the new form.

Habituation potential

Both barbiturate and benzodiazepine tranquillisers have the potential to lead to severe dependence. This dependence will often be both physical and psychological and can be very profound. The higher the dose taken and the longer the period of use, the more risk there is of dependence developing. It can reach a point where the user becomes totally dependent on the drug to cope with their life and feels afraid to attempt to decrease or cease use.

Withdrawal effects

The withdrawal effects of heavy or long-term use of tranquillisers can be very unpleasant to experience or observe. It has been suggested that such withdrawal is more difficult and more unpleasant than withdrawal from heroin.

Sudden withdrawal can be dangerous; in the case of barbiturates, it can result in convulsions, fits and sudden death. Withdrawal from tranquillisers can be achieved if it is managed and carried out over a period of time, but if sudden withdrawal is attempted the user may experience unpleasant bouts of psychosis, depression, agitation, fitting, insomnia, panic attacks, hallucinations and confusion. They may also experience heavy, unpleasant levels of perspiration, nausea and vomiting, which may be accompanied by a high degree of weight loss.

Withdrawal from heavy or long-term misuse of tranquillisers should never be attempted without seeking professional help.

Overdose potential

Both forms of tranquillisers can be very dangerous if taken in overdose. This danger is exacerbated by the fact that the difference between the high doses needed to achieve the desired effects of misuse are very close to the overdose levels of these drugs. It is easy to overdose accidentally, particularly if the user's judgement is impaired by other depressant drugs or alcohol at the time. Similarly, if the user has been tranquilliser-free for a period of time, their tolerance level will have reduced, and returning to their usual dose can lead directly to overdose. The effects of overdose include extreme drowsiness, depression of the breathing reflex leading to very slow and shallow breathing, a very weak pulse, and cold and clammy skin. If untreated, this can lead quickly to coma and death.

Street names

Tranquillisers: tranx, benzos, barbs, barbies, blockers, blockbusters, downers, tueys, chewies, traffic lights, goof balls, moggies

Temazepam in jelly capsules: jellies, jelly beans, M&Ms, yellow eggs, green eggs, rugby balls

Slang associated with use

Freaking, pill popping – Use of tranquillisers

Losing the plot – Being heavily under the influence

Tranquillisers: benefits and drawbacks

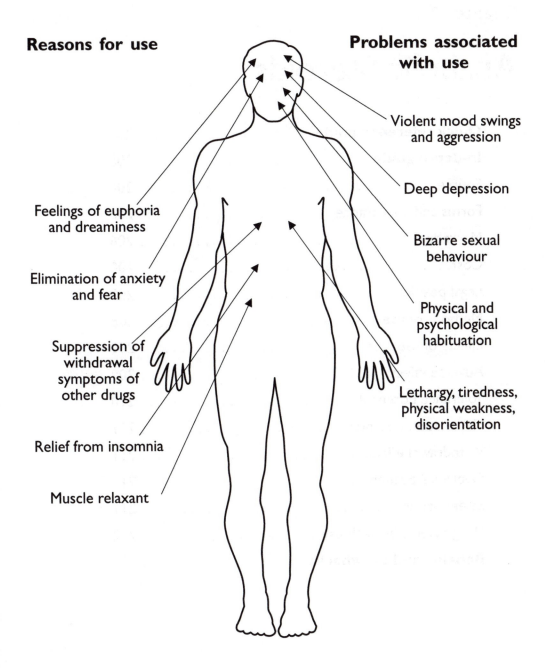

Reasons for use

Feelings of euphoria and dreaminess

Elimination of anxiety and fear

Suppression of withdrawal symptoms of other drugs

Relief from insomnia

Muscle relaxant

Problems associated with use

Violent mood swings and aggression

Deep depression

Bizarre sexual behaviour

Physical and psychological habituation

Lethargy, tiredness, physical weakness, disorientation

Chapter 9

Anabolic Steroids

Anabolic steroids: quick reference guide

Source

Group of synthetic products formulated to imitate natural hormones produced within the human body.

Forms and appearance

Produced in capsule and tablet forms in a variety of colours and in injectable liquid form.

Marketing

The solid and liquid forms are usually marketed in their original packaging. Many of them will have been manufactured outside the UK, with little control being applied to quality and purity. A large proportion of the anabolic steroids used for non-medical purposes have been produced specifically for veterinary use.

There is little or no street trade in steroids. The street drug dealer is not the usual supplier of these substances: most users buy them from someone they know who shares their interest in body-building, body-sculpturing or sport. Another major source is the Internet, with large numbers of websites offering a wide range of anabolic steroids for sale. By following up advertisements in certain body-building magazines, it is sometimes possible to obtain steroids by mail order.

Cost

Due to the limited nature of the market for steroids, no established prices exist. Vendors of these drugs will set their prices to suit the customers that they are in contact with. A typical price for steroids in the UK would be in the region of £20 for 100 tablets. The price for vials and bottles of injectable liquid varies according to type and price. A single-dose vial in the UK costs £8–10.

There have been many instances in which steroids have been supplied free of charge by unscrupulous sports coaches to young people engaged in competition.

Legal position

Anabolic steroids are controlled by the Medicines Act 1968, which makes it an offence to supply pharmaceutical forms of the drugs without a prescription but not to possess them. Anabolic steroids are class C drugs under the Misuse of Drugs Act 1971, which makes it an offence to possess or to supply non-pharmaceutical forms of the drugs.

Methods of use

Steroids can be taken orally in the form of tablets and capsules, but the most common form of misuse is to inject the liquid form intramuscularly.

Effects of use

Most users experience an increase in muscle growth and body bulk, together with greater stamina and strength.

Adverse effects

There is a long list of problems associated with excess use. These include bone-growth irregularities, high blood pressure, heart disease, liver and kidney dysfunction, liver and kidney cancers, hepatitis, shrinking of the testes, uncontrollable erections, impotence, mood swings, aggression and irritability, disruption of fetal development, development of breasts in males, and irreversible enlargement of the clitoris.

Tolerance potential

Tolerance develops with continued use.

Habituation potential

There is little evidence of a purely physical dependence developing with continued use, but many users experience a profound psychological dependence upon these drugs.

Withdrawal effects

Some users experience a catastrophic collapse of muscle strength and stamina together with extreme irritability and mood changes.

Overdose potential

Overdosing with steroids can lead to collapse, coma, convulsions and death.

Anabolic steroids: in-depth guide

Source

Anabolic steroids are produced by the pharmaceutical industry for use in the treatment of certain human health disorders and for veterinary purposes. They are designed to imitate naturally occurring hormones with anabolic and androgenic properties. The anabolic properties help in the formation of muscle tissue and body bulk, which give the user extra strength and stamina. The androgenic properties control the development of the sexual organs in both sexes and the development of other masculine or feminine features.

The synthetically produced steroids that are misused are almost always those designed to imitate the anabolic properties of the natural hormones. Although this is the intention when the anabolic steroid products are manufactured, it is impossible to completely eliminate the androgenic properties, and all anabolic steroids will also have an effect on the sexual development of the user. The term 'anabolic steroid' does not include the wide range of corticosteroids, which have a number of uses in the treatment of conditions such as asthma and eczema.

Forms and appearance

The steroids that are misused normally will have been produced commercially for medical and veterinary use and will be found in tablet and capsule form in a wide range of colours. Anabolic steroids are also manufactured in liquid form for injection. It is in this form that most misusers administer their steroids. The liquid forms are often in single-dose vials or multi-dose bottles, with a self-sealing rubber membrane at the top that allows the insertion of a hypodermic needle (see Figure 9.1).

Marketing

Anabolic steroids are not normally available through the normal channels of supply that apply to other street drugs. The trade in anabolic steroids is established within a fairly tight circle of like-minded people. Most misuse of steroids occurs by people engaged in body-building or body-sculpturing, for competition or recreational purposes. Body-builders are interested in developing their physique to a form that is

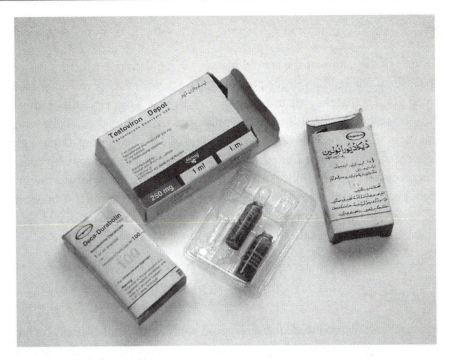

Figure 9.1 Anabolic steroids

seen by those involved in the sport as being ideal. Body-sculptors are interested in achieving a body form that they see as being beautiful or attractive to others, or as expressing the image that they wish to create of themselves. It is the muscle-building effect of anabolic steroid products that these people are seeking, and they will almost always be supplied with their drug of choice by someone connected with the gymnasium, sporting establishment or club that they are part of. There have been many instances of these drugs being supplied to young people involved in sport by their coaches.

A lot of the steroids in use have been manufactured in the former Eastern Bloc countries, where standards of purity and quality control often are poor. The instructions and dosages often are not written in English, and it may be difficult to determine the strength of a particular product. A large proportion of these imported steroids were manufactured for use in veterinary medicine and were never intended for human use. Dosage instructions therefore will not relate to human use.

Sources such as these also supply large quantities of counterfeit steroids, i.e. steroids that carry recognised trade names of pharmaceutical products but have been produced by unauthorised manufacturers to dubious purity standards. Other counterfeit products sold as steroids may in fact contain no genuine steroids at all.

Cost

Because of the nature of the steroid market, no regular price structure has become established. The vendor sets the price according to what they perceive the particular group of users that they are in contact with will bear. The price will be affected by the relationship that exists between supplier and user. Many users will get together and share steroids that have been obtained by one of their group. Other users will have their drugs supplied at reduced cost or even without charge by coaches or other members of the same team. When ordered by mail order or via the Internet, anabolic steroid tablets typically cost around £20 per 100 in the UK; injectable liquid costs around £8–10 for a single-dose vial. Much larger bottles of liquid are available, and as always there are savings to be made by buying in bulk.

Legal position

Pharmaceutically produced anabolic steroid products are available only on prescription or through a veterinary surgeon in the UK and thus are controlled by the Medicines Act 1968. To import, purchase or possess them for personal use is not an offence. It is an offence, however, under the Medicines Act for an unlicensed person to supply them to another, either by sale or as a gift. This offence carries a maximum penalty of six months' imprisonment and a £5000 fine.

Non-pharmaceutically produced anabolic steroids, i.e. counterfeits of genuine drugs, are controlled under class C of the Misuse of Drugs Act 1971; possession of such drugs carries a maximum sentence of two years' imprisonment and a £5000 fine.

Most professional and amateur sports and body-building coaches have to be licensed by the governing body of their particular sport. These organisations have very firm anti-drug policies, and any coach supplying or allowing the use of steroids by people under their supervision will risk instant revocation of their licence.

Methods of use

The tablet and capsule forms of the drug are usually taken orally, but sometimes they are prepared for injection. The use of steroids in this form is very much overshadowed by the use of the liquid injectable forms. The drug is much more effective when injected into the muscle tissue, and this method is favoured by regular users. Many users obtain their steroids in large multi-dose bottles that contain a large number of doses. The bottle has a rubber membrane at the top, which allows the repeated insertion of a hypodermic needle to draw up each dose. The use of such multi-dose packs reduces the cost of the drug but introduces a potentially deadly risk. Many of these bottles are shared by groups of users, who each take their dose from it. It is not unknown for such groups to share the same injecting equipment. There is a common belief among such users that they are not at risk of contracting diseases such as HIV/AIDS or hepatitis or developing septicaemia, because they are all fit and live healthy lifestyles. Users often believe, mistakenly, that body-builders and sports-people are always 'straight' and therefore not likely to have been exposed to such problems through unsafe homosexual practices. These falsely held beliefs can expose users to the risks of contracting and then spreading dangerous and potentially fatal diseases by sharing infected injecting equipment.

Effects of use

The use of anabolic steroids is usually combined with a strict regime of diet and strenuous exercise in order to build the type of muscle tissue that the user is seeking. The drug will encourage the body to convert a high-protein diet into muscle, which is further toned and strengthened by the exercise.

Many steroid users achieve a marked increase in body bulk and develop powerful and clearly defined muscles all over their bodies. This leads to a considerable increase in strength and stamina, which, combined with the correct regime of exercise, can result in a useful increase in sporting performance.

Adverse effects

Little is known about the effects of long-term and regular use of anabolic steroids. Many of the products misused were never intended for use in humans, and little research has been carried out concerning this. From the knowledge that we do have, it is clear that misusers of steroids run very grave risks with their bodies' natural development and long-term health.

Because of the androgenic properties of steroids, many adolescents who use anabolic steroids will experience changes in their sexual drive. In young males, the penis may enlarge and the user may suffer problems with frequent and uncontrollable erections. These erections can last a very long time and become extremely painful. Adult male users often experience shrinking of the testes and difficulty in achieving erection. They may also develop breasts of a distinctly female nature, with nipples that become very pronounced and often painfully inflamed.

Female adolescents may suffer disturbance of the menstrual cycle; prepubescent users may fail to develop a proper menstrual cycle at all. In others, the clitoris may become painfully enlarged and inflamed. Some female users experience deepening of the voice and excessive growth of dark facial and body hair, while others develop patterns of irreversible baldness normally seen only in men. Pregnant users run the risk of the drug interfering with the proper development of the fetus, with the result that a miscarriage may occur or the child may be stillborn or may have physical or mental abnormalities.

Both adolescent and adult users may experience severe personality changes, which may take the form of an increase in irritability, aggression and the potential for violent behaviour, known as 'roid rage'. This may be coupled with an increase in sexual drive, leading some users into inappropriate sexual behaviour or committing violent sexual crimes.

When use of steroids has been heavy or prolonged, the user may develop clear signs of mental illness. Bizarre behaviour, extreme paranoia and delusions may become apparent and lead to the user requiring inpatient treatment in a psychiatric hospital.

Dysfunction of the liver and kidney can occur; in some cases, complete failure of these organs can result, leading to serious illness and death. Cancers of the liver and kidney have been reported in some long-term users.

There may be visible signs of use in some heavy steroid users. The skin and the pupils of the eyes take on a yellow colour, with the skin showing frequent outbreaks of acne or rashes of red spots. The breath develops a powerful and unpleasant odour.

The development of groups of abnormally large and powerful muscles in certain parts of the body may put an unnatural pressure on other muscle groups and lead to strains and other injuries that take an unusually long time to heal.

When used by young people who have not achieved full growth, anabolic steroids may cause premature closure of the bone ends in the legs, which will prevent them growing to full length. This condition will lead to a loss of height potential in the person and is irreversible.

Tolerance potential

As with most drugs, the body learns to adapt itself to steroids, and the user will find that they achieve less and less from them as time passes. This will mean that they will have to increase the individual dose taken or the frequency of use. At the same time, the body bulk will be increasing, and so more of the drug may be needed for equivalent effect. This may lead to a pattern of constantly increasing use, which exposes the user more and more to the adverse effects that the drugs can cause.

Habituation potential

There is little evidence of the development of any physical dependence on steroids. Many users become psychologically dependent on the drug due to their 'need' to maintain the body shape and performance that they see as being so important. They have used the drug to achieve a body that gives them the status and self-image that they desire, and consequently they are afraid to stop using the drug in case this leads to a loss of muscular definition, strength and performance, with a subsequent loss of status and self-image.

This dependence can be very powerful, and the user may become locked into a pattern of use that they feel unable to break out of, even when they become aware of the adverse effects of steroids.

Withdrawal effects

Sudden, unsupervised withdrawal from heavy or long-term use of anabolic steroids can be dangerous. The user may suffer complete muscular collapse, leading to an almost total loss of strength and stamina. This has resulted in hospitalisation in many cases and confinement to a wheelchair for long periods before the body can be rehabilitated in some.

Other users suffer considerable psychological problems during withdrawal, experiencing violent mood swings and periods of severe depression and anxiety.

No regular or heavy user of steroids should attempt to withdraw from their use without seeking professional help.

Overdose potential

Heavy doses of steroids can lead to a dangerous increase in body temperature and blood pressure. This will increase the possibility of heart failure and stroke. Overdose can also lead to convulsions, collapse, coma and the possibility of sudden death.

Street names

Roids

Also a large number of generic and brand names, including Sustanon, Deca-Durabolin (nandrolone), Anavar, Anadrol, Equipose, stanozolol, Dianabol

Slang associated with use

Roid rage – Aggression and violence associated with long-term steroid use

Stacking – Combination of using fast- and slow-acting steroids to achieve particular effects over a specific timescale

Anabolic steroids: benefits and drawbacks

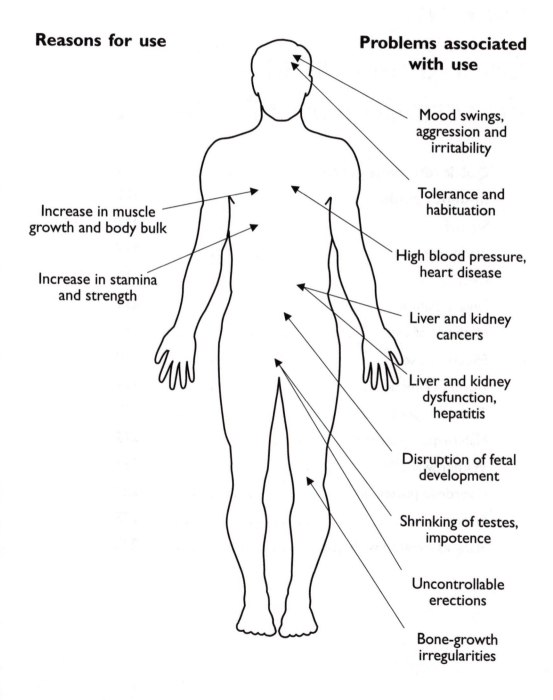

Reasons for use

Problems associated with use

Mood swings, aggression and irritability

Tolerance and habituation

Increase in muscle growth and body bulk

High blood pressure, heart disease

Increase in stamina and strength

Liver and kidney cancers

Liver and kidney dysfunction, hepatitis

Disruption of fetal development

Shrinking of testes, impotence

Uncontrollable erections

Bone-growth irregularities

Chapter 10

Over-the-counter and Prescription-only Medicines

Over-the-counter and prescription-only medicines: quick reference guide

Source

Wide range of medicines available with or without prescription. They fall into three basic groups: opiates, antihistamines and sympathomimetic.

Marketing

Medicinal preparations that are sold under a number of brand and generic names from pharmacies, drug stores, supermarkets and general stores. They are also sold via the Internet and sometimes on the street.

Cost

Prices vary from product to product, but in general terms the misuse of these preparations costs less than that of street drugs.

Legal position

Some of these preparations contain substances that are controlled by the Misuse of Drugs Act 1971 or the Medicines Act 1968, but some are free from control.

Methods of use

The vast majority of misused over-the-counter medicines are taken orally, although some are injected occasionally.

Effects of use

The effects achieved vary from product to product and according to the dose taken.

Adverse effects

These differ according to the product being used and the dose taken.

Tolerance potential

Tolerance will develop with continued use of many of these drugs.

Habituation potential

All of these products have the potential to create physical or psychological dependence with repeated or long-term use.

Withdrawal effects

Withdrawal from many of these products can produce unpleasant effects.

Overdose potential

Serious overdose of many of these products can be dangerous and may be fatal.

Over-the-counter and prescription-only medicines: in-depth guide

Source

A wide range of medicinal products are available to treat a variety of medical conditions. Some of these preparations are available only by means of a doctor's prescription. Others are available without prescription but can only be sold by registered pharmacists. Many others can be purchased without restrictions from general stores and similar outlets.

Marketing

The list of preparations that can be misused is long and includes a large number of products sold under various brand and generic names. It would not be practical to produce a comprehensive list of products that can be misused in this way, as new products are constantly being added to those already available. Most of the products that are misused fall into three basic groups, which we will look at in more detail.

Opiate products

A number of products contain opiate substances. Most of these are naturally occurring opiates, such as morphine and codeine, which are obtained from the opium poppy, but some contain opiate-like products that have been produced synthetically.

These products are intended for use as painkillers, cough treatments and medicines for stomach disorders and diarrhoea. All opiates have good analgesic (painkilling) properties and are often added to other substances in preparations intended to provide pain relief. The most powerful of these contain dihydrocodeine tartrate, a potent synthetic form of codeine. This drug is sold on its own, marketed under names including DHC and DF 118 Forte, and in combination with other analgesics, such as paracetamol, and marketed under names including Co-dydramol and Remedeine. These are available legally in the UK only on prescription, but a thriving street trade in these drugs exists. They are also widely available through a number of Internet sites.

A wide range of codeine phosphate-based painkilling preparations, usually in tablet or capsule form, are available without prescription from pharmacies in the

UK. Such remedies usually contain a mixture of either paracetamol or ibuprofen and codeine phosphate. A number of websites sell these preparations.

Opiate substances have a calming effect on the nerves that produce the coughing reflex. Many cough medicines contain preparations of codeine or morphine and are available in the UK from pharmacies without a doctor's prescription. These can usually be identified by the manufacturer's warning that the product may cause drowsiness and cautioning the user against driving, using machinery and drinking alcohol while using the medicine. These types of cough remedy are commonly misused, for example Gee's linctus, which until recently was one of the UK's most popular cough medicines.

Many stomach and diarrhoea treatments contain morphine or codeine. The analgesic effects of these substances alleviate the pain of stomach disorders and also slow down the action of the bowel, therefore easing the debilitating effects of constant diarrhoea. Although now considered old-fashioned in these days of branded medicines, kaolin and morphine mixture is still available from pharmacies without prescription. It can be sold only under the supervision of a pharmacist, but it is relatively inexpensive and contains a substantial level of tincture of morphine, sometimes called 'opiate squill'. If the mixture is allowed to settle, the purified kaolin falls to the bottom of the bottle, leaving above it a clear brown liquid high in morphine. It is this liquid that the misuser is seeking.

Antihistamine products

A large range of medicinal products are available containing antihistamines in one form or another. Some of these products are available only on prescription, while others are available without prescription from pharmacists. They are commonly used to alleviate the symptoms of hay fever, allergic reactions to certain insect bites and other allergic conditions. They are also used to treat a range of skin rashes, such as nettle rash, in some cough preparations, in many travel-sickness remedies and to aid sleep.

Sympathomimetic products

The term 'sympathomimetic' is used to describe a range of substances whose actions mimic a number of naturally produced substances within our bodies. They are included in several products used to alleviate the symptoms of colds and 'flu. They are used particularly in the 'cold-cure' products that dry up a runny nose and clear a congested chest. Similar substances are also found in many laxative products.

Some people use laxatives habitually and in large doses in order to assist them in losing weight. This use is often associated with people with anorexia nervosa. Many of these products contain substances that are chemically similar to amphetamine and have similar effects. Most are available without prescription but must be purchased from a pharmacy.

In the UK, the Council of the Royal Pharmaceutical Society issued advice in 2004 to pharmacists that they should be alert to anyone buying any opiates, antihistamines or sympathomimetics either regularly or in large quantities.

Cost

Most of the products discussed above can be obtained from a number of Internet sites at widely ranging prices. Painkilling tablets containing codeine retail from pharmacies in the UK for as little as £2 for 20 tablets, while some of the cold remedies retail at around £2.50 for 20 tablets. Where available, both Gee's linctus and kaolin and morphine retail at around £2.50 for a 250ml bottle.

Legal position

Preparations that use opiate products are controlled by the Misuse of Drugs Act 1971. As opiates, they are class A substances in schedule 5. Their place in this schedule allows them to be sold over the counter without prescription, but only by registered pharmacists. Having purchased them lawfully, it is an offence to supply them to another person other than for a medical purpose. If they are supplied to another person for misuse, then the full penalties of any class A drug can be applied.

Antihistamine and sympathomimetic preparations are controlled by the Medicines Act 1968, which regulates their availability through pharmacies and other retail outlets. Supplying these products for misuse could make the supplier liable to a maximum fine of £5000.

Methods of use

All of these preparations have been designed to be taken orally, and it is by this method that most misuse occurs. Some users who are seeking extreme effects or are experimenting crush the tablet forms and prepare them for injecting or inject the liquid forms.

Effects of use

The effects that the preparations were intended to produce are very rarely those that the misuser is seeking. The sought-after effects can usually be produced only by taking very much higher doses of the products than are recommended for medicinal purposes.

Opiate products

When taken in high doses, opiate products will produce the effects of opiates such as heroin but in a much milder form. The user will not experience the hit or rush that heroin produces, but they will feel relaxed, calm and free from worries and physical and emotional pain. Many users of heroin turn to other opiate-based medicinal products, such as those detailed above, to control the withdrawal effects of heroin when they are unable to obtain or afford their usual drug of choice. Some users, however, will never use heroin but will exclusively use over-the-counter opiate products as a matter of choice.

Antihistamine products

Most antihistamine products cause drowsiness if taken to excess. This effect is increased if alcohol is used at the same time. This drowsy state can be very relaxing and allows the user to feel free from the responsibility of facing their problems. Most antihistamine products also have an antiemetic effect, controlling feelings of nausea and preventing vomiting. Most opiates produce nausea in some users, and users sometimes take large doses of antihistamine to control these effects. Some users crush antihistamine tablets, particularly those intended for travel-sickness, and mix the resultant powder with their heroin and inject both substances at the same time, thus achieving the effects that they desire while avoiding the nauseous effects.

Sympathomimetic products

Because of the chemical similarity of some sympathomimetic products to amphetamine, the most sought-after effect of their misuse is to achieve stimulation. The user takes high doses of the product to achieve feelings of uplift and exhilaration, together with an increase in energy and stamina. Some people use these products when supplies of their usual stimulants are not available to them, but some users use only over-the-counter products through choice and never use their street equivalents.

Adverse effects

Most misusers of over-the-counter medicines use them in much higher doses than the manufacturers recommend in order to achieve the effects that they are seeking. This can also mean that they experience adverse effects that people using the products at their normal dosages do not suffer.

Opiate products

Most misusers of opiate-based products experience the normal adverse effects of street opiate use, such as depression of breathing and heart rate together with the risk of vomiting. They are likely also to suffer psychological problems and changes in their personality.

Heavy users of opiate-based medical preparations also run the risk of suffering from other problems such as serious kidney disease. This can become so severe that total kidney failure can occur, placing the user's life under serious threat and requiring a great deal of medical care to overcome. They may also suffer serious digestive problems, such as extreme constipation, ulceration of the stomach lining and internal bleeding. Long-term use may also lead to anaemia and problems with the immune system.

Many misusers of opiate-based painkilling products suffer serious health problems caused by the other ingredients in the product. These opiates commonly are combined with paracetamol, which can cause serious and even fatal damage to the liver if used heavily and over a prolonged period.

Antihistamine products

The excessive misuse of preparations containing antihistamines can lead to serious eye problems, including blurred and double vision. These can be very long-lasting and difficult to treat. This may be accompanied by persistent headaches, nausea and vomiting. Long-term use also can lead to problems with the digestive system, with alternating bouts of constipation and diarrhoea. This can be debilitating and may lead to a serious reduction in general health.

Sympathomimetic products

Excessive and prolonged use of sympathomimetic products exposes the user to the risks associated with the use of amphetamine-like drugs. There may be profound psychological changes and the appearance of latent mental problems. Many of these products can cause heavy and continuous diarrhoea, which can lead to the loss of vital vitamins and trace elements from the body, leading to a serious deterioration in health. It can further lead to the user becoming prone to many disorders that normally the body would be able to resist. The stimulant effects acting on a severely weakened body can lead to cardiac arrest and sudden death.

Tolerance potential

All of these products have the potential for tolerance to develop within the misuser. This will result in more and more of the product being required to achieve the effects that are sought. As the dose rises, so does the risk of adverse effects being experienced, and serious damage to general health may occur.

Habituation potential

Products that contain opiates have the potential to cause serious physical dependence in their misusers. This dependence can become so severe that the misuser's whole life becomes built around their use of the product. This is commonly seen when codeine-based cough mixtures, or morphine based Gee's linctus or kaolin and morphine are misused. It can reach the point where up to five bottles of the preparation are used each day. The misuser may have a particular preference for one type over another, but most misusers will use whichever is available if necessary. As these products can be purchased only from a pharmacy, misusers may spend a great deal of time travelling around from one pharmacy to another, buying a bottle in each so as to avoid arousing suspicion. On one occasion we know of, a user's car was searched by the police and 22 empty bottles of Gee's linctus were found scattered on the floor. From the labels affixed to the bottles, it was deduced that they had been sold over the course of a week or so, from eight different pharmacies in the area around the user's home. Another misuser of Gee's linctus, who was in his mid-thirties, while looking at his history of drug use with his drug counsellor estimated that he had consumed 30,000 bottles of the product in his lifetime.

These and the other types of over-the-counter medicines described earlier all have the potential to create psychological dependence. Misusers feel that life is too difficult or unpleasant to face without the chemical prop provided by their substance of choice.

These dependencies can be very difficult to treat and require a great deal of skilled help and support if there is to be any chance of success.

Withdrawal effects

The opiate-based products produce the withdrawal effects that are experienced by users of street heroin (see page 154).

Most heavy and prolonged misusers of other over-the-counter medicines experience problems of anxiety and panic when they stop using their chosen drug. They may also experience abrupt and unpleasant reactions, including vomiting, constipation and diarrhoea, as their body tries to adapt to going without the large amounts of drug that previously were being used. Anyone who has been regularly misusing products of this nature over any length of time is well advised to seek professional help before trying to withdraw abruptly.

Overdose potential

All of these preparations are being used in overdose, when misused in the ways that have been described. It is often only by taking them in overdose that the desired effects can be achieved. In extreme overdose situations, many of the products can produce very real risks. Heart, breathing and circulation problems can occur, which could lead to collapse, coma and death.

Street names

Dihydrocodeine tablets: DFs, diffs, doofers

Slang associated with use

The nod – Effect of dihydrocodeine

Chapter 11

'Date-rape' Drugs

The expression 'date-rape drug' is a recent addition to the drug-related lexicon in the UK. It is generally applied to the practice of plying an unsuspecting woman or, more rarely, man with a stupefying, amnesia-inducing or mood-altering substance in order to facilitate non-consensual sex. The practice itself is, of course, very old: men have been plying women with alcoholic drink in the hope of gaining 'consent' for sex for centuries. In more recent times, however, we have seen an increasing use of more powerful drugs, either on their own or in combination with alcohol, to achieve the same outcome.

In this chapter, we examine in detail two of the drugs most commonly used for this purpose, Rohypnol (flunitrazepam) and gamma-hydroxybutyrate (GHB). Reference should also be made in this regard to ketamine, a full description of which can be found in Chapter 5.

Rohypnol (flunitrazepam)

Rohypnol: quick reference guide

Source

Flunitrazepam, a sedative drug produced under the trade name Rohypnol.

Forms and appearance

Seen as dull-green caplets with a blue core, or more rarely as small white tablet scored with an imprinted groove or cross and the manufacturer's name 'ROCHE' together with an encircled '1' or '2' imprinted on the reverse. The US Drug Enforcement Administration have reported the seizure of some counterfeit examples in Egypt, which were pinkish brown in colour.

Marketing

Besides its use as a sedative, flunitrazepam is used both to facilitate non-consensual sex and as a 'parachute drug' for people coming down from prolonged or excessive stimulant use. The only legal source of supply in the UK is through a doctor's private prescription. Manufacturers of Rohypnol have ceased commercial distribution of this product in the UK. A small street trade exists for people seeking the drug, sourced through surpluses of the drug sold on by those who have been prescribed it by their doctor and through supplies bought over the Internet.

Cost

Around £1–2 per tablet in the UK.

Legal position

Flunitrazepam is a class C drug under the Misuse of Drugs Act 1971. Possession and supply other than by prescription is an offence.

Methods of use

Rohypnol is taken orally. When administered to someone without their knowledge, it is usually placed in a drink.

Effects of use

Sedation and feelings of euphoria.

Adverse effects

Sleepiness, numbness, loss of muscle control, confusion and amnesia.

Tolerance potential

Tolerance develops in people taking regular doses.

Habituation potential

In people using the drug regularly, and especially in large doses, a powerful physical dependence can occur.

Withdrawal effects

Withdrawal from habituated use can lead to anxiety, tension, restlessness and irritability and, in extreme cases, hallucinations, delirium, convulsions, shock and cardiovascular collapse.

Overdose potential

Overdose can lead to serious illness and death.

Rohypnol: in-depth guide

Source

Rohypnol is the trade name of a sedative called flunitrazepam, which belongs to the benzodiazepine family of sedatives, including familiar drugs such as Valium and Librium. Rohypnol is some ten times more potent as a sedative than either of these. It is manufactured in many different countries worldwide and is licensed in Europe, including the UK, for medical use as a short-term treatment for severe forms of insomnia and as a pre-anaesthetic medication. It is not licensed for medical use in the USA.

Forms and appearance

Rohypnol is currently manufactured as a 0.5mg caplet which is dull green in colour with a distinct blue core that can be seen when the caplet is broken in half. Rohypnol has in the past been manufactured in 1mg and 2mg tablets, both of which are white and around the size of a paracetamol tablet, imprinted with either a bisecting groove or a cross on one side and the word 'ROCHE' on the reverse. Also imprinted on the reverse were the numbers '1' or '2' enclosed in a circle, indicating whether the tablet was of the 1 or 2mg strength. Rohypnol is supplied by the manufacturer in blister packs clearly marked on the reverse with the makers's name, the word 'Rohypnol', and the size of the dose.

Marketing

Due primarily to its use as a 'parachute drug' to ease the more unpleasant symptoms experienced following withdrawal from prolonged or heavy use of stimulants such as amphetamine, ecstasy or cocaine, Rohypnol has built up a small following in the UK in the dance club scene. The street trade in Rohypnol that has developed to service this scene is also the source of supply for people wishing to use it to facilitate non-consensual sex. This trade obtains its supplies from those who have been lawfully prescribed the drug and are willing to sell their surplus, and to an increasing extent though supplies purchased in bulk over the Internet or smuggled into Europe from Asia. A large and increasing number of Internet sites offer the drug for sale.

Cost

At street level, the drug can be purchased for as little as £1–2 per tablet in the UK.

Legal position

Rohypnol under its generic name flunitrazepam is a class C drug under the Misuse of Drugs Act 1971. The possession or supply of the drug is lawful only under the authority of a prescription, otherwise the usual class C penalties apply:

- *Simple possession*: maximum penalty on indictment of two years' imprisonment plus an unlimited fine.

- *Possession with intent to supply to another*: maximum sentence on indictment of 14 years' imprisonment, plus an unlimited fine, plus seizure of drug-related assets.

- *Supplying to another*: As above.

- *Administration to another person to facilitate non-consensual sex (date rape)*: maximum sentence of life imprisonment.

Methods of use

Rohypnol is almost always taken orally. When administered to another person without their knowledge, it is usually dissolved in their drink. For date-rape purposes, an alcoholic drink is preferred, because the sedative effect of the drug is enhanced when mixed with alcohol. Rohypnol in the form first seen in the UK dissolved in liquid without altering its taste, colour or appearance. In January 1998, the manufacturer altered its formulation to make the drug far slower to dissolve and to release a powerful blue dye on dissolving, turning any drink a bright blue colour. To counter the problem of detecting such a colour change in a drink that is already a dark colour or served in a dark glass or in a dimly lit room, a non-dissolving substance was also added that would create a white scum-like residue floating on the surface of the drink. Of the various counterfeit forms of the drug that have been seized around the world, none has had any of these safely features.

Self-protection

Following the reformulation of Rohypnol, it is possible for an alert person to protect themselves from having their drink 'spiked' by being watchful for colour changes to their drink or the presence of a floating white residue. Such alertness becomes more difficult following a number of alcoholic drinks or in the dimly lit surroundings of a dance club or pub. The problem is exacerbated further by the popular habit of consuming drinks directly from the bottle. Many of these bottles are highly coloured or packaged in an opaque covering, rendering careful monitoring of the drink almost impossible.

The best advice we can give to anyone wishing to give themselves the greatest chance of avoiding this sort of problem is first and foremost to trust no-one that they do not know well. Never accept a drink in a glass or in an already opened bottle from someone you do not trust. Open your own drinks and keep them under close supervision at all times. If you have to leave a drink unsupervised, then abandon it: never return to finish it later. Many club-goers have told us that they keep their thumb firmly over the open neck of the bottle when it is not in their mouth. Resealable tamper-proof bottles are becoming available, which enable the drinker to close the top of the bottle when they are not drinking. However, even with this type of bottle, it would not be wise to leave it unattended and then return to it.

A number of companies now market Rohypnol-detection devices in the form of test strips that can be dipped into a suspect drink. Such devices will detect the presence of any benzodiazepine drug.

The final piece of advice we would offer is not to become intoxicated to the point where you are incapable of exercising the necessary caution to stay safe. Any night out, however pleasurable, is not worth getting raped for.

How can you tell whether you have been a victim?

As the effects of the drug wear off, perhaps eight or more hours after ingestion, the victim will experience feelings of a hangover, profound confusion and an inability to remember events that occurred while the drug was affecting them. They may also be aware of having had dream-like hallucinations of being involved in sexual activity. There may also be physical signs of sexual activity, such as bleeding, tearing and bruising to the vaginal and/or anal areas, bruising to the inside or outside of the thighs or on the arms or wrists, bite marks anywhere on the body, traces of semen or vaginal fluid on the body or clothing, or evidence that they have been undressed, such as torn clothing or clothing having been replaced or fastened incorrectly.

Traces of Rohypnol can be detected within the body up to 72 hours after ingestion, and anyone who suspects that they have been the victim of the drug should report the occurrence to the police and/or a rape crisis centre (see Appendix 2 for details).

Effects of use

When used deliberately, flunitrazepam provides a calming, euphoric, sedative effect that will help the person cope with the come-down or withdrawal effects, such as anxiety, agitation, panic, paranoia and hypervigilance, that can follow prolonged or excessive use of stimulant drugs. The effect is felt about 30 minutes after ingestion of the drug, peaks within two hours, and can last for up to eight hours. The US Drug Enforcement Administration in 2005 reported that such use was gaining in popularity in the USA among young club-goers. There is increasing evidence of such use, termed 'roaching out', in the UK.

Adverse effects

When used deliberately and repeatedly, the user may have to cope with a number of adverse effects, including problems associated with abnormally low blood pressure, such as dizziness, particularly when rising from a prone or sitting position, fainting and collapse.

Other physical symptoms of repeated use include gastrointestinal problems, such as vomiting and urinary retention. Contrary to expectations with a sedative drug, a number of regular users have reported problems of excitability and aggressive behaviour.

In a person to whom the drug has been administered without their knowledge, someone may have had non-consensual vaginal or anal sex with them, possibly without the use of a condom. Thus, the adverse effects could include unwanted pregnancy and/or the acquisition of a sexually transmitted disease, such as HIV/AIDS, viral hepatitis, gonorrhoea or syphilis.

When the drug is administered without the person's knowledge, the effects appear within 30 minutes of ingestion and can include severely impaired memory to the point where they remember nothing of what happens to them for several hours until the effects of the drug wear off. The victim may also suffer symptoms of intoxication, sedation, loss of inhibitions, loss of motor control, dizziness and confusion. It is during this period that the victim is at their most vulnerable to sexual attack.

Tolerance potential

In regular users, tolerance to Rohypnol develops rapidly. The drug is intended for only short-term medical use in order to avoid this problem.

Habituation potential

A profound physical dependence develops with regular use of Rohypnol. Its habituation potential matches its potency as a sedative.

Withdrawal effects

Withdrawal from habituated use of Rohypnol can lead to very unpleasant symptoms. The withdrawal effects can include severe headache and muscular pain, extreme anxiety, tension, restlessness, confusion, irritability, hallucinations and delirium. These problems can be accompanied by amnesia to such an extent that the sufferer may feel that they have lost their identity and have no knowledge of who they are or how they came to be in the circumstances that they are in. More acute dangerous and life-threatening symptoms such as cerebral convulsions and cardiovascular collapse can occur in extreme cases. Such withdrawal seizures can occur a week or more after the cessation of drug use. As with all benzodiazepine-type drugs, cessation of use should be done in a tapered, gradual fashion, preferably under medical supervision.

Overdose potential

All benzodiazepine drugs carry a risk of fatal overdose. This potential is made worse by the sedative nature of the drug, which may lead the user to become confused as to how much they have taken. The use of other depressant substances, such as alcohol, will exacerbate these risks.

Street names

Roofies, roopies, ruffies, rophy, roach, rope, R2s, circles

Slang associated with use

Being roached out – Being under the influence of the drug

Spiking – Adding the drug to an unwary person's drink

Rohypnol: benefits and drawbacks

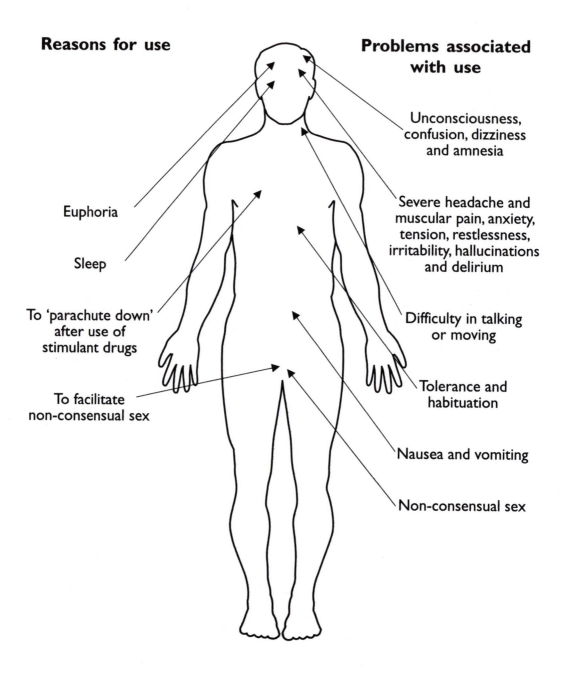

Reasons for use

Euphoria

Sleep

To 'parachute down' after use of stimulant drugs

To facilitate non-consensual sex

Problems associated with use

Unconsciousness, confusion, dizziness and amnesia

Severe headache and muscular pain, anxiety, tension, restlessness, irritability, hallucinations and delirium

Difficulty in talking or moving

Tolerance and habituation

Nausea and vomiting

Non-consensual sex

GHB (gamma-hydroxybutyrate)

GHB: quick reference guide

Source

Gamma-hydroxybutyrate was developed and used initially as an anaesthetic. It is no longer licensed for medical use in Europe, but it is still licensed in the USA as a treatment for narcolepsy.

Forms and appearance

Usually seen as a colourless clear liquid. Seen much less commonly in the form of tablets or powders of various colours.

Marketing

GHB is used widely as a mood-altering drug within the dance club scene, has some users within the body-building community and on occasion is used on unwary women or, more rarely, men to facilitate non-consensual sex. It is available widely in the UK in liquid form within the dance club scene and from a large number of Internet sites, usually in small (about 30ml) plastic bottles. It is also available from some shops dealing in pornography and drug and sex paraphernalia (sex and head shops).

Cost

Around £10–15 for a 30ml bottle of liquid, with no established price for the much rarer tablet or powder form.

Legal position

GHB is a class C drug under the Misuse of Drugs Act 1971.

Methods of use

GHB is taken orally. When administered to someone without their knowledge, it is usually placed in a drink.

Effects of use

Euphoria, relaxation, lowering of inhibitions, increase in libido.

Adverse effects

Nausea, vomiting, drowsiness, low blood pressure, respiratory depression, confusion, hallucinations, amnesia, convulsions, coma.

Tolerance potential

Tolerance develops in people taking regular doses.

Habituation potential

There is no clear evidence for the development of any physical or psychological habituation.

Withdrawal effects

No known withdrawal symptoms.

Overdose potential

Overdose can lead to respiratory depression and death.

GHB: in-depth guide

Source

GHB is a totally synthetic product. It was first developed in a pharmaceutical form as gamma-hydroxybutyrate and used as an anaesthetic, mostly in obstetric, maxillofacial (face and jaw) and laryngeal surgery. It is not licensed for medical use in Europe, although it is licensed in the USA as a treatment for certain forms of narcolepsy. The GHB that reaches users in Europe has been manufactured in Asia, Europe and the USA. The recipe for its manufacture, together with the necessary chemicals and equipment, are easily available on the Internet. The strength and purity of GHB vary, and this aspect of the drug makes it potentially very easy to overdose on it.

Forms and appearance

The liquid form of GHB is best described as looking like water. It is clear, odourless and colourless, with a slightly salty taste. In this form, it is usually supplied in small plastic bottles of around 25–30ml. The bottles are typically white and labelled 'GHB' or sometimes 'liquid ecstasy'.

The more rare powder and tablet forms are usually white, but they have been seen in a variety of colours.

Marketing

GHB is used as a recreational drug to achieve an altered mood state with feelings of euphoria and intoxication. It also has a small following among body-builders and body-sculptors, as its use is believed to enhance the production of natural growth hormones within the body and to encourage the sort of deep sleep that is best for the building of muscle protein. This is usually combined with the use of anabolic steroids. It is also used on occasion as a 'date-rape' drug to facilitate non-consensual sex with an unwary person. The connections between GHB and date rape are illustrated by street names such as 'Easy lay' and 'Scoop her'. In 2003 in the USA, Andrew Luster, heir to the Max Factor cosmetic empire, was sentenced to a total of 124 years' imprisonment for a series of three rapes of women in which he had used

GHB to render them insensible. In 2003 in the UK, David Meachen was sentenced to ten years' imprisonment for the offences of indecent assault and grievous bodily harm committed against a woman whom he met in a bar and whose drink he laced with GHB. Evidence presented at his trial showed that when arrested, he was in possession of sufficient GHB to render 16 adults unconscious.

In the UK, GHB is available widely within the dance, club and pub scenes and from street dealers supplying young customers who frequent such scenes. It is also widely and easily purchased from a large and increasing number of Internet sites dedicated either to GHB itself or to drugs in general.

More rarely, since its inclusion in 1993 in the Misuse of Drugs Act 1971, the drug is available from sex and head shops, i.e. outlets that retail soft (and not so soft) pornography and a range of sex toys and drug-related paraphernalia.

Cost

As with all drugs, prices vary considerably. Dealers will price the drug as high as they think the market will bear. From street and club dealers, a 30ml bottle of liquid GHB typically will cost in the UK around £10–15. Supplies of liquid GHB over the Internet are usually priced in US dollars and are around half the UK street price.

Legal position

GHB, under its generic name gamma-hydroxybutyrate, is a class C drug under the Misuse of Drugs Act 1971, and the usual class C penalties apply:

- *Simple possession*: maximum penalty on indictment of two years' imprisonment plus an unlimited fine.

- *Possession with intent to supply to another*: maximum penalty on indictment of 14 years' imprisonment, plus an unlimited fine, plus seizure of drug-related assets.

- *Supplying to another*: as above.

- *Administration to another person to facilitate non-consensual sex (date rape)*: maximum sentence of life imprisonment.

Methods of use

When used deliberately, the liquid is taken orally, often by being sipped using the cap from the bottle as a measure. One capful is usually considered sufficient for one dose. The tablet forms are also used orally; the much rarer powder forms are sometimes prepared for injection.

When administered to another person without their knowledge, GHB is usually added to a drink, which is often alcoholic.

Self-protection

The guidance given in relation to Rohypnol (see page 230) applies equally to GHB. A further problem with GHB is the lack of any safety features, such as the blue dye and non-dissolving residue seen with genuine Rohypnol. A number of companies market testing kits that detect the presence of GHB. Such kits are becoming readily available through a number of Internet sites.

How can you tell whether you have been a victim?

The guidance given in relation to Rohypnol (see page 230) applies equally to GHB.

Effects of use

When used deliberately and in small doses, the effects of GHB will be those of any central nervous system depressant, i.e. euphoria, relaxation, dreaminess, intoxication and elevated libido. These effects will begin to be felt within 10–15 minutes of ingestion and will rise rapidly to a peak over the following 30 minutes. The effects from a low to moderate dose will generally last for around three to six hours. This period can be doubled or even trebled if the drug is taken with moderate to large quantities of alcohol.

Adverse effects

When taken in low doses, the most problematic side effects are usually drowsiness, dizziness, nausea and vomiting, sweating and, occasionally, hallucinations. With increasing doses, the adverse effects worsen alarmingly. This problem is complicated further by the uncertain strength of much of the GBH that reaches the market. Many of the bottles that we have seen are clearly marked with the caution not to exceed the stated dose, which is usually quoted as a capful. This has always seemed to us a ludicrous instruction, as the strength of any two bottles can vary by a factor of as much as five.

The effects of excessive use can include respiratory depression, tremors, convulsions, unconsciousness, amnesia, coma and death from respiratory failure.

As with Rohypnol, the experiences of a person to whom the drug has been administered without their knowledge could include someone having non-consensual vaginal or anal sex with them, possibly without the use of a condom. Thus, the adverse effects could include unwanted pregnancy and/or the acquisition of a sexually transmitted disease such as HIV/AIDS, gonorrhoea or syphilis.

The anaesthetic effects of GHB are strengthened by administering it mixed with alcohol. Provided the dose administered is not excessive, the victim will within a few minutes feel highly intoxicated and drowsy. They may pass out and remain unconscious for up to three or four hours. When the effects of the drug wear off, they may be left feeling hungover, confused and disoriented. They may suffer profound amnesia as to what happened to them while under the influence of the drug.

Tolerance potential

As with most drugs, the body adapts to the use of GHB, and its effects diminish with repeated use. The user will then need to increase the dose of the drug to achieve the effects that they desire. This tolerance vanishes quickly when use ceases.

Habituation potential

No clear evidence exists as to whether a physical or psychological dependence can develop with continued use of GHB. To date, users known to us do not seem to have developed any such dependency.

Withdrawal effects

There is no clear evidence of any significant withdrawal symptoms when abstaining from GHB.

Overdose potential

There is a danger of taking an overdose of GHB, which could result in serious conse-quences, including respiratory collapse, convulsions, unconsciousness, coma and death. As discussed earlier, this danger is exacerbated by the uncertain strength of any one supply of the drug.

Street names

Names that illustrate its mood-altering qualities: GBH, liquid ecstasy, liquid X, chemical X, clear X, X rater, liquid dream, goop

Names that illustrate its date-rape potential: easy lay, EZ lay, scoop her, get-her-to-bed

Slang associated with use

Spiking – Adding the drug to an unwary person's drink

GHB: benefits and drawbacks

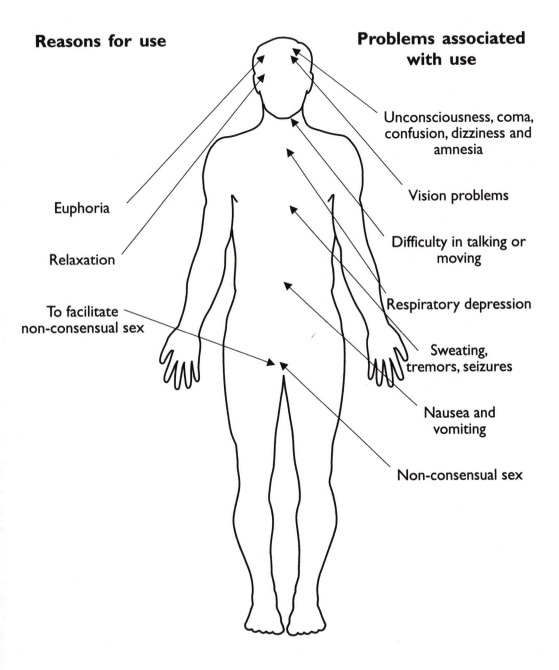

Reasons for use

Euphoria

Relaxation

To facilitate
non-consensual sex

**Problems associated
with use**

Unconsciousness, coma,
confusion, dizziness and
amnesia

Vision problems

Difficulty in talking or
moving

Respiratory depression

Sweating,
tremors, seizures

Nausea and
vomiting

Non-consensual sex

Part II

Part II

Chapter 12

Signs and Symptoms of Substance Misuse: Things you need to look out for

The misuse of substances in the UK is, due to its antisocial and illegal nature, mostly a covert activity, carried out in privacy and away from direct public gaze or in venues where others also are indulging in the activity and thus where the practice is tolerated, accepted or even encouraged.

Research into the drug-misuse activities of 16- to 19-year-old students in Hampshire showed that the majority used their drugs at their friends' homes while parents were absent, or in parks and other such open spaces.[1]

Detection and recognition of such misuse therefore is extremely difficult for untrained and uninitiated observers. They may never witness the effects of direct drug misuse, and they may easily overlook the physical and behavioural symptoms of such activity or pass them off as being due to some other cause. Perhaps only the symptoms of withdrawal may be seen; these may be very similar to behaviours brought on by other circumstances, such as the general stresses and pressures of being young, and therefore maybe easily discounted.

Even the paraphernalia and detritus of substance misuse can be easily overlooked, for much of it utilises everyday materials and objects that in their own right would not give rise to suspicion.

1   Hettiaratchy, S.W. and Baines, S. (1993) *Survey of Young People.* Basingstoke: London NHS Trust.

It is therefore necessary, if you are to be able to recognise instances of substance misuse, to have an appreciation and understanding of certain behavioural signs and physical evidence that may be apparent. It is worth stating again that many of these behavioural symptoms may mimic those of other causes, and consequently these alone should never be used as the basis for making assumptions or accusations that somebody is misusing harmful or illegal substances. Further investigation is always advisable.

Marked and uncharacteristic mood swings, aggression or apathetic behaviour

Substance misusers usually administer their chosen drug or solvent in order to bring about (what is to them at least) a positive change in their mood or activity. Regular usage may quickly cause a tolerance to the substance to build up, requiring ever-increasing amounts of that substance in order to achieve the hoped-for result each time. As the effect of each use fades, the user will most probably begin to suffer the onset of withdrawal symptoms. Unless a further dose of the drug or an alternative is used, there are likely to be changes in the person's mood and behaviour that are visible to outside observers. What goes up must come down, and the high gained from using a particular substance may result in a corresponding low once its use ceases.

Because continued substance misuse may lead to a succession of highs and lows, the user may appear to be on an emotional rollercoaster. At one point they may be energetic, confident, happy, friendly or just at peace with the world, and then they may change to being drained, apathetic, emotionally withdrawn, morose, irritable, depressed, isolated, paranoid or even aggressive, over a short period of time.

Marked mood swings may be a characteristic of some forms of substance misuse, but they may also be the usual signs of adolescence, mental health problems, or simply a reaction to pressures in that person's life. Therefore, they should never be used as a guaranteed pointer to the use of drugs or other substances.

Truancy and lateness for school, college or work

Many users will not exhibit these symptoms in public, preferring to readjust as best they can to a state of near-normality before allowing themselves to be seen in public. If they are unable to achieve this readjustment within the necessary timescale, they may report that they are sick and therefore unable to attend school, college or work. Others may truant or arrive late, without giving any real explanation, in order to give themselves valuable time to return to a reasonable state of equilibrium. Leaving work or school early to obtain drugs to offset the withdrawal symptoms may also happen.

Deterioration in personal hygiene and dress

Due to the debilitating effects of many substances and the lack of recovery time available to the user, attention to personal hygiene and grooming may suffer badly. Many users who previously kept up a good standard of personal appearance and cleanliness become unkempt, dirty or unshaven. Many fail to change their clothes or bedding or wash themselves, and they may well in time begin to smell unpleasant.

Covering suspicious behaviour by lying or being vague

Working standards, reliability and time-keeping may be put at some risk due to the debilitating effects of the come-down from some substances. Users will often adopt strategies of deception to cover their mistakes and their odd behaviour. There may be evidence of deteriorating relationships with peers, workmates, siblings and other family members.

Unusual conflict with authority figures

Conflict may erupt with parents, teachers or other authority figures where none existed before.

Sudden and marked change of habits, loss of purpose in life, and lack of motivation or goals

Favoured tasks, hobbies, activities and personal goals that previously were considered to be important to a user may quite suddenly lose their appeal and be dropped from their daily routine. This loss of purpose in life has proved in many instances to be an important indicator of drug and other substance misuse. Again, it must be stressed that the pressures and strains of ordinary life, or even mental states such as depression or schizophrenia, may offer another explanation for this sort of behaviour. The exhibition of such behaviour is in any case worthy of further investigation, so that the exact cause and possibly a remedy may be found.

Excessive borrowing of money

Once a regular drug habit has become established, funding it may become a real difficulty. This will be particularly true if a tolerance level has been reached that necessitates the use of ever-increasing quantities of the substance. Regular users, and particularly young users, may never seem to have any spare finances despite having a regular salary, pocket money or other source of money. Their continuing habit may force them into patterns of excessive begging or borrowing from family members, friends, colleagues and even complete strangers, without any real hope or intention of paying back the amounts borrowed.

Stealing from family, friends, school, shops, work

The stealing of money or goods to sell on from home, shops, work or school may become commonplace. Users may become involved in stealing goods to order for other people, and they may reach the point where they are so desperate for money that nothing and nobody is sacred. Many users realise the inevitability of being found out or caught in the act, but the lure and promise of a drug can wipe these thoughts from the mind, leaving them without any feelings or conscience.

Selling of own property, with little or nothing to show for it

One of the more obvious pointers to possible substance abuse, especially among young people, who generally do not have much in the way of expensive saleable goods, is the selling of one's own property. Even items of great sentimental value or that have brought the owner much previous pleasure and pride may be disposed of. Items such as televisions, DVD and video recorders, CDs, computers, computer games, bicycles, guitars, MP3 players, stereos and jewellery may be disposed of at a fraction of their true value without a flicker of remorse, as a result of the person's desperate need to raise the necessary cash to buy more drugs. In some cases, goods of this nature may be exchanged directly for drugs. This kind of behaviour can be taken to extremes at times, and we have known cases where users have disposed of their cars, houses and even businesses in order to realise the funds needed to finance a long-term drug habit. We once dealt with a 21-year-old unemployed heroin addict who confessed to selling irreplaceable family heirlooms with great sentimental value at prices that did not begin to approach their true market value, in order to fund his habit. Perhaps the saddest case that has ever come to our notice was that of a young mother addicted to amphetamine who, after selling most of her own property and committing a number of frauds, was ashamed to admit that she had been reduced to selling her seven-year-old daughter's toys in order to pay for her drugs.

Young people do sell their own property for genuine reasons, but in most of these cases they will use the money raised to buy something else. If the items are sold to buy drugs, there will be nothing to be seen in replacement for the goods sold. The money that was raised may quite literally have gone up in smoke.

Another issue to be aware of is that of the user becoming involved in the selling or supplying of drugs in order to generate profits that can be used to fund their own habit. This may occur in only a minor way to begin with, bringing in just enough to cover the user's own habit; however, because it can be an easy and quick way to raise quite large sums of money, it can easily escalate into a much more serious business activity. Funding a drug habit by dealing generally involves buying drugs from more major suppliers in larger quantities than an individual would normally need for themselves, in order to obtain the discounts that are commonly available for buying in bulk. The excess drugs are then offered for sale to friends and acquaintances at normal street prices, thus recouping the whole of the original outlay. Some user–dealers will attempt to increase their profit margins by adulterating or 'cutting' the drugs that they sell with other substances to increase their bulk and weight.

Furtive telephone calls and use of drug slang

Even small-time dealers will need to advertise when they have drugs for sale and what drugs they have. They may make and receive a large number of furtive telephone calls. It is likely that the use of drug-related slang will be prevalent during these telephone calls, in order to try and conceal their real purpose to anyone overhearing them. As with many other forms of language, drug-related slang is used in order to exclude those who do not understand it while bestowing credibility on those who can use it in the right context.

Frequent short visits from new or older friends, and many short excursions away from home

These telephone calls may be followed up by a succession of brief visits by a large number of familiar and unfamiliar people, many of whom may be outside the normal age range or social group of the dealer. There may also be frequent occasions when the dealer will have to go out to see someone for a short while, usually straight after a telephone call. It is not easy to recommend eavesdropping on another person's private telephone calls, but in some cases this can be the only way to find out exactly what is going on.

As most substance misuse is carried out in private, the only signs and symptoms that become apparent to the observer may be those of withdrawal or come-down. It will, therefore, be necessary to understand certain characteristics that are peculiar to certain drugs.

Wearing dark glasses even in dull weather

Cannabis may cause a condition known as red eye, in which the user's eyes become very bloodshot. This condition may be particularly noticeable in the morning following use of the drug, and this may prompt the user to wear dark glasses in order to hide their eyes from the view of others. They may wear the dark glasses at very inappropriate times, such as in dull weather or even indoors.

Short-term memory loss and deterioration in performance, loss of concentration and loss of coordination

Cannabis use may lead to the loss of short-term memory and a marked reduction in the user's powers of concentration. This together with generally apathetic behaviour on the part of the user may make tasks such as driving or operating machinery difficult and, in many cases, very dangerous, not to mention illegal.

Poor appetite and weight loss or eating binges

Eating binges after cannabis use are very common and are affectionately known in drug slang as 'the munchies'. Indeed, so effective is cannabis at stimulating the appetite of most people that some consider its use beneficial in the alleviation of some symptoms of wasting diseases, such as AIDS and multiple sclerosis, in which the appetite is severely reduced.

At the other end of the scale, many drugs, especially stimulants, can powerfully suppress the appetite. Both cocaine and amphetamine have this effect. They also speed up the user's metabolism, giving them feelings of energy and stamina. Usage on a regular basis or over an extended period of time inevitably will lead to a loss of body weight, making some users lean and thin.

Suffering a succession of colds and episodes of 'flu, which may persist for an unusually long time

Disruption to the normal intake of nutrients may go on to cause damage to the body's immune system, leaving the user open to many ailments such as colds and 'flu. Having developed these illnesses, the user may be unable to shake them off, and the condition may go on for an unusually long time.

Depression, shyness and poor self-image

Some people use substances as a way of self-medicating away their problems, without ever being aware that they have a medically recognisable condition. Depression, anxiety, lack of confidence and some other mild psychiatric disorders may be dealt with in this way, but also the reverse can be true: disorders such as these may arise as a direct result of the use of certain substances. This is especially true of cannabis and amphetamine, which can cause paranoia and psychosis and bring to the fore latent mental illnesses, such as schizophrenia, which otherwise may have remained dormant.

The remedy for adverse withdrawal symptoms in the view of some users is simply to administer another dose of the drug. However, carrying on in this way could very soon lead to the development of a high level of tolerance or a full-blown psychological and/or physical addiction. All this means more business for the dealer, but it is bad news for the user, whose general health and wellbeing undoubtedly will suffer.

Spending time away from home, usually overnight

Seeking out and using drugs may necessitate the user being away from home overnight or for even longer periods. To avoid detection, the reasons given to explain away this time may be vague, misleading and muddled, if any explanation is forthcoming at all.

Excessive sleeping, usually after time away from home

On returning home, the user may seem antisocial and need to sleep for long periods, especially in order to offset the effects of stimulant drugs and recover from strenuous activity.

Drunken behaviour and slurred speech

If depressant drugs have been used, this may affect the user's coordination and speech, making them appear out of control and sluggish.

In order to verify your suspicions of possible drug use, it is necessary for you to back up your observations with some form of physical evidence, if possible.

Behavioural signs and symptoms of possible drug use: summary

- Marked and uncharacteristic mood swings, aggression and apathetic behaviour.

- Truancy and lateness for school, college, work, etc.

- Deterioration in personal hygiene and dress.

- Covering suspicious behaviour by lying, being vague, etc.

- Unusual conflict with authority figures.

- Sudden and marked change of habits, loss of purpose in life and lack of motivation or goals.

- Excessive borrowing of money.

- Stealing from family, friends, school, shops, work, etc.

- Selling of own property with little or nothing to show for it.

- Furtive telephone calls and use of drug slang.

- Many short visits from new or older friends, and many short excursions away from home.

- Wearing dark glasses even in dull weather.

- Short-term memory loss and deterioration in performance.

- Loss of concentration and coordination.

- Poor appetite, weight loss or eating binges.

- Suffering a succession of colds and episodes of 'flu, which may persist for an unusually long time.

- Depression, shyness and poor self-image.

- Spending time away from home, usually overnight.

- Excessive sleeping, usually after time away from home.

- Drunken behaviour and slurred speech.

Note: Many of these signs may simply be normal signs of adolescence or may be due to some other cause rather than drug use. It is wise to make further investigations before reaching conclusions.

Chapter 13

Physical Evidence of Possible Drug or Substance Use

The paraphernalia and detritus of drug and substance misuse, such as needles, syringes and tablets, will be evident to most people, but things may not always be quite so easy. Many everyday objects can be utilised for taking drugs and therefore can easily be passed off as innocuous, insignificant and totally unrelated to drug or substance misuse. To detail all of the varying forms of substance misuse paraphernalia would call for a much larger book than we have here. In addition, new ways of using substances are constantly being dreamt up, so this chapter is confined to those items that are most likely to be seen.

Cigarette lighters, matches and candles (especially if the person is a non-smoker)

A large number of illegal drugs can be smoked, using a wide variety of methods and equipment. First, there has to be a source of heat, and so matches, cigarette lighters and candles may be possible evidence of drug use. This is especially true if the person in possession of them is not known to be a tobacco smoker.

Knives, metal foil, drink cans and bottle tops discoloured by heat; funnels, outer covers of matchboxes and large straws

Many substances can be smoked simply by heating them gently and inhaling the resultant fumes that are given off. Cooking foil, metal bottle tops and drink cans can all be used for this purpose, the fumes produced being directed into the user's mouth or nose by use of a straw, paper or cardboard tube. Other users favour the use of a funnel made by cutting the top part off a plastic bottle or the outer sleeve of a matchbox to collect and direct the fumes. The holding of a matchbox cover in the mouth to collect fumes is known as 'playing the mouth organ'.

Heated knife blades can be used to smoke certain substances. Heating the blade of a knife and pressing it directly on to the substance will make the substance smoulder and produce vapours that can then be inhaled. This can also be done by heating two knife blades and holding the substance between them both. These practices are known as 'hot-knifing' and are often used by cannabis users who wish to smoke their drug without the use of tobacco.

Long-stemmed pipes (chillums)

Cannabis smokers sometimes use special long-stemmed pipes made from stone, wood, clay, ceramic, metal or glass. These pipes are known as chillums. They help to cool the cannabis smoke in order to prevent burning of the user's lips, tongue and throat, because cannabis burns at a higher temperature than tobacco.

High-tech pipes

A vast array of high-tech cannabis-smoking pipes have appeared on the market. These are often made from metal and take a variety of forms from something the size of a rather thick credit card to a finger-sized cylinder. All these pipes feature extended internal smoke passages leading from the burning bowl to the mouthpiece. This extended pipework allows the hot cannabis smoke to cool. Many of these modern designs would not be recognised by uninitiated people as being connected to drug use. An Internet search for 'cannabis pipes' will reveal a large number of websites dedicated to their sale and will educate the reader in what to look out for.

Home-made hubble-bubble pipes (bongs) and similar devices

Other devices for cooling cannabis smoke are home-made versions of the hubble-bubble or hookah water pipe, known as 'bongs'. These are generally made from watertight containers such as glass or plastic bottles or metal or plastic cans with tight-fitting lids. They are half filled with water and have a tube inserted at an angle through the side of the container, far enough to have its lower end below the level of the water. At the outer end of the tube will be some form of heat-proof metal bowl, sometimes fashioned from a milk bottle top, in which to burn the cannabis. Using the neck of the bottle or a vertical pipe fitted to the top of the watertight container, the user draws the smoke through the water by sucking. As the smoke bubbles through the water, it is cooled, and some of the tar and other impurities are removed. This cooled and less irritating smoke can then be taken deeper into the lungs and held there for a longer period of time, resulting in more of the drug's active ingredient (THC) being able to pass into the bloodstream.

These devices are usually quick and easy to produce and therefore may be discarded after use, especially when the user is under the influence of the drug and not thinking clearly. Other devices, however, are created painstakingly and will be elaborate and durable affairs intended for long-term use. It has been known for bongs to be fashioned from buckets and other large containers for use by many smokers at once, and we have seen a fully automatic electric bong. There are a large number of websites dedicated to the sale of cannabis-smoking paraphernalia, which market an enormous array of different bong designs.

Another device for smoking cannabis, known as a 'lung', consists of a small plastic bottle with the base removed. To this open end is then attached a plastic bag; a smoking bowl is fitted to the top of the bottle. Some cannabis is placed in the bowl and lit. The bag is pumped to draw the smoke down into it; once the bag is full, the smoking bowl is removed. The user inhales the smoke through the top of the bottle by pumping the bag.

No object, therefore, should be overlooked as a possible device for the smoking of drugs.

Large cigarette papers and short cardboard tubes (roaches)

Cannabis cigarettes, known as 'spliffs', 'joints' and 'reefers', are in the main constructed or 'built' with the use of extra-large cigarette papers or multiple smaller papers. When smoked in this way, it is still necessary to cool the cannabis smoke, and so a small cardboard tube about the size of a commercial cigarette filter is inserted in the end that is to be placed in the mouth. This tube, known as a 'roach' or 'roach end', keeps the burning material from spilling out of the cigarette and distances the lips and mouth from the burning material.

Packets of cigarette-rolling papers with pieces torn from them

Many roaches are simply made from pieces of the cigarette-paper packet, and therefore the finding of roaches or such torn packets is a good indication of cannabis use. In recent years, the authors have seen a large range of 'roach cards'. These are cards printed with an advertisement for a musical event or some item of drug paraphernalia and that have been perforated in order to enable the smoker to break them up into pieces suitable for use as roaches. Finding such printed cards with sections missing is a good indicator of cannabis smoking. Some ex-cannabis users still use roaches out of habit when hand-rolling ordinary tobacco cigarettes.

Razor blades, modelling knives and scalpel blades

Herbal or resinous cannabis can be inserted into a factory-produced cigarette by slitting the cigarette with a modelling knife, scalpel or razor blade, adding the drug, and then resealing the cigarette with a cigarette paper. In these cases, the filters are always removed before lighting, as they filter out most of the active ingredient of the cannabis if left in place.

Cigarette filters and cotton-wool

Cigarette filters are of great benefit to injecting drug users, who use them to filter out undissolved solids from powdered drugs or crushed tablets in solution. If this is not done, these solids may clog the needle and syringe or block small blood vessels, causing serious medical problems, including loss of limbs.

Spoons discoloured by heat, often with a bent stem

Drug injecting often involves a great deal of ritual. The usual method is to dissolve a quantity of powdered drug or crushed tablets in a small amount of water in the bowl of a spoon, known as a 'cooking spoon'. The stem of the spoon may have been bent to allow it to stand or be held on a flat surface without spilling any of the contents.

Lemon juice, vinegar and ascorbic and citric acids

A few drops of a mild acid, commonly vinegar, ascorbic acid (vitamin C) or lemon juice, are often added to help break down the drug. The spoon is then heated from below to speed up the dissolving process. This is known as 'cooking up'. When the drug has dissolved completely, a cigarette filter or a small piece of rolled cotton-wool is dropped into the solution. The needle attached to the syringe, or sometimes just the syringe, is inserted into the filter and the liquid drug drawn up into the barrel of the syringe. The drug is then ready for injecting into a vein, known as 'shooting up', or under the skin, known as 'skin-popping'. The undissolved solids, with luck, remain in the filter.

Some users save their old filters for use when they are unable to obtain or afford their drug. They use any residue left in the filter for their hit by reheating the filter in a small amount of water.

Tourniquets, syringes, needles, swabs and water ampoules

Tourniquets are used to raise the profile of the veins in order to facilitate injection. Many injectors clean the injecting site on their skin with a spirit swab; some users use ampoules of sterile water produced especially for injection. Many pharmaceutical drugs are produced in ampoules ready for injection, and the discovery of any of these items would be indicative of an injecting user.

Folded 5cm squares of paper (wraps or deals)

Drugs sold in powder form, such as heroin, cocaine and amphetamine, generally are marketed in small quantities, usually fractions of a gram. They are commonly marketed in small pieces of folded paper, measuring about 5cm^2, known as 'wraps' or 'deals'. The paper is folded in such a way that the powder inside will not come out, despite rough handling. Due to their small size, once folded, the wrap can be easily transported and concealed. Wraps may measure as little as 3 x 1.5cm when folded. The discovery of empty wraps is a good indicator of drug use, while the discovery of quantities of full folded wraps may indicate drug dealing.

Powdered drugs and crushed tablets can be taken by mouth. This is commonly done by 'dabbing', i.e. lifting the powder into the mouth on a wet finger. These drugs may also be added to drinks. Sometimes they are swallowed wrapped in a piece of cigarette paper: the powder is placed in the centre of the paper, which is twisted together to hold the drug in a shape known as a 'bomb' and then swallowed.

Coloured powders and sets of scales

People who deal street drugs in powder form may, in order to increase their profit margins, adulterate the drug with other substances to increase its bulk and weight. Indeed, this may already have been done much further back in the dealer chain, long before it reaches the street dealer. Other powdered substances such as coffee, talcum powder, glucose and rat poison may be used, depending on the colour and consistency of the drug being adulterated. It has even been known for brick dust to be mixed with street heroin.

The discovery of quantities of such powdered substances in abnormal circumstances may therefore be important.

Small, portable, accurate sets of scales, together with a set of small weights, usually in fractions of a gram, are often used by drug dealers. The possession of such items can often be used to successfully prosecute a person suspected of dealing in illegal substances.

Lighter fuel, lighter gas, hairsprays, spray deodorants, solvent glues, spray polishes, correcting fluids and dry-cleaning fluids

Volatile substances, lighter fuels and gases, and aerosol cans of hairspray or deodorant may need to be viewed with some suspicion. This is especially true if empty containers are found, particularly in more than usual quantities or if an attempt has been made to conceal them. A search of a playing field used by young people from a nearby school in our area yielded over 150 empty aerosol cans, indicative of the size of this problem.

Plastic bags, crisps packets, drinks cans and clothing that smell of solvents

Solvents can be used in a number of different ways. Some users spray the substances directly into the mouth. Others spray the solvents into plastic bags or crisps packets, which are then held over the nose and mouth. It is not unknown for much larger plastic bags containing solvents to be placed completely over the user's head, a method known as 'space-helmeting'.

Drinks cans also can be used for sniffing solvents. The solvent is poured into an empty can held in the hand. The heat from the hand causes the solvent to evaporate, so that it can be sniffed through the ring-pull opening.

It is possible to sniff directly from rags, clothing and paper towels, and it is therefore important to view with some seriousness any such items found that smell of solvents.

Use of strongly scented products

In order to mask the smells produced by smoking drugs or solvent abuse, some users utilise other strong-smelling items, such as air-fresheners, aftershaves and incense sticks in large quantities. Such behaviour should be investigated in order to establish the reason for their use.

Tablets, capsules, powders, dried plant material, very small often dried mushrooms, small stamp-like paper squares with coloured motifs printed on them

We cannot emphasise enough that the discovery of any piece of equipment unfamiliar to you, along with any form of capsule, tablet, powder, crystal, plant material or solvent, must be regarded very seriously and should be investigated thoroughly, perhaps with expert assistance from a local community drugs service, doctor, pharmacist or police officer. These services usually will be helpful and sympathetic in these matters and can be approached anonymously.

Physical evidence of possible drug use: summary

- Cigarette lighters, matches and candles (especially if the person is a non-smoker).

- Knives, metal foil, drinks cans and bottle tops discoloured by heat.

- Funnels, outer covers of matchboxes and large straws.

- Stone, clay, wooden, metal, glass or ceramic long-stemmed pipes (chillums).

- High-tech metal pipes ranging in appearance from rather thick credit cards to finger-sized cylinders.

- Home-made hubble-bubble pipes (bongs) and similar devices.

- Large cigarette-rolling papers and short cardboard tubes (roaches).

- Cigarette-rolling paper packets with pieces torn from them.

- Razor blades, modelling knives and scalpel blades.

- Cigarette filters and cotton-wool.

- Spoons discoloured by heat, often with a bent stem.

- Lemon juice, vinegar, ascorbic acid and citric acid.

- Tourniquets, syringes, needles, swabs, filters and water or drug ampoules.

- Folded 5cm squares of paper (wraps or deals).

- Coloured powders and sets of scales.

- Lighter fuel, lighter gas, hairsprays, spray deodorants, solvent glues, spray polishes, correcting fluids and dry-cleaning fluids.

- Plastic bags, crisps packets, drinks cans and clothing that smell of solvents.

- Use of strongly scented products.

- Tablets, capsules, powders and dried plant material.

- Very small, often dried, mushrooms.

- Very small stamp-like paper squares with coloured motifs printed on them (trips or tabs).

Note: there may be perfectly legitimate explanations for possession of some of these items. You should check out your findings with an expert before making any assumptions or accusations.

Chapter 14

Managing Drug-related Incidents

Since the use of illegal drugs in our society has become extensive, few people in positions of responsibility for others, particularly young people, will never find themselves at some point having to deal with an incident that is in some way related to drug use. This applies to parents, teachers, social workers, youth leaders and many other professionals.

This chapter is not intended to lay down strict rules for the management of such incidents. Rather, it is intended to provide a set of guidelines that will help the person concerned approach and deal with the incident with a degree of confidence. Many professionals will already have policies laid down by their organisations that outline approved courses of action, and they will have to give due regard to such policies when considering the guidance in this chapter. There may be times, however, when an incident is being dealt with by someone, such as a parent, relative or even a stranger, who has no official policy to guide them at all, or the circumstances are such that an organisation's policy does not apply. It is at these times that most people would feel at their most inadequate in dealing with incidents and when these guidelines may be of most help to them. It is worth adding that these guidelines have been formulated as a result of many years of experience assisting various individuals and organisations in managing drug-related incidents. We have created a number of scenarios that describe typical drug-related incidents of the sort that readers may find themselves having to deal with. The guidelines for dealing with each scenario are outlined in some detail and are accompanied by a simplified flowchart that takes the reader step by step through the actions to be taken. Both the notes and the flowcharts should be referred to together when considering each scenario.

Scenario 1: Person displaying behavioural signs and symptoms of possible drug use

Note 1

By reading Chapter 12, you will become familiar with most of the behavioural clues that drug users display, and the reasons for them. These are mostly the sorts of clue that would be noticed only by someone in fairly regular contact with the person. You may see behavioural changes that initially are very small but that grow and accumulate until you begin to suspect that they are the result of drug or other substance use.

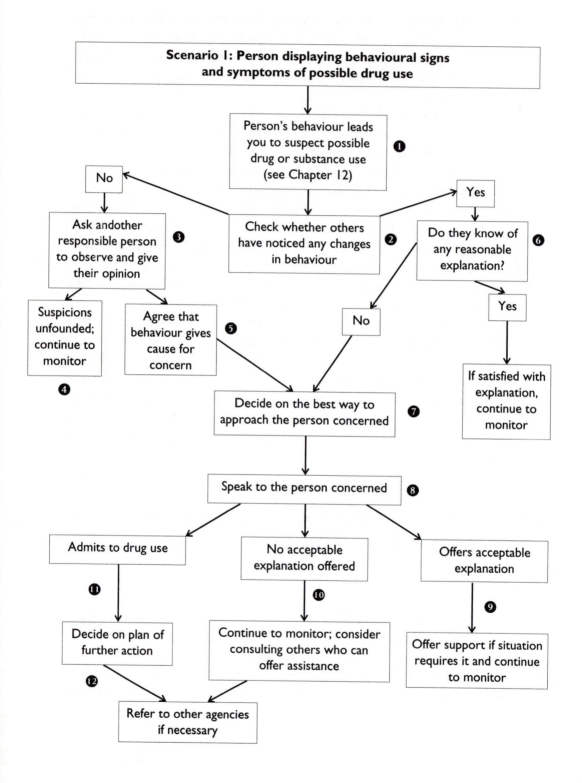

Scenario 1: Person displaying behavioural signs and symptoms of possible drug use

Person's behaviour leads you to suspect possible drug or substance use (see Chapter 12) ❶

No

Ask andother responsible person to observe and give their opinion ❸

Check whether others have noticed any changes in behaviour ❷

Yes

Do they know of any reasonable explanation? ❻

Suspicions unfounded; continue to monitor ❹

Agree that behaviour gives cause for concern ❺

No

Yes

If satisfied with explanation, continue to monitor

Decide on the best way to approach the person concerned ❼

Speak to the person concerned ❽

Admits to drug use ⓫

No acceptable explanation offered ❿

Offers acceptable explanation ❾

Decide on plan of further action ⓬

Continue to monitor; consider consulting others who can offer assistance

Offer support if situation requires it and continue to monitor

Refer to other agencies if necessary

Note 2

Having begun to suspect that someone is behaving in a way that could indicate drug use, an obvious first step is to talk to other people who have dealings with the person in question in order to ascertain whether they have noticed anything out of the ordinary and whether they have similar suspicions.

Note 3

It may be that no-one else has had the opportunity to observe the person closely or noticed anything unusual. If this is the case, it would be a good idea to ask someone responsible to observe the person for a while and to give their opinion as to whether your suspicions are well-founded. If that person is someone with previous experience of dealing with drug incidents, then so much the better.

Note 4

The observer may not agree with you and may reassure you that your suspicions are unfounded, in which case it will be up to you to decide whether to take further action. If you decide not to take it any further at this stage, then it would be advisable to continue to monitor the situation.

Note 5

If the person you have asked to carry out the observations agrees with your assessment of the situation, then you are in a much better position to plan your course of action.

Note 6

It may be that other people have already noticed the behaviour that has aroused your suspicions and, indeed, other signs that perhaps have not been apparent to you. There may be a non-drug-related explanation for the person's behaviour; other people may have information not known to you that satisfactorily explains the matter. One of the authors of this book was approached by the mother of a 16-year-old boy after a parents' drug information evening. She described a set of behavioural changes that she had observed in her son. From the description given, it seemed possible that drug use was involved, and suitable advice was given. The mother contacted the author a few days later to say that she had followed the advice and had a conversation with her son. The behavioural changes were not a result of drug use: in fact, the boy's girlfriend was pregnant, and he did not know how to deal with the situation.

This is perhaps a classic example of drug-type behaviour arising as a result of other problems in a young person's life. However, even if information is offered that appears to explain the behaviour, it is prudent to continue to monitor the person in question.

If other people have noticed the behaviour and have no reasonable explanation for it, then it is necessary to investigate further.

Note 7

Having tried to find an explanation for the behavioural clues observed, but without success, there is little more that can be done other than to approach the person concerned. Consideration needs to be given as to the best way of doing this. You will need to consider whether it would be best to see the person alone or whether it would be best to have somebody else present. It very much depends on your relationship with the person concerned. You may judge that you are more likely to get to the truth if you speak to them alone, or it may be that you decide that it would be more prudent to have a witness or someone else to provide a second opinion. Only you can be the judge in these cases. It is well worth trying to work out exactly what you are going to say to the person beforehand, and what are you hoping to achieve. What exactly is it that has led you to the suspicions that you have? What do you suspect the person of doing? You may need to seek advice and support from someone with experience in these matters before you decide on the best method of dealing with this.

Note 8

Having decided on the best way of approaching the person, it is worth taking a moment to consider how you will speak to them. It is never a good idea to adopt an accusatory or confrontational style; it has been our experience that if a user is confronted too fiercely at this stage, then they may simply run off. Then you have not only a drug user but also a missing person. Remaining calm is vital. Try to show by the tone and style of your conversation that it is your wish to help and not to provide the person with yet another problem. Explain the things that led to you forming the suspicions that you hold, and produce any evidence that you might have to back up your suspicions. Unless you have a clear grasp of drug slang, it is better to use the correct terms when talking about drugs. Nothing makes a non-drug-user look more foolish than using the wrong slang. Remember the slang belongs to their world, not yours, and they may react unfavourably if you try to use it and get it wrong.

Note 9

The person may offer a perfectly reasonable explanation at this point for the behaviour that you have noticed. This explanation may indicate that they have another, non-drug-related problem that you can perhaps help with. You may be in a position to offer support, advice and practical help that will assist the person in coping with this problem. Even if you are satisfied with their explanation, it would be prudent to continue to monitor the situation.

Note 10

If the person denies all drug use but offers no satisfactory explanation for their behaviour, you may not be in a position to substantiate your suspicions at this stage and may be unable to take it any further. You will clearly need to monitor the situation further, and you may consider consulting with others who can advise you as to the steps available to you. It may be that you feel that you have done all that you can and need to refer the matter on to others to deal with (see note 12).

Note 11

If your suspicions are well-founded and your approach is well thought out, the person may admit to you that they are involved in the use of drugs or some other substance. It is especially important at this time to remain calm and to consider carefully the next step. It would be prudent for you to inform the person that you may find it necessary to pass on the details of your conversation to others, should you consider it the correct course of action.

It is useful to gather some more vital information at this point. What drug or substance are they using? What method of administration are they using? How much and for how long have they been using? This will help you to judge whether it is likely that they have become habituated to the drug, and what their financial position might be as a result. It will be useful to find out where they use their drug and with whom. This information may not be forthcoming, but if it is, it may enable you to take action to help bring such use to an end.

The last and perhaps most vital questions that you should seek answers to are why they are using drugs in the first place, what they get out of it, and whether they require help. It may be that you can take steps that will help to eliminate their need to use drugs. You may be able to help bring about a change in their lives that will make drug use unnecessary.

Most drug users in the early stages of use will not perceive that they have any sort of problem. They believe that they are in control of their drug use, not that the drug is controlling them. This may of course be wrong, and it may be your task to make them understand this. Invariably, you will not be able to provide any support or influence if the user does not accept that they have a problem. If they accept that they do need help, it will then be necessary to work out with them a plan of action to resolve the situation.

Note 12

It may be that, after listening to all that the person has to say, you decide that it is best if you refer the person on to others. This could be a community drugs service, which will offer confidential help and support to the person, or it may be that you feel the situation is such that you need to refer the matter to a higher authority, such as senior colleague, parents or the police. There will almost always be the need to refer the matter to a higher authority if the person does not cooperate with you.

Scenario 2: Person under the influence of, or withdrawing from substance use

Note 1

The physical signs of drug or substance use vary considerably from person to person, and from drug to drug. They will also depend on how much was taken, how recently and what previous experience the user has had of that drug or substance. For the non-expert, it is sufficient to be aware that a person who displays signs of intoxication, loss of control, unsteadiness, lethargy or hyperactivity, or is suffering from hallucinations, is possibly under the influence of a drug or other substance. However, all of these signs also have other causes. They could be the symptoms of an illness or accidental poisoning or a side effect of a prescribed medicine. It is the responsibility of the observer to check out the reasons for the behaviour that they are witnessing. If the person is going through withdrawal from drug use, they are likely to display signs of disorientation, depression, mood swings, aggression, lethargy or tiredness. They may also, in extreme cases, show signs of suffering physical pain.

Note 2

Having observed behaviour that leads you to suspect drug or substance use, the most useful thing that you can do is to consult with others to see whether anyone else has noticed the same behaviour.

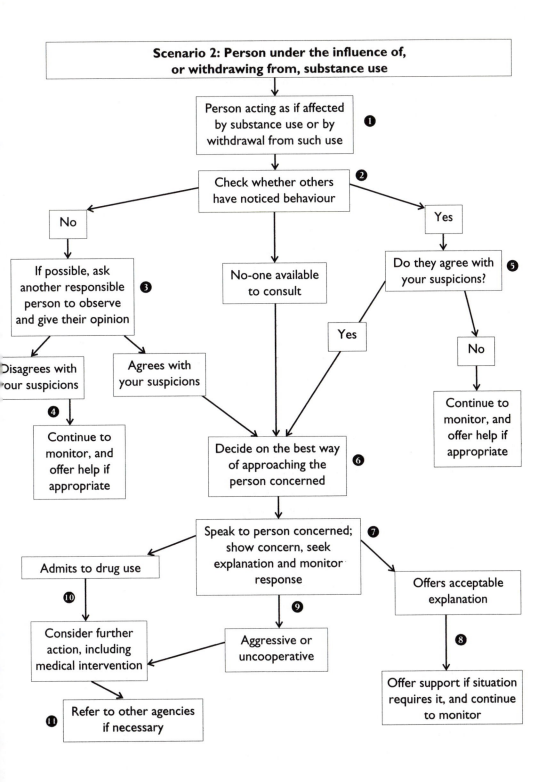

Scenario 2: Person under the influence of, or withdrawing from, substance use

Person acting as if affected by substance use or by withdrawal from such use ❶

Check whether others have noticed behaviour ❷

No

Yes

If possible, ask another responsible person to observe and give their opinion ❸

No-one available to consult

Do they agree with your suspicions? ❺

Yes

No

Disagrees with your suspicions ❹

Agrees with your suspicions

Continue to monitor, and offer help if appropriate

Continue to monitor, and offer help if appropriate

Decide on the best way of approaching the person concerned ❻

Speak to person concerned; show concern, seek explanation and monitor response ❼

Admits to drug use ❿

Offers acceptable explanation

Consider further action, including medical intervention

Aggressive or uncooperative ❾

Offer support if situation requires it, and continue to monitor ❽

Refer to other agencies if necessary ⓫

271

Note 3

If no-one has noticed anything out of the ordinary or has not had an opportunity to observe the person, it would be useful to ask someone to monitor the person and then give their opinion. Of course, some discretion must be exercised here: it would not be wise to seek an opinion from an unreliable person or someone who is closely connected with the person you are observing, for they may give you an incorrect answer in the belief that they are protecting their friend.

Note 4

The person asked to monitor the situation may be able to satisfy you that the behaviour that aroused your suspicions is not drug-related. If so, there may be other forms of help that you can offer the person in question. Of course, it is still advisable to keep an eye on the situation, in case it recurs.

Note 5

The behaviour may already have been noticed by someone else, and they may be of the opinion that it is not related to drug or substance use. If you are satisfied with that opinion, then proceed in the same way as for note 4.

Note 6

If no-one is available to give you an opinion, or if those that you have asked share your opinions, you then have to decide on the best way to approach the person concerned. It is worth sounding a note of caution here: if the person is unknown to you, or if you are in any doubt about your own safety, then it is essential to seek help from others before any approach is made; it may be necessary to call in the police.

If you are satisfied that you are not at risk, then you need to decide on the best way to talk to the person. Depending on your previous relationship with them, it may be best to speak quietly to them away from others, or you may judge that it would be best to have someone with you.

Note 7

Having decided on the best way of approaching the person concerned, it is worth spending a moment considering how you are going to speak to them. It is never a good idea to adopt an accusatory or confrontational style. It has been our experience that if a user is confronted too fiercely at this stage, then they may run off. Then you have not only a drug user but also a missing person. Keeping calm is vital. Try to show by the tone and style of your conversation that it is your wish to help them, not to provide them with yet another problem. Explain the things that led to you forming the suspicions that you have, and produce any evidence that you might have to back up your suspicions.

Monitor closely any responses, for this may enable you to judge how deeply affected they are and whether it is likely that they are going to need medical help.

Note 8

It may be that the person offers an explanation of their behaviour that satisfies you that it is not connected with drug or substance misuse. By taking a non-accusatory and helpful tone initially, it will be easier for the person to confide in you if they have some other problem. There may be some form of help or support that you can offer.

Note 9

However carefully you plan your approach, the person may react badly to it and become uncooperative or aggressive. If you are unable to calm them and gain their co-operation quickly, it may be best to withdraw from the situation and refer it on to others. Depending on the circumstances of the individual case, you may be able to pass on the matter to someone in a position of authority, or it may be necessary to inform the police.

Note 10

A careful, non-confrontational approach may lead the person to admit that they have been using drugs or other substances. They may be experiencing very unpleasant feelings and be frightened by the situation they find themselves in, and they may want someone to help them. It will be important to ascertain, if you can, what substance they have been using, how much and how recently. You will need to decide whether it is necessary to seek medical assistance. If you are satisfied that immediate medical help is not needed, you can then consider what further action is called for. Again, this will depend on your relationship with the person and the particular circumstances of the case. It may be the very first time that they have ever tried drugs and they may have been put off by the experience. If, on the other hand, it is part of an ongoing situation, then this will need to be handled carefully. Only you can be the judge of this.

Refer to Scenario 1, note 11 for further guidance.

Note 11

After listening to all that the person has to say, you may decide that it is best to refer them to someone else. This could be a community drugs service, which will offer help and support to the person in a confidential manner. However, you may feel that you need to refer the person to a higher authority, such as senior colleagues, parents or the police. There will almost always be the need to refer the matter to a higher authority if the person will not cooperate with your offers of help.

Scenario 3: Person found unconscious

Note 1

You may be the first person on the scene of someone who has lost consciousness as a result of their use of drugs or other substance. Your actions at this stage can make the difference between full recovery and death.

Note 2

The first rule of all emergency aid is not to panic. This is easier to say than carry out in real life, but somehow you must remain calm. By preparing yourself for such an eventuality, you will make staying calm easier to achieve.

You will need to make an initial assessment of the situation in order to check whether the person is breathing and the heart is beating. Ensure that the airway is open and clear it of any obvious obstructions. Unless it is necessary for you to perform immediate cardiac massage and/or mouth-to-mouth resuscitation, you should place the person in the recovery position; this prevents the tongue from falling back and blocking the airway, and allows liquids such as vomit to drain freely from the mouth. The following instructions for placing an unconscious person in the recovery position can be practised with a partner until both of you are familiar with them:

1. Kneel on the ground next to the person and straighten and place together their legs. Put the person's arm that is nearest to you out at right-angles to their body, and then bend it at the elbow, laying it down with the palm uppermost.

2. Take hold of the person's other arm and draw it across their chest, bending the elbow so that the back of the person's hand is laid in contact with the side of their face nearest to you. Hold the hand in that position.

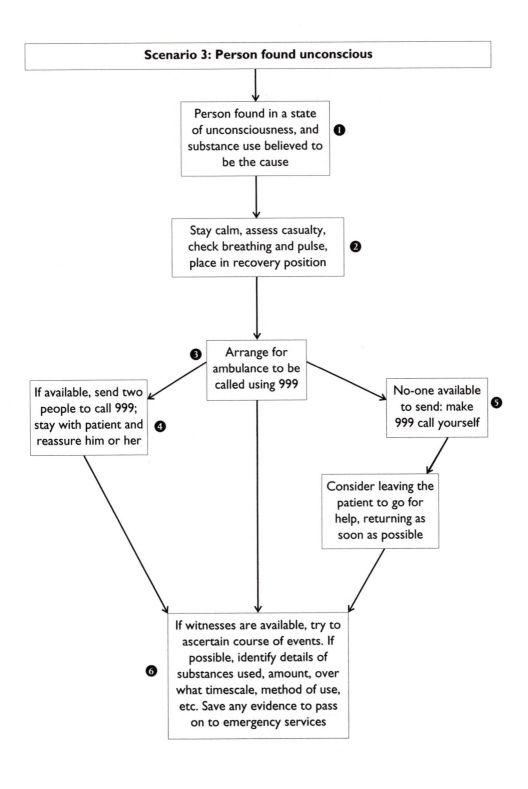

Scenario 3: Person found unconscious

Person found in a state of unconsciousness, and substance use believed to be the cause ❶

Stay calm, assess casualty, check breathing and pulse, place in recovery position ❷

❸ Arrange for ambulance to be called using 999

If available, send two people to call 999; stay with patient and reassure him or her ❹

No-one available to send: make 999 call yourself ❺

Consider leaving the patient to go for help, returning as soon as possible

❻ If witnesses are available, try to ascertain course of events. If possible, identify details of substances used, amount, over what timescale, method of use, etc. Save any evidence to pass on to emergency services

3. With your other hand, take hold of the person's leg that is furthest from you. Hold it above the knee and pull until the person rolls on to their side. They should now be lying on their side facing you, with their face supported on one hand and with the upper leg sticking out at right-angles, with the knee bent to support the weight of the body.

4. Tilt the person's head back to ensure that the airway stays clear, and adjust the position of their hand if necessary. The person is now in a stable and safe position.

In the UK, the St John Ambulance organisation, among others, offers full first-aid training to organisations and individuals. Their website www.sja.org.uk/swyorks/halifax/training/recovery.htm offers a step-by-step pictorial guide to placing a casualty in the recovery position. More extensive first-aid training can be arranged through their website at www.sja.org.uk, which also provides links to their world-wide branches. The Red Cross also provides such training; in the UK, details can be found at www.redcross.org.uk/firstaid and in the USA at www.redcross.org/services/hss/course/community.html.

Note 3

If a person is unconscious and you suspect that drug or substance use is the cause, you must summon medical help as soon as possible. In circumstances such as these, it is never safe to wait to see whether the person comes round of their own accord. Delay could have fatal consequences.

Note 4

Once you have assessed the situation, if there is someone in the vicinity, get them to summon help by dialling 999 or your local emergency number for an ambulance. This can be being done while you are stabilising the person in the recovery position. If a mobile phone is not available to call an ambulance, and it is necessary to send someone to find a telephone, if possible send two people, for experience has shown that this ensures that it will be done. Nothing can be more frustrating for the person caring for the casualty than having to wait in vain for an ambulance that has not been called.

As you wait for medical help, continue to monitor the person, as their condition may change and call for more first-aid treatment from you. Their state of unconsciousness may lighten, and you will then need to reassure them that you have the situation under control. On the other hand, the state of unconsciousness may deepen and they may stop breathing, in which case you will need to commence re-suscitation.

Note 5

You may find that you are the only person in the vicinity, without a mobile phone and with no-one who you can send to summon help. In this case, you may need to consider leaving the person to summon help yourself. Once you have put the person in the recovery position, it should be fairly safe for you to leave them for a short time. If you can stabilise them further by placing a cushion or similar to prevent them rolling on to their back, then so much the better.

Note 6

Once you are satisfied that help is on the way, you may have time to enquire as to whether anyone witnessed the course of events that led to the person becoming unconscious. Information of this nature could be invaluable to the medical staff who will treat the casualty. Similarly, have a look around to see whether there is any physical evidence that could help in the identification of the substances taken. Hand over anything found to the ambulance crew before the casualty is taken away.

Scenario 4: Self-disclosure of substance use

Note 1

This scenario deals with the case in which a person discloses to you that they are using drugs or other substances. Clearly, there may be many reasons why a person admits their substance use to you. They may have become concerned about what they are doing, they may have been frightened by a bad experience, or they may feel that they are losing control and need help. It may be simply that they want to sound you out, to gauge your attitude to what they are doing. Whatever the reason, one thing is clear: they have chosen to talk to you, and that puts you in a very important and responsible position. If you respond in the right way, you may be able to do a great deal of good. If you respond in the wrong way, you may make the situation worse.

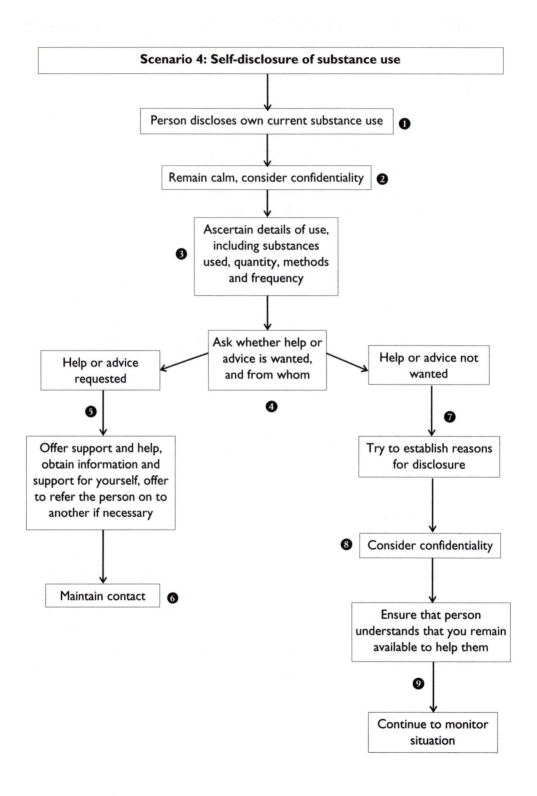

Scenario 4: Self-disclosure of substance use

Person discloses own current substance use ❶

Remain calm, consider confidentiality ❷

❸ Ascertain details of use, including substances used, quantity, methods and frequency

Ask whether help or advice is wanted, and from whom ❹

Help or advice requested

Help or advice not wanted

❺ Offer support and help, obtain information and support for yourself, offer to refer the person on to another if necessary

❼ Try to establish reasons for disclosure

Maintain contact ❻

❽ Consider confidentiality

Ensure that person understands that you remain available to help them

❾ Continue to monitor situation

Note 2

The first thing that you must do is remain calm. This may depend on your relationship with the person. If your relationship is personal, then staying calm will not be as simple as if your relationship is on a more professional level.

At this point, you will need to consider whether you can keep confidentiality for this person. This will depend on your relationship with them and the details that they have told you. You will need to make it clear to them that you may find it necessary to relate to others what is said to you.

Note 3

You must respond to the disclosure in such a way that the person feels able to go further and tell you exactly what they are involved in. You need to ascertain certain information if possible, including what substances they are using, in what quantities, for how long and by what method. If you are going to help them to make the right decisions about their substance use, you will need as full a picture as possible of what they are doing.

Note 4

It may become clear very quickly that the person is seeking your help. You will need to find out exactly what sort of help they are looking for. Is it from you, or do they want you to refer them elsewhere? You will need to explore gently with them the sort of help that might be the best for them (see Chapter 15 for details of treatment options).

Note 5

If help is requested, it is vital that you do not try to promise more than you can deliver. It does no harm to say to the person that you are willing to support them but you feel that they need more help than you can provide. There is a whole range of other agencies that can offer confidential help and to which you can refer them.

If you are going to try and provide the help personally, it is important that you get help and support for yourself before you become too involved, as it is easy to get into a position where you feel that you are out of your depth and failing to provide the help that you had promised.

Note 6

If you refer the person on to another agency, it is important that you maintain contact with them if possible. They will greatly appreciate your continuing support, and it may help them to feel that they are not on their own as they try to deal with their problems.

Note 7

It may be that the person maintains that they do not require help and refuses offers that you make. Now is the time to find out why the disclosure was made in the first place. In many cases, disclosures are made to test out the person receiving the information. It may have been made to shock you or to show off. It could also be that the person wants help but cannot bring themselves to admit it. Careful questioning at this stage may make the reasons for the disclosure more clear.

Note 8

You may need to remind the person of the limits of confidentiality that you are able to offer them.

Note 9

Even if the person refuses all offers of help, it is important that they understand that you remain available if they change their mind. The way in which you respond to them may lead them to return later to take up your offer of support and help.

Scenario 5: Third-person disclosure

Note 1

You are offered information that another person is misusing drugs or some other substance.

Note 2

Clearly, there will be implications of confidentiality in this situation. Information that is offered on the basis of 'Don't tell anyone I told you' is often nothing more than gossip. You may need to make it clear from the outset that whatever the person

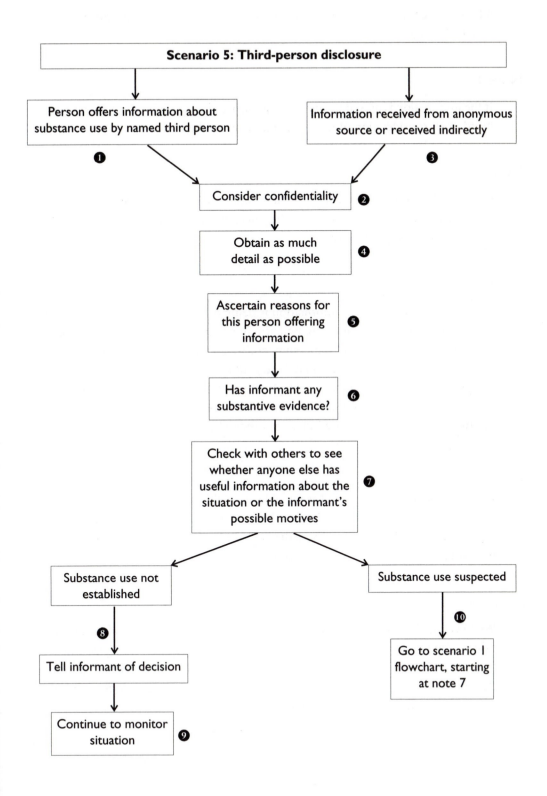

Scenario 5: Third-person disclosure

Person offers information about substance use by named third person ❶

Information received from anonymous source or received indirectly ❸

Consider confidentiality ❷

Obtain as much detail as possible ❹

Ascertain reasons for this person offering information ❺

Has informant any substantive evidence? ❻

Check with others to see whether anyone else has useful information about the situation or the informant's possible motives ❼

Substance use not established

Substance use suspected

❿

❽ Tell informant of decision

Go to scenario 1 flowchart, starting at note 7

Continue to monitor situation ❾

tells you may lead to some action on your part, or to you passing the information on to somebody else.

Note 3

If the information is passed to you anonymously or is something that you have over-heard, then consideration of confidentiality may not be necessary.

Note 4

However the information reaches you, it is important that you obtain as much detail as possible. Half a story is of little use. You need more information if you are to deal with it in the best possible way.

Note 5

You must consider why this information is being offered to you. What are the motives of the informant? They may be entirely genuine if the informant is worried about what is happening and wants someone to help the person they are telling you about. On the other hand, they may be trying to divert attention from themselves and perhaps their own drug use, or maybe they simply wish to cause trouble for the person they are naming. You will need to be satisfied that you are being given good information and not being used in some other way.

Note 6

Having obtained as much detail as possible, it would be wise to ask whether the informant has any substantive evidence to back up what they are saying. Perhaps they know where the drugs or paraphernalia are kept by the person in question or they have something else that can back up their story.

Note 7

Whatever the level of information and back-up evidence, it is worth checking with others who know either the informant or the person being named, to see whether they can add anything to what you have already been told. They may have information that will throw light on the possible motives of the informant or that will support or negate the information given.

Note 8

It may be that having listened to all that the informant has to say, and gathered what other information is available, you are still not satisfied that this is a case of drug or substance misuse. If this is so, then you will need to tell the informant of your decision in whatever way seems appropriate.

Note 9

Even if you are satisfied that drugs are not involved, it would be prudent to monitor the situation.

Note 10

If you are satisfied that drugs or other substances are being misused, then you will need to think carefully about your next step. For more information on what approaches you can make, see scenario 1, note 7.

Scenario 6: Person believed to be in possession of substance or paraphernalia

Note 1

This scenario deals with a situation in which you become aware that a person is in possession of what you have good cause to believe is an illegal drug or some other substance of misuse and/or items that are connected with their use. It may be that you have been given information that has led to this belief or that you have actually seen the person using or handling something that has aroused your suspicion.

Note 2

The first thing that you have to decide is whether it is possible for you to take possession of these items. This depends very much on your relationship with the person. If the relationship is personal, such as a parent/child relationship, then you may decide that you are going to take possession of the items regardless of whether the person agrees. If your relationship is on a more professional level, however, you will need to decide whether you can persuade the person to hand over the items. You have no right to search the person against their will, but there is nothing to stop you asking them to turn out their pockets or bags. It is often possible to persuade people

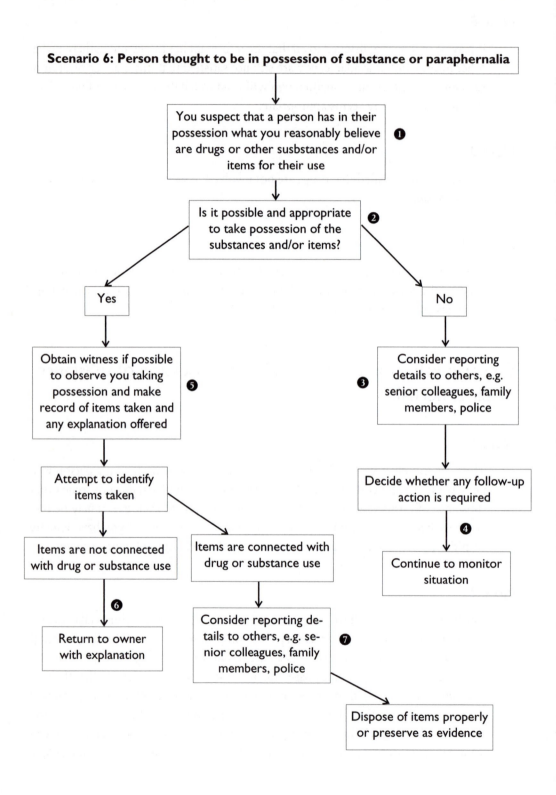

Scenario 6: Person thought to be in possession of substance or paraphernalia

You suspect that a person has in their possession what you reasonably believe are drugs or other susbstances and/or items for their use ❶

Is it possible and appropriate to take possession of the substances and/or items? ❷

Yes

No

Obtain witness if possible to observe you taking possession and make record of items taken and any explanation offered ❺

Consider reporting details to others, e.g. senior colleagues, family members, police ❸

Attempt to identify items taken

Decide whether any follow-up action is required ❹

Items are not connected with drug or substance use

Items are connected with drug or substance use

Continue to monitor situation

❻

Return to owner with explanation

Consider reporting details to others, e.g. senior colleagues, family members, police ❼

Dispose of items properly or preserve as evidence

to do what they would rather not do, but this will depend on your confidence and skill.

Note 3

If it is not possible to take possession of the items, then you will need to decide on what action you are going to take. You may decide to refer the matter to a higher authority. You could consider telling a senior work colleague, a member of the person's family or the police. The police have the power to carry out searches of persons and property, providing you can give them sufficient information to satisfy them that your suspicions are reasonable.

Note 4

Depending on the results of passing the situation on to others, you will need to consider whether there is any further action that you need to take. The situation may be taken out of your hands, but, depending on your relationship with the person, there may be some follow-up action that you can usefully take. Whatever happens, it is prudent to continue to monitor the situation.

Note 5

If you are able to take possession of the items, try to get a witness to your action if possible. This may prevent the person making unfounded allegations against you of assault or similar later on. Take note of any explanation that they offer for the items you have taken possession of. They may come clean with you and admit that the items are drugs or drug- or substance-related. On the other hand, they may deny it flatly, leaving you to prove it.

It is worth at this stage covering two important points. Have you the right to take possession of an illegal substance? And how do you do it safely?

In the UK you are completely within your rights under common law to take possession of an illegal substance if you are doing so to prevent the commission of a criminal offence. In this case, you are seizing the items to prevent them being possessed by the other person, and you are clearly acting within the law. Having seized the items, you now need to act in such a way that you stay within the law. In order to do so, you need to do one of two things as soon as possible. You must either hand the items to the police or destroy them. Do not just dispose of such in household waste. It is wise to have a witness present at the destruction if possible. What you must not do is put away the items for 'safekeeping', as you will then be in illegal possession of them.

Handling the items correctly is largely a matter of common sense. The following advice is intended to assist you to keep yourself safe and to preserve the evidential value of the items if you intend to pass them on to the police.

Drugs in solid, powder, tablet or capsule form

Such things may be found in wrapping or packaging that is either commercially produced or home-made from, for example, folded paper, cooking foil or clear plastic film. This wrapping should be preserved along with the substance, as this could help in its identification.

When opening a suspect wrapper, take care not to spill any of the contents. If any is spilled, it should be gathered up and placed in an envelope rather than the original wrapping, as this could contaminate the remains of the sample.

Great care should be taken to avoid spilling any of the contents on to the skin. Rubber gloves will provide adequate protection.

No attempt should be made to identify the substance by sniffing or tasting it. You are not a part of a detective film: this is real life, and such actions can be extremely dangerous.

LSD trips and tabs

The small paper squares impregnated with LSD and called 'trips' or 'tabs' are commonly wrapped in clear plastic film to prevent deterioration. Do not open the wrapping. If the wrapping is opaque, open with care but do not touch the contents. It is possible for LSD to be absorbed through the skin if it is handled for a sufficiently long time. Rewrap the LSD and dispose of it, or store it until you hand it over to the authorities.

Needles, syringes and 'cooking spoons'

These can present possible health risks to anyone handling them. If they have been used, you are open to the risk of infection if the needle pierces your skin. They should be handled with great care and placed in a secure, puncture-proof container to await disposal. If a suitable 'sharps' box is not available, then a strong metal or plastic box will suffice.

Paraphernalia, bongs, pipes, tin-foil, etc.

There are few health risks with these articles if they are handled with care. They should be wrapped in clean paper and placed in a large envelope to await disposal.

If you intend to hand over the items to the police, they should be stored in sealed clean envelopes to await collection. If more than one item has been found, they should be placed in separate envelopes. Details should be recorded of the circumstances of each find or seizure.

Anyone who has handled an item that is suspected of being involved in drug use is advised to wash their hands thoroughly as soon as possible afterwards.

Note 6

Having taken possession of the items, it may become clear to you that they are not connected with drug or substance use. If this is the case, then there is little you can do but return them to their owner with an explanation as to your actions.

Note 7

If you are convinced that the items are connected with drug or substance use, then you have to decide what action you are going to take next. You may decide that you can deal with the incident yourself, in which case you should dispose of the items, as detailed in note 5. You may, however, feel that the matter should be referred on to some higher authority or the police. If this is the case, you should preserve the items as evidence, as detailed in note 5.

Scenario 7: Discovery of substance and/or paraphernalia

Note 1

This scenario deals with the finding of drugs or other substances of misuse or related paraphernalia. They could be found concealed or simply abandoned.

Note 2

In cases such as this, it is always worth making general enquiries to ascertain whether anyone has any information that can give you a clearer picture of how the items got to be where you found them.

Note 3

You are about to take into your possession something that could be an illegal drug (see scenario 6, note 5 for your rights in relation to taking possession of drugs). It is a

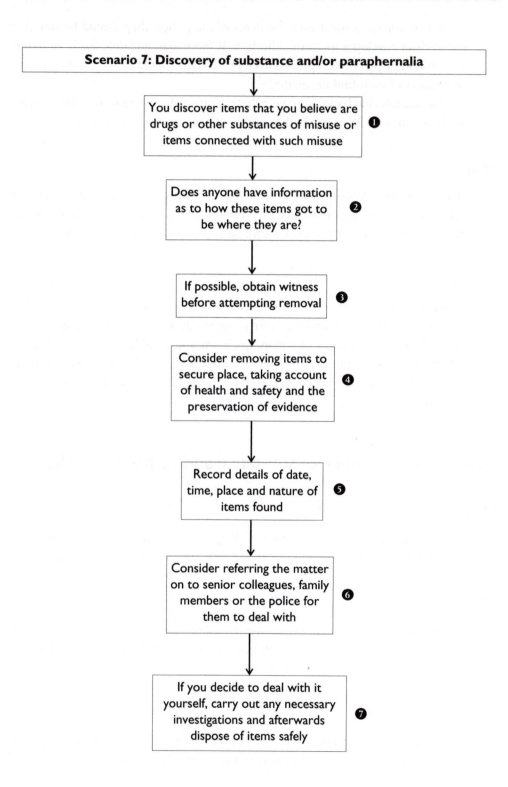

Scenario 7: Discovery of substance and/or paraphernalia

You discover items that you believe are drugs or other substances of misuse or items connected with such misuse ❶

Does anyone have information as to how these items got to be where they are? ❷

If possible, obtain witness before attempting removal ❸

Consider removing items to secure place, taking account of health and safety and the preservation of evidence ❹

Record details of date, time, place and nature of items found ❺

Consider referring the matter on to senior colleagues, family members or the police for them to deal with ❻

If you decide to deal with it yourself, carry out any necessary investigations and afterwards dispose of items safely ❼ good idea to get a witness to your actions if possible, as this may well prevent someone making allegations of wrongdoing later.

Note 4

Before you remove the items, give some consideration to your own health and safety and the need to preserve the evidential value of the items if you intend to involve the police. If the items are in a reasonably secure place, and you intend to refer the matter to the police, it is best to leave them where they are, not to touch them or allow anyone else to do so, and call the police as soon as possible. If you intend to deal with the matter yourself or you want to consider your possible courses of action, it will be necessary for you to remove the items to a secure place. Take all necessary precautions for safety, as detailed in scenario 6, note 5.

Note 5

Having removed the items to a secure place, make a record of the incident, including a description of what was found, location, time and witnesses.

Note 6

Once the items are secure, you have to decide what to do next. In most cases, you should consider referring the matter on to a higher authority for them to decide on what course of action to follow. This higher authority could be a senior colleague, family member or the police.

Note 7

If you intend to deal with the matter yourself, you will need to make as many enquiries as you can to establish the source of the items. The discovery of the items may be connected with enquiries that you are already involved in, and it may be possible to identify the person or people responsible for them. If this is the case, then you should refer to the flowchart for scenario 1, starting at note 7, before approaching the person concerned.

Chapter 15

Common Reasons for Drug and Substance Misuse, and Details of Available Treatment

Common reasons for drug and substance misuse

There are almost as many reasons for using drugs as there are users, but many recur with great regularity. Depending on the drug being used, drugs can change or lift your mood, increase your energy levels, change your perspective, aid sleep, help you relax, remove emotional or physical pain, reduce your appetite and weight, lower inhibitions, increase libido, and give you feelings of great physical and mental prowess. Drugs can also be used in order to change your self-image, provide entry into certain groups, rebel, or simply to fill time and relieve boredom.

Substances may be used to mask a person's problems, but this will work only temporarily. Drugs are a short-term solution: they do not remove or resolve difficulties, but rather change the user's perception of the immediate circumstances.

Some people who use drugs and other substances do so simply because of their availability or for social reasons, and there may be no discernible underlying problems. Many, however, do have problems, even if they are not aware of them, and some people are simply self-medicating these problems away. Such problems may be of a complex and deep psychological nature, caused by earlier life traumas, e.g. abuse or bereavement, or they may be much simpler, such as boredom or low self-esteem. By using drugs to relieve these problems, users can unwittingly be putting themselves into situations that actually increase and exacerbate them, for regular use may lead to other health, legal and social difficulties.

To keep things in perspective, however, most people will not use substances at all. Many people who start out using drugs or other substances do so for only a short period, and of these only a small percentage go on to develop any medium- or long-term problems as a direct result. However, these users can cause damage to society well out of proportion to their numbers.

In a survey of tertiary college students, which we carried out in our local area, participants were asked to list all of the reasons that they were aware of as to why they or their peers had ever used drugs. One surprising result came from a young man, who stated that almost every aspect of his life was controlled or manipulated by adults and that he used drugs because it was one of the few areas of his life over which he felt he had complete control. His stated reason for his own use of drugs was his feelings of powerlessness over his own actions and decisions.

The students' responses are listed below:

- addiction
- to rebel
- attention-seeking
- because they are available
- to look good
- because of insecurity
- to give confidence
- for experimentation
- to increase intelligence
- for enjoyment of experience
- peer pressure
- to expand horizons
- to mask illness
- to escape reality

- to relieve boredom
- due to ignorance
- to remove worries
- to make your hair grow
- because they are illegal
- to stay awake
- to increase strength and stamina
- to change character and image
- out of curiosity
- culture and religion
- to forget
- recommended by friends
- to be happy
- to impress

- for stimulation
- to get high
- for inspiration
- by mistake
- to cause trouble
- to remove inhibitions
- as a joke
- out of desperation
- because they are cheap
- why not?
- out of choice
- to increase self-esteem
- to relieve stress
- to relax
- for enjoyment
- for convenience
- to get in the mood
- to be sociable
- to get in with the right crowd
- for sexual purposes
- to relieve pain
- to relieve depression

- when drunk
- for nostalgia
- to self-medicate
- for the experience
- because everyone does
- for fun
- for danger and excitement
- to remain alert
- instability
- a quick fix for problems
- to relieve insomnia
- to lose weight
- for research
- to gain weight
- to commit suicide
- as a reward
- for a dare
- to cope
- to increase performance
- to celebrate
- because they are prescribed
- giving in to temptation

Treatment options for people with drug problems

For some people, their use of drugs or other substances may not, in their eyes at least, constitute a problem. They may be using only recreationally or in order to be sociable, may be able to afford easily what they use, may not be habituated either physically or psychologically, and may not be suffering from any side effects or withdrawal symptoms. Indeed, they may appear to have the entire situation under control, and for them it may remain this way. Certainly the majority of users start out like this. But situations have a tendency towards change after a time, and for many users it may turn out to be quite a different story. Substance use for them may have reached a point where it is adversely affecting their physical and mental health, finances, employment, relationships, education, legal position and living accommodation. Also affected, of course, will be many of the people around them, such as partners, family, friends and the victims of any drug-related crimes with which the users might be involved in order to fund their habits.

Even at this advanced stage, many users still will not see their substance use as a problem and may simply transfer any problem on to others who may be affected or who are showing concern, insisting that they are making something out of nothing. Even further along this road, the user may reach a point at which, despite wishing to ignore the facts, there is no alternative but to admit to having a problem for which they may require help, support and understanding.

Depending on the degree and length of time of their usage, the particular drug or drugs being used, and any other life problems faced by the user, a range of services are available to users and to others connected with them who are also involved or affected in some way. But, however good these services are, they can succeed in helping only if the user is willing to cooperate and be totally honest with themselves and others.

If recognised at an early enough stage, some users respond well to simple interventions such as being spoken to by a parent, friend or partner who shows care and concern for them. Others may respond better after being spoken to by their GP, a social worker, teacher, police officer or some other authority figure who they respect.

However, some users will need more than just a good talking or listening to. This is particularly true in cases where substance misuse is carried out in order to mask other problems in the user's life, whether consciously or not. The fear of having to cope without using substances as a psychological prop can be too great to contemplate.

Local drug services

In the UK, most major towns and cities have drug and substance misuse services. These may be statutory or voluntary in nature, are staffed or supported by trained personnel, and offer a range of services to users and other people. Many such services have trained counsellors, therapists and medical staff, one of whom may be assigned as key worker to the user after an initial assessment interview to determine their needs. Counselling may be offered on a one-to-one or group basis, and in some cases this proves to be all that is needed to overcome the user's problems and help them to become substance-free. Relapse-prevention counselling may then follow to ensure that the person remains substance-free. Some agencies even offer alternatives to counselling, such as acupuncture, stress-management and relaxation classes, and sport and exercise sessions.

Detoxification

Further help may be required in the form of prescribed medicines to help the person cope with the possible withdrawal symptoms or as a substitute for the original drug of choice. This medication may then be reduced gradually, over an agreed period of time, so that eventually the person is able to become totally substance-free.

This detoxification process, which clears drugs from the user's system and allows the body to adjust accordingly, may be achieved quite quickly, especially if the user is committed to becoming 'clean'. This commitment may be due to the influence of other people, the desire to remain in a job, for travel or legal purposes, or because of pregnancy or illness. The process, however, may take much longer and may never be achieved totally. This could be as result of relapse or panic as the end of the course of medication gets closer.

Detoxification can take place at home, especially if support is given by the user's family and friends or if it would be impractical, as in the case of a parent who is unable to leave their children. Many drug services support this kind of venture, making frequent home visits to the user and enabling them to remain in the familiarity and safety of their own surroundings. Other services require the user to enter an outpatient day-detoxification clinic or specialist residential detoxification unit, sometimes located within psychiatric hospitals, for which they may first need to be referred by their GP.

If committed to prison, some users have to detox against their will; the regime may be unsympathetic, with the reducing period being short and painful, with little backup or support. This situation is becoming less common, as many prisons are now changing their regimes, allowing their new inmates to become drug- and substance-free in drug-free wings and under the help of dedicated substance misuse workers.

To work well, detoxification programmes have to be planned carefully. The pros and cons need to be discussed at length with the user, and questions such as 'Why now?', 'Is this the best time?', 'Have I enough support services?' and 'What happens afterwards?' will have to be addressed. If, during this process, some of the user's other problems, which may well have led to their substance misuse in the first place, are not dealt with, then they may simply be setting themselves up to fail. Such failure inevitably will lead to the user going straight back to their usual way of coping, by using substances.

Similarly, large lifestyle changes may have to be considered. Changing one's circle of friends or even moving house may be thought to be necessary, in order to keep clear of familiar people, places and circumstances, any of which may trigger off thoughts of former drug use and lead to a new bout of craving. It is clear, therefore, that detoxification is best carried out with professional and medical help in order for it to have a chance of success, although some brave souls have managed it on their own.

For some users of class A drugs in the UK who have come to the notice of the courts due to committing crime to fund their habits, drug treatment and testing orders (DTTOs) can be enforced, requiring the user to attend specialist centres for many hours each week in order to change their offending and drug-using behaviour, rather than receiving a custodial sentence.

Rehabs

Residential rehabilitation facilities, known as 'rehabs', exist for users who seriously want to get away from substance misuse and get their lives back together. This option is time-consuming, usually expensive and in great demand. There are four main types of rehab, each with its own regime or working method.

The first is 'general rehab', which acts rather like a small community. Its residents may be able to decide on their own communal needs and rules. Counselling is carried out both individually and in group sessions. The average length of stay in this type of establishment is between six and eight months.

The second type is the Christian-based establishment, which normally offers one-to-one counselling rather than group work. Residents here may be expected to adopt a Christian outlook in order to help them overcome their drug problems. This may involve regular Bible study groups, prayer sessions and religious services, which may be unacceptable to some users. The average length of stay in such establishments may be up to a year.

The third type, known as 'concept rehabs', are highly structured establishments where the residents' time is filled to capacity. Therapeutic sessions are intense and somewhat confrontational, allowing users to get in touch with and express their feelings openly. The user's self-image and lifestyle may be taken to pieces systematically in order to rebuild them in a more acceptable way. As this way of working can prove to be too much for some residents, the dropout rate can be quite high, wasting precious resources. The average length of stay, for those who last the course, is between 9 and 18 months.

The final type of rehab uses the 'Minnesota method', a programme based on the 12 steps to sobriety used by Alcoholics Anonymous. Substance misuse is considered by advocates of the Minnesota method to be a lifelong illness that requires constant counselling in order to avoid relapse. The residents' days are long and organised, with an individual's progress measured and assessed by both peers and rehab workers. The average length of stay at this type of establishment is quite short, being perhaps only six to eight weeks. However, halfway houses run by the rehab may then offer ongoing placement to former residents for up to 12 months. During this time, they are offered further support before being totally integrated back into everyday society, where they must then fend for themselves.

Rehab is not for the faint-hearted, and the different regimes must be studied carefully before the correct choice can be made. As residential establishments, they may well be situated far from the user's familiar haunts. This may be considered an advantage by some people, who may want to get away from their previous lives. Others, however, may not wish to be so far from home due to commitments to children, family and friends.

Funding for referral to a rehab establishment usually is in the control of the relevant local authority from their community care budget, and therefore restrictions may be placed on them at times of high demand. In some cases, depending on the financial circumstances of the user or their family, the user may be asked to contribute towards the costs of their treatment.

Before being accepted to any rehab, all potential residents are assessed for suitability and then interviewed to ensure that they have the right level of commitment. Similarly, it must also be decided as to whether the particular rehab can meet the person's needs. These procedures, together with the issue of securing adequate funding, mean that there may be substantial delays between the user deciding to go to a rehab and actually being admitted.

In the UK, fewer rehabs cater specifically for women than for men, possibly reflecting the greater use of drugs and other substances by men. Even fewer establishments cater for people with mental health problems, pregnant women and women with dependent children.

It is worth stating that residential rehabilitation is not always totally successful. This may be due to many factors, not least the determination and cooperation of the user and the degree of support available to them once they leave. Some users may have to make several attempts before they can say that they have totally conquered their drug habits and dealt with the reasons that led to them being there in the first instance.

Prescribing

Among the substance-using population, there is a percentage for whom drug taking has become simply a way of life, which they have no wish to change. Financial, social or medical considerations, or perhaps the threat of a prison sentence, may be the only reason for them seeking out agencies that offer prescribing services. A good number of users addicted to illegal heroin will be looking to obtain a daily maintenance dose of legal methadone, a synthetic opiate, as a substitute for their drug of choice. Others may be trying to obtain daily prescriptions for dexamphetamine or buprenorphine, used as a substitute for amphetamine or to treat opiate addiction, respectively, especially in the short term or after a period of methadone use. These forms of medication have to be taken orally, usually on a daily basis. The amount prescribed is calculated by a doctor, who equates it to match the person's current use of street drugs. Urine samples may be taken at this time in order to confirm that the user is actually using the substance that they claim.

Oral forms of medication are especially useful, as a daily dose of oral medication may well make the practice of injecting heroin or amphetamine unnecessary. Prescribed drugs, unlike their street counterparts, are of a known strength and purity, and their effects may well last for much longer. For example, street heroin may produce an effect that lasts six hours or so, whereas the corresponding dose of methadone or buprenorphine may last for more than 24 hours, thus preventing the onset of withdrawal symptoms.

For many users, prescribed drugs are preferable and may keep at bay various medical, legal and social problems that otherwise may adversely affect their lives. Prescribing obviates the need for the criminal activities that usually are necessary in order to fund a drug habit, and reduces the amount of physical and mental harm that can be caused by the use, especially intravenously, of street drugs.

Once a prescription is secured, the user will generally be in contact with a voluntary or statutory drugs worker, who in time may well be able to help them to consider changing their lifestyle for the better.

For heroin users who prefer to carry on injecting, perhaps due to a needle fixation in which they derive pleasure from the use of the needle itself, some services offer injectable forms of a synthetic opiate as a substitute.

Users of cocaine, ecstasy and other hallucinogenic drugs are not catered for easily, as there are no medical alternatives. Control of withdrawal symptoms and other side effects by using drugs such as antidepressants, tranquillisers, painkillers or sleeping pills may be necessary in these people. However, many tranquillisers, painkillers and sleeping pills can themselves lead to addiction problems, and so they must be prescribed carefully and their use monitored. For users who present with addiction to these types of drug, alternatives can be offered, usually on a gradually tapering basis, in order to break the dependence.

Needle and syringe schemes

For many years now, in the UK the prevention of HIV transmission within intravenous drug-using populations has been aided by needle- and syringe-exchange schemes. The UK government's Advisory Committee on the Misuse of Drugs believed that HIV infection could prove to be a far more devastating problem for society than drug use itself, which led to the establishment of a number of needle- and syringe-exchange schemes. The schemes provide injecting users free of charge with clean injecting equipment, such as needles, syringes, medical swabs, sterile water, vitamin C powder, filters and safe disposal facilities, in order to reduce or stem the transmission of bloodborne diseases within the injecting population and thus prevent wider transmission into the general population. The schemes reduce or remove the need to share or reuse dirty or contaminated injecting equipment, which could be contaminated with HIV or hepatitis virus.

The schemes are in no way intended to condone the injecting of drugs but simply to safeguard public health. At the same time, they are saving much public money, which the health service can ill afford to lose, for the cost of needle and syringe provision to users is minimal compared with the cost of treating the many more cases of HIV, AIDS and viral hepatitis that may result if such schemes were withdrawn.

Needle- and syringe-exchange schemes also provide a means of contacting injecting users who normally would not access health-based services, including users who inject steroids in order to reshape their bodies.

As with local drug services, most areas of the UK have needle- and syringe-provision schemes, which exist to facilitate easy collection and disposal of equipment from pharmacies, surgeries, mobile and static drug services, and other outlets.

For details of all the available services in your locality, contact directory enquiries or look in the telephone directory. You can also get details from local doctors and hospitals, chemists, the police, social services, Citizens' Advice Bureaux or your local drug action team.

Chapter 16

The Language of Drug and Substance Abuse

Slang abounds in drug-using circles, just as it does in any other exclusive area of society. Its purpose is just the same as anywhere else: the use of slang in the correct context can send to the listener important messages about the person speaking to them. It may, for instance, give the speaker immediate credibility, inferring that they are familiar with and knowledgeable about the subject matter, that they are neither a spy in the camp nor a time-waster. Their status may then rise as the listener gains a degree of confidence and reassurance from what he or she is hearing, being able to deduce from the information given whether they are listening to a seasoned or relatively new user of substances, a dealer, or simply a genuine customer looking for a supplier.

This process must work both ways before any real degree of trust can be built up and the conversation allowed to continue. Therefore, if the correct and acceptable responses are forthcoming, the original speaker will also learn much about their conversation partner; if they are not satisfied, then the conversation will be brought to an abrupt halt.

More importantly, the use of slang gives users the ability to exclude the uninitiated non-drug-taking majority, keeping them ignorant of the true nature of conversations going on around them, while allowing those involved to get on with their dealings unhindered and without arousing any suspicion.

Thousands of slang words are in common use in the various drug scenes today. Some may well be restricted to only one country, to particular areas of a country or to particular types of user, while others are universally understood and accepted. A particular word or expression may mean one thing in some places and something entirely different in others. New words appear from time to time, perhaps to introduce or advertise new substances or to give old substances a new image. New paraphernalia also appear and will be given new slang names.

The terminology is of a varied nature, some being quite obvious as to its origins but other words being more obscure. Slang can convey all of the aspects of drug and substance misuse and may be indicative of colour, effect, place or country of manufacture or cultivation, size, appearance, shape, weight, design, chemical composition, method of use, paraphernalia of use, trade name, quality or purity, associated danger, cost or historical usage; alternatively, it may be based simply on rhyming slang, for example:

Colour: white lady, snow (cocaine powder)

Effect: speed or whiz (amphetamine); Easy lay (GHB when used as a 'date-rape' drug)

Place of origin: Bolivian marching powder (cocaine powder)

Size: microdots (small pills of LSD)

Shape: Nepalese temple balls (ball-shaped cannabis resin)

Weight: eighth (eighth of an ounce of cannabis)

Design: doves (ecstasy tablet with bird imprint); Mercedes (ecstasy tablet with Mercedes car symbol imprint)

Chemical makeup: acid (LSD); base (form of amphetamine)

Method of use: puff, blow, draw (cannabis for smoking)

Paraphernalia: spike (hypodermic needle); barrel (syringe)

Trade names: roopies (Rohypnol); moggies (Mogadon)

Quality or purity: shit (poor-quality heroin); snideys (fake drug)

Associated danger: M25s (ecstasy)

Cost: champagne (cocaine)

Historical: hash, hashish (cannabis; from Haschishin, a nineteenth-century group of assassins who made use of the drug)

Rhyming slang: Bob Hope (dope, cannabis)

Slang terms may drop out of use and then be resurrected. For instance, 'reefer' was once the accepted term for a cannabis cigarette; it then went out of fashion, particularly in the UK, to be replaced by the terms 'joint' and 'spliff', but recently it seems to have made a comeback. Perhaps the influence of the Internet is at work here: with so many sites dedicated to extolling the pleasures of cannabis use being American in origin and using the term 'reefer' commonly, the expression is catching on with a whole new generation of UK users.

It can be difficult for the non-user to understand fully how and when to use drug slang correctly, and it is better therefore to use it only if you are totally sure of the meaning, pronunciation and correct context in which it should be used. If not, then it is better to stick to known technical descriptions and commonly accepted terms to avoid losing face when talking with users.

Below is a list of the more common drug slang currently in use, which may help you to understand this secret 'language':

Acid	LSD
Acid head	LSD user
Adam	Ecstasy (from MDMA)
Afghan black	Cannabis resin
Amp	Ampoule of drugs
Amytal	Barbiturates
Artillery	Injecting equipment
Backtrack	To draw blood back into the syringe
Bad trip	Frightening or unpleasant LSD trip
Bag	Small quantity of drugs, usually in powder form
Bagging	Inhaling solvents from a bag
Bang up	To inject drugs
Barb	A form of tranquilliser or sleeping pill
Barbie	A form of tranquilliser or sleeping pill
Barrel	Syringe for injecting
Base	Putty-like form of amphetamine or cocaine
Basuco	Cocaine paste

Batman	LSD 'tab' design with an image of Batman
Bennies	Benzedrine tablets
Benzo	A form of tranquilliser or sleeping pill
Bernice	Cocaine
Bhang	Herbal cannabis
Billy	Amphetamine
Billy whiz	Amphetamine
Bindle	Number of packages of drugs fastened together
Biscuit	Pale brown, coarse-grained ecstasy tablet
Black	Cannabis resin
Blocker	A form of tranquilliser or sleeping pill
Blockbuster	A form of tranquilliser or sleeping pill
Blotter	LSD paper square
Blow	Herbal cannabis
Blue star	Mythical LSD design with an image of a blue star
Bolivian marching powder	Cocaine
Bomb	Small quantity of drugs wrapped in a cigarette paper for swallowing
Bong	Home-made water pipe for smoking cannabis
Boot	'Hit' of heroin
Bottling or hot-bottling	Version of 'hot-knifing', in which a bottle with no bottom is used to concentrate the smoke
Brown	Heroin
Buddha	LSD 'tab' design with an image of the Buddha

Buds	Flower tops of the female cannabis plant, added to tobacco to produce a high-strength mixture
Building	Making a cannabis cigarette
Burger	Large brown ecstasy tablet
Bush	Herbal cannabis
Busted	Searched (either a person or a house) or being arrested
Buzz	Effects of a stimulant drug
Buzzing	Feelings after use of ecstasy
Cabbaged	Becoming intoxicated using ecstasy
Cannabis red eye	Bloodshot eyes after heavy cannabis use
Cat Valium	Ketamine
Champagne	Cocaine
Charge	Cocaine
Charlie	Cocaine
Chasing	Inhaling the fumes of burning heroin
Chasing the dragon	Smoking heroin on a piece of foil
Chemical X	Gamma-hydroxybutyrate (GHB); sodium oxybate
Chewies	Tuinal tablets
Chi	Chinese heroin
Chill out	Period of cooling down after overheating from ecstasy use
Chill room	Room provided at a rave or club for cooling down after ecstasy use
Chillum	Clay, glass, metal or wooden smoking pipe

China white	Heroin; fentanyl, a synthetic opiate found most commonly in the USA
Circles	Rohypnol tablets
Clean	Not using drugs
Clear X	Gamma-hydroxybutyrate (GHB); sodium oxybate
Cocktail	Mixture of drugs, often taken experimentally
Cog	Can of liquid petroleum gas (LPG)
Cogging	Inhaling solvents, particularly gas
Coke	Cocaine
Cold turkey	Withdrawing from drugs, particularly heroin, without medical help
Colombian	Cannabis resin
Come-down	Withdrawal from the effects of drugs
Connection	Drug supplier
Cook up	To prepare a drug for injection
Cooking spoon	Metal used to heat and dissolve powder drugs for injection.
Crack	Freebase cocaine
Crack baby	Baby born with an addiction to crack cocaine because of crack use by the mother during pregnancy
Crack head	User of crack cocaine
Crash	Come down from amphetamine
Crystal splitter	Very strong ecstasy tablet with a crystalline coating
Cut	To mix other substances with a drug to add bulk and weight
Dab	To pick up a drug on a wet finger and lick it off

Deal	To sell drugs
Dealer	Supplier of drugs
Deck	Small package of drugs
Detox	To withdraw from drugs under medical supervision
Dex	Dexedrine; dexamphetamine
Dexies	Dexedrine, a form of amphetamine
DF	DF-118
DF-118	Opiate painkiller in tablet form
Diesel	Cannabis oil
Diff	DF-118
Dike	Diconal, a synthetic opiate
Disco biscuit	Brown, coarse-grained ecstasy tablet
Ditto	Drug treatment and testing order
Doll/Dolly	Methadone
Dollar	Ecstasy tablet with image of dollar symbol
Doofs/Doofers	opiate painkillers in tablet form
Dope	Resin and herbal cannabis
Dope head	Person who uses drugs and also deals to finance the habit
Dots	LSD in the form of small pills or tablets
Double Bart/ Double Dutch Bart Large	LSD 'tab' design showing the cartoon character Bart Simpson
Dove	Ecstasy tablet with image of bird
Downer	A form of tranquilliser or sleeping pill
Draw	Cannabis

Draw up	To load a syringe
Drop	To take a drug by mouth
Drought	Local shortage of drugs
E	Ecstasy
Easy lay	Gamma-hydroxybutyrate (GHB); sodium oxybate
Eighth	One-eighth of an ounce of cannabis
EZ lay	Gamma-hydroxybutyrate (GHB); sodium oxybate
Five-skinner	Cannabis cigarette made from five papers
Fix	Injection of drugs
Flashback	Tripping out again some time after LSD use. Can be days, months or even years later. Usually a bad trip
Flintstones	LSD tab design showing images of the Flintstones cartoon characters
Flush	To draw blood in and out of a syringe
Flying	Feeling obtained soon after cocaine use
Fold	Paper packaging for drugs
Freebase	Freebase cocaine
Fun candy	Confectionery containing cannabis
Ganga/Ganja	Cannabis
Gas	Liquid petroleum gas used for sniffing
Gasman/gasboy	Liquid petroleum gas user
GBH	Gamma-hydroxybutyrate or sodium oxybate, liquid hallucinogenic stimulants also used as 'date-rape' drugs
Gear	Any illegal drug, but most commonly heroin
Get her to bed	Gamma-hydroxybutyrate (GHB); sodium oxybate

GHB	Gamma-hydroxybutyrate (GHB); sodium oxybate
Gold	Cannabis resin
Goof ball	A form of tranquilliser or sleeping pill
Goop	Gamma-hydroxybutyrate (GHB); sodium oxybate
Gorbies	LSD tab design showing the face of Mikhial Gorbachev
Gouching	Falling asleep while very stoned
Gravy	Heroin powder
Green eggs	Temazepan in jelly capsules
Gun	Needle and syringe
Grass	Herbal cannabis
H	Heroin
Habit	Addiction
Harry	Heroin
Hash	Cannabis resin
Hash cake	Cake containing cannabis
Hashish	Cannabis resin
Hash oil	Cannabis oil
Head rush	Sensation of injected drugs reaching the brain, or sometimes loss of sensation or mini-blackout lasting a few seconds while dancing
Head shop	Shop dealing in drug paraphernalia, legal mind-altering substances and, in many cases, pornography
Hemp	Herbal cannabis
Hemp sucker	Lollipop containing cannabis
Henry	One-eight of an ounce of cannabis (Henry VIII)

Herb	Herbal cannabis
High	Feeling of being up while under influence of drugs
Hit	To buy or to inject drugs; the initial effect felt of a drug
Home-grown	Herbal cannabis grown in the UK
Honey	Cannabis oil
Hookah	Water pipe for smoking cannabis
Hooked	Addicted
Horse	Heroin
Hot-knifing	Smoking a drug by touching it with a heated knife blade and then inhaling the resultant smoke
Hubble-bubble	Water pipe for smoking cannabis
Huff	To inhale solvents
Indian hemp	Cannabis
Indica	Variety of cannabis plant, grown mostly in countries away from the tropics, but with warm climates. Needs less light than *Sativa* but grows more slowly
Iranian	Heroin
Jack up	To inject drugs
Jellies	Temazepan in jelly capsules
Jelly beans	Temazepan in jelly capsules
Joint	Hand-rolled cannabis cigarette
Joker	Type of cannabis joint made by arranging five papers into a large triangle shape to produce a cone-shaped joint
Junk	Heroin
Junkie	Drug user

K	Ketamine
Karma	State of being high on drugs
Khat	Leaves of the plant *Catha edulis*, a mild stimulant is chewed in some African cultures
Kick	To stop taking drugs
Kulfi	Sweets containing cannabis, rarely found in the UK
Leaf	Cocaine
Lebanese	Cannabis resin
Liberty cap	Species of hallucinogenic mushroom
Line	Narrow line of cocaine arranged for snorting
Liquid dream	Gamma-hydroxybutyrate (GHB); sodium oxybate
Liquid ecstasy	Gamma-hydroxybutyrate (GHB); sodium oxybate
Liquid gold	Poppers
Liquid X	Gamma-hydroxybutyrate (GHB); sodium oxybate
Locker room	Poppers
Looking through the window	Use of LSD paper or gel tab by placing under the eyelid
Louis	16th of an ounce of cannabis
Lose it	To become detached from reality through drug use
Lose the plot	To become disoriented after repeated or long-term drug use
Love dove	Ecstasy showing image of bird
Lung	Device for smoking cannabis comprising a small bottle and a plastic bag
M&Ms	Temazepan in jelly capsules
Magic mushroom	Any of the species of hallucinogenic mushroom

Main line	To inject drugs
Marijuana	Herbal cannabis
Mesc	Mescaline
Meth	Methamphetamine; methadone
Mexican Valium	Rohypnol
Microdots	LSD in the form of small pills
Microfine	1ml syringe with a very fine needle
Mike	Microfine syringe
Mindset	Mood of LSD using at time of use
Mixing the gravy	Smoking cocaine mixed with other drugs
Moggies	Mogadon sleeping pills
Monged out	Being heavily under the influence of drugs, usually cannabis
Moroccan	Cannabis resin
Moroccan gold	Cannabis resin
Mule	Person who smuggles drugs for a third party
Munchies	Eating binge induced by cannabis
Mushies	Hallucinogenic mushrooms
Nederweed	Hybrid cannabis variety with a high THC level grown in northern climates
Needle fixation	Obsession with needle and syringe use
Nitro	Poppers
Nod	Effect of codeine or dihydrocodeine
Oil	Cannabis oil

Om	LSD tab design showing the Hindu word 'om', a mystic word regarded as summing up all truth
Paste	Putty-like form of amphetamine
Percy	Cocaine
Phy-amps	Methadone in ampoules (Physeptone)
Pistol	Needle and syringe
Playboy	Ecstasy tablet showing image of rabbit
Poppers	Amyl/alkyl/butyl nitrite
Pot	Cannabis resin
Pot head	Cannabis user
Psychonaut	LSD user
Puff	Herbal cannabis
Purple om	LSD tab design showing the Hindu word 'om' in purple
Push	To encourage others to use drugs
R2	Rohypnol tablet
Reader	Prescription for methadone
Red leb	Cannabis resin
Red rock	Methadone
Red seal	Cannabis resin
Reefer	Cannabis cigarette
Resin	Cannabis resin
Rizla	Brand of cigarette rolling paper, commonly used for rolling cannabis cigarettes; also available in king size
Roach/Roach end	Cardboard tube inserted in the mouth end of a cannabis cigarette, often made from a piece of the cigarette paper packet; Rohypnol tablet

Roach card	Printed advertising card perforated for use as roaches
Roached out	Being under the influence of Rohypnol
Roast	To heat resin cannabis to make it easier to crumble
Rock	Freebase cocaine
Rocky	Cannabis resin
Roid Rage	Aggression and violence associated with steroid use
Roids	Anabolic steroids
Roofies	Rohypnol tablets
Roopies	Rohypnol tablet
Rope	Rohypnol tablet
Rophy	Rohypnol tablet
Ruderalis	Variety of cannabis plant grown mostly in European countries. Needs only low light levels and will tolerate cool climates. Produces low levels of THC
Ruffies	Rohypnol tablets
Rugby balls	Temazepam in jelly capsules
Runner	Person who acts as a go-between for the user and the supplier
Rush	Rapid onset of the drug effect
Saddam Hussein	LSD 'tab' design showing the face of Saddam Hussein
Sativa	Herbal cannabis
Scag	Heroin
Scat	Heroin
Scoop her	Gamma-hydroxybutyrate (GHB); sodium oxybate
Score	To purchase drugs

Script	Prescription for drugs given as an alternative to illegal drug use or for the management or treatment of withdrawal symptoms
Sense	Sinsemilla: the flower of the cannabis plant
Sensi	Sinsemilla: the flower of the cannabis plant
Set	State of mind of the user before taking drugs
Shit	Cannabis resin; heroin
Shoot up	To inject drugs
Shrooms	Hallucinogenic mushrooms
Skag	Heroin
Skagging	Smoking heroin from a piece of foil
Skin	Paper used for making cannabis cigarettes
Skin popping	Injecting subcutaneously
Skin up	To make a cannabis cigarette
Skunk/skunk weed	Herbal cannabis
Slate	Cannabis resin
Smack	Heroin
Smiley	LSD 'tab' design showing a smiley face
Snidey	Substance sold falsely as a particular drug
Sniffer	Solvent abuser
Snort	To sniff cocaine or another drug up the nose
Snow/snowflake	Cocaine
Snowball	Heroin mixed with cocaine
Soap	Cannabis resin

Space cake	Cake with cannabis as an ingredient
Spaced	Feeling calm while under the influence of drugs
Spark up	To light a cannabis joint
Special K	Ketamine
Speed	Amphetamine
Speedball	Heroin/cocaine mix
Speed freak	User of amphetamine
Spike	Hypodermic needle
Spiking	Adding a drug to an unsuspecting person's drink or food
Spliff/splith	Hand-rolled cannabis cigarette
Spot	To smoke cannabis without using tobacco by burning small quantities on the end of a pin and inhaling the smoke
Stack	To combine shorter-acting oral steroids with longer acting injectable steroids
Stag	Poppers
Stash	Amount of drugs, usually hidden
Strawberry	LSD 'tab' design showing image of a strawberry
Strung out	Coming down from drugs
Stuff	Heroin powder
Sucking	Inhaling gas or aerosols
Sulphate/sulph	Amphetamine
Super skunk	add to existing entry for skunk/skunk weed but change definition to read 'high strength herbal cannabis'
Swab	Alcohol pad used to clean skin before injecting

Swallower	Person who smuggles drugs in swallowed condoms
Tab	LSD paper square
Teenth	16th of an ounce of cannabis (see Louis)
Temazies	Temazepam tablets
Ten-pound bag	Amount of drugs costing £10
Thai stick	Herbal cannabis wound around a stick and secured with thread
THC	Tetrahydrocannabinol, the active ingredient of cannabis
Three-skinner	Cannabis cigarette made from three papers
Toke	Puff of cannabis, usually from someone else's joint
Toke can	Home-made smoking pipe made from a drinks can
Toot	Cocaine
Tootsie roll	Methadone
Track mark	Injection scar
Tranx	A form of tranquilliser or sleeping pill
Traffic lights	A form of tranquilliser or sleeping pill
Trip	Hallucinogenic experience induced by LSD; LSD paper square
Tuey	A form of tranquilliser or sleeping pill
Vitamin K	Ketamine
Wacky backy	Herbal cannabis
Wash	Crack cocaine
Washing	Using amphetamine by rubbing it into the gums or on to the teeth; producing crack cocaine from cocaine hydrochloride powder

Weed	Herbal cannabis
White	Cocaine; pharmaceutical-grade heroin
White dove	LSD 'tab' design showing an image of a white dove
White lady	Cocaine
White stuff	Morphine
Whizz	Amphetamine
Window	LSD gelatine square measuring about 5 x 5mm
Wired up	Being tense as a result of drug use
Works	Syringes and needles
Wrap	5cm square of paper folded in order to hold drugs
X-rater	Gamma-hydroxybutyrate (GHB); sodium oxybate
Yellow eggs	Temazepan in jelly capsules
Yellow Mercedes	Ecstasy tablets
Zoom	Mixture of cocaine, heroin and amphetamine that is sniffed or injected

Chapter 17

The Legalisation Debate

Increasingly, the question of whether certain drugs should be legalised raises its
head. Cannabis is the predominant subject of much of this debate, as it was in the
UK in 2004, when cannabis was reclassified to a class C drug. This debate has been,
and still is, led largely by those who wish to see a further relaxation of the present
law, such as current and prospective users, people who stand to make profits from
the sale of the drug, and people who feel that it is a question of freedom of choice.

We have been engaged in considering this question in great detail over a number
of years. Despite the many arguments put to us in favour of total legalisation, we are
still firmly of the opinion that a change in the current legal position of cannabis
would be a grave, highly damaging, irretrievable blunder for which future generations would not thank us.

Our work has brought us into contact with many self-confessed users of cannabis and countless others who believe that cannabis is an innocuous, natural and, in
some circumstances, beneficial substance. However, despite the arguments and
opinions put forward, we have heard nothing to date that convinces us that we
should change our stance. We are concerned primarily with the undisputable evidence linking cannabis use with numerous mental health problems, especially in
heavy users. This view is supported strongly in an article published in 2005 by Dr
Philip Milln[1], a consultant psychiatrist at the Priory Hospital, Marchwood, UK, a
leading drug-treatment and rehabilitation centre. The article refers to a 15-year
study into adolescent cannabis use conducted by the Institute of Psychiatry, which
shows that young people who use cannabis regularly at the age of 15 are four and a
half times more likely than non-users to suffer significant mental health problems

---

1   Milln, P. (2005) *Mindworks: Adolescent Cannabis Use*. Leatherhead Surrey: Priory Group.

including schizophrenia by their mid-20s. The report produces evidence that by age 26, ten per cent of people who had used cannabis on three or more occasions at age 15 had a diagnosis of schizophrenia, compared with only three per cent of all other study participants.

Many readers of this book will become involved in discussions on this issue, and you will need to be fully aware of all aspects of the debate, in order to participate fully and come to your own informed decisions. To assist you in this, this chapter sets out the arguments that are commonly put forward by people in favour of legalisation and follows this with counter-arguments that are based on our knowledge and experience of the drug scene.

Is cannabis a harmless natural substance?

It is often claimed, especially by young people, that cannabis is a harmless natural substance. During a presentation on the subject to a group of tertiary-level biology students, one of them said to us: 'How can cannabis be harmful? It is a naturally oc-curring herb. God would not have put it on the Earth if it was harmful.' We would not presume to speak for God, but the Earth contains many natural 'herbs' that are not only harmful but also deadly. Tobacco, deadly nightshade and the death-cap mushroom are just three examples. Such a statement from an 18-year-old student may seem ludicrous, but it is backed up by all sorts of literature aimed at young people. There is even a T-shirt available showing a picture of a cannabis leaf and the slogan 'God doesn't make mistakes'.

Such statements are based on a lack of any real knowledge or understanding of the drug and its potentially damaging effects. Cannabis is a complex substance, which we are only just beginning to understand. The reader is advised to study Chapter 3 on cannabis, especially the section on adverse effects.

Is cannabis good for people with certain medical conditions?

It is often argued that cannabis is harmless and has many uses in medicine. A number of research studies are being carried out in the UK and other countries into the use of cannabis in the treatment of certain medical conditions, including to alleviate the nauseous effects of chemotherapy, to control pain and reduce muscle spasm in people with multiple sclerosis, and to encourage appetite in patients suffering certain wasting conditions, such as AIDS or HIV infection. Early results of this research include a report[2] published in 2003 into the use of whole-plant cannabis extract to control pain and muscle spasm in MS patients. The results of this study indicate significant beneficial effects for some such patients. This research is ongoing and is unlikely to be copmpleted for some time. Many drugs have appeared useful at first only to lead to disastrous consequences later, thalidomide being one example.

There do appear to be some beneficial properties of cannabis, and it may be that some medical uses will be found. However, that is not a reason to believe that it is harmless. Many illegal drugs have medical uses. Heroin in pharmaceutical form (morphine) is used to treat extreme pain, often in people with terminal illnesses. Cocaine has been used as an anaesthetic, and forms of amphetamine are used in the treatment of sleep disorders and for hyperactivity in children. But this does not mean that they are harmless.

Is cannabis addictive?

The answer to this depends on what we mean by 'addictive'. If we mean a solely physical dependence, in which the user has undergone physiological changes that will necessitate further doses of the drug in order to stem withdrawal symptoms, then generally the answer is no. However, while it is unusual for a cannabis user to develop a true physical dependence, it is becoming increasingly recognised that heavy use of the more potent forms of cannabis, such as skunk and super-skunk, has the potential to precipitate a true physical dependence. On the other hand, it is extremely common for regular users of any form of cannabis to develop a profound psychological dependence. We have worked with an enormous number of cannabis users over many years, and many of them live their entire lives based around their cannabis use. We have known users who could not get out of bed in the morning and face the world without first using the drug. One user kept a fully charged bong by his bed and smoked this as soon as he awoke. Regular users often get themselves into a state in which they are afraid to face life without using cannabis.

People have been using cannabis for thousands of years

While it is certainly true that people have grown cannabis for many thousands of years, most of that growing has been to produce plants for use as a source of fibre for

---

2   Wade, D.T., Robson, P., House, H., Makela, P. and Aram, J. (2003) 'A preliminary controlled study to determine whether whole-plant cannabis extracts can improve intractable neurogenic symptoms.' *Clinical Rehabilitation 17*, 18–26.

cloth and rope. Examples exist of the use of cannabis as a mood-altering drug going back throughout recorded history, but its use in this way is very irregular. There has never been widespread recreational use of cannabis, even in countries where the plant occurs naturally. Its use as a drug has occurred within fairly restricted groups and never seems to have lasted for a prolonged period. Its use fades and then recurs in other groups years later. Unlike opium and coca, there exists no long-term history of mass use of cannabis, merely a series of separate examples of smaller-scale use. Today's cannabis users are the first in history to use cannabis on such a substantial scale. They have volunteered to take part in the largest field trial of a disputed drug ever held. Our experience and our reading of the latest scientific research evidence suggests to us that the outcome may well be detrimental to many users individually and to society as a whole.

Cannabis has many non-medical uses

A figure often quoted in publications that support the legalisation of cannabis is that there are 50 thousand non-medical uses for the plant. We have been unable to discover how this figure is arrived at and who first quoted it. It seems to have become part of the mythology that surrounds cannabis. We would suggest that it is unlikely that there are 50 thousand different uses for wood or plastic, let alone cannabis. It is certainly true that cannabis fibre can be turned into cloth and rope. Hemp-based ropes are still produced and have a valued use in many industries. Hemp cloth is more rare and has almost disappeared from the normal clothing trade. Other than these two examples, there is very little non-drug use of the plant anywhere in the world.

With over four million regular users in the UK, should it be made legal?

This is a curious question. It is being suggested that if enough people do something illegal, then it ought to be legalised. We would suggest that there are many examples of laws that are broken constantly by people without anyone suggesting that they ought to be repealed because of such non-compliance. It is likely that many millions of people in the UK drive above the legal speed limit at some point. This is not a reason to do away with speed limits. Given a chance to, a large number of people would choose not to pay their income tax, but no-one suggests that is a reason to scrap the income-tax laws. Something may remain undesirable, however many people choose to take part in it.

The counter-argument to this is that cannabis use is a victimless crime. Users may claim they are not hurting anyone but themselves, and so it should be allowed. This common argument provides a glimpse of the essentially selfish nature of all drug use. Many drug users refuse to recognise the validity of the feelings of people around them, particularly those who care about them, and refuse to accept that their families and friends have any right to be concerned, frightened, angry or ashamed of their drug use. It is the user's business and no-one else's. In our experience, cannabis use by many people has seriously and adversely affected families, relationships, colleagues, employment, education and physical and mental wellbeing. The majority of these factors will also have a financial implication for the rest of society.

Why do we criminalise an accepted social activity?

The first thing to say is that this cannot be an accepted social activity because it is an illegal act. It turns logic on its head to suggest otherwise. Even if there are some four million cannabis users in the UK, that still leaves millions of others to whom it is unacceptable. We live in a democracy, and society has the right to decide what is acceptable and what is not. Just because a minority of people wish to do something that most do not, that is not a reason to suggest that society has to change its views in order to accept theirs.

Is cannabis attractive to people just because of its illegality?

There is no doubt that many people, especially young people, are attracted to cannabis use precisely because it is forbidden. There is an extra attraction to doing something that is against the rules. However, to think that by legalising it we will stop the problem is to misunderstand what drug use is all about. If cannabis is legalised, then all we will have dealt with is the drug, not the users. They will still have their desires to break the rules and do something risky and illegal. With cannabis legalised, they will not be able to exercise that desire by its use. What then? Perhaps they will move on to break the law with other drugs that the majority of us consider even more dangerous.

If you legalise cannabis, will you get rid of the dealers?

First we need to decide how cannabis is to be marketed should it ever be legalised. Some people have suggested that it should be sold at local pharmacies to people over a certain age. Suggested ages vary, but 16 (the same age as for buying tobacco legally) and 18 (the same as for buying alcohol legally) are favourites. With this model of marketing, we still leave the dealer to satisfy the needs of people under age and those for whom the pharmacy is too far away or open at inconvenient times.

Another suggested model is to sell cannabis at places where tobacco is currently available, such as newsagents, public houses, convenience stores, garages and so on, but still only to people over a certain age. This fails to remove the dealer, who will still serve the needs of young users.

If we legalise cannabis totally and allow it to be sold to anyone, of any age, and through any retail outlet, including vending machines, then the cannabis dealer will have little trade available to them. What will the dealer do then? Will he or she give up and seek honest employment or sign on as unemployed? We doubt it. We suggest that they will carry on doing what they know best. They will carry on dealing drugs – potentially even more dangerous drugs.

The only way in which the dealer could be taken completely out of the picture is to legalise all drugs and sell them everywhere and to anybody. Are we really ready to contemplate that? Does anyone really believe that such a move would result in fewer drugs being used, and a safer, healthier society?

Would there be less crime if cannabis was legalised?

If cannabis were legalised, it would be left to the private sector to supply and market it. It is unlikely that any responsible government would consider becoming involved in the production and supply of cannabis for street use. Private enterprise would set the price at what the market could bear. When the sale of alcohol was legalised in the USA following the end of Prohibition in 1933, the new breweries set their prices to match what the public had been used to paying for their illegal liquor in the speakeasies. This is what would be likely to happen with cannabis. Perhaps competition between suppliers would bring the price down a little, but that can happen only if sales rise because more people are using the drug. In addition, it is likely that any government would place a tax on legalised cannabis in the same way as they do with alcohol and tobacco. This may mean an overall rise in the price, with the potential for crimes being committed in order to pay for the extra cost.

Currently, tobacco and alcohol products are common targets during burglaries and similar crimes. Such targeting would likely switch to cannabis. Similarly, cannabis may, in the same way as tobacco and alcohol, be smuggled from other countries to avoid paying taxes.

Would legalising cannabis save police and customs resources?

If cannabis were legalised, clearly police and customs officers would save valuable time investigating its importation, supply and use. However, if legalisation then led on to a rise in the use of other drugs for the reasons outlined earlier, then it is likely that no overall saving would be made. In addition, we need to consider the effects of mass use of cannabis on public safety and order. There is already a substantial and increasing problem on our streets caused by the antisocial behaviour of large numbers of people affected by alcohol. Are we ready to add cannabis to this situation?

Some other things to think about

It is our view that to change the law in relation to cannabis, such that it is available legally, would inevitably lead to an increase in the use of it and potentially other drugs. Such an increase in drug use would lead to an increase in the requirements of the already overstretched UK health service. Who would pay for that? Not the regular drug users, as many of them would not be in gainful employment or making any financial contribution to the treasury.

And where would we get enough cannabis to meet this increase in demand? It is likely that UK growers would try to produce as much as they could, but, given the climatic conditions in the UK, the majority would have to be imported. We would need to think about where we would import cannabis from. It is unlikely that other countries would follow the UK in legalising the drug, and thus they would be unhappy about supplies travelling through their territory to reach us. In the worst-case scenario, it may be necessary for governments to overlook the activities of organised international criminals importing the required amounts of cannabis to satisfy demand.

What would happen to educational standards if the majority of young people, and indeed those educating them, were using cannabis regularly? We know that it affects short-term memory and long-term motivation, and it is difficult to see how standards could do anything other than decline. The same may happen to production in industry and commerce, with workers at all levels suffering from the effects of cannabis use.

If cannabis's availability were unrestricted in the UK, we could become the centre for massive drug tourism, with many thousands of people being attracted here to obtain their supplies. We would also see the arrival of foreign suppliers trying to muscle in on the lucrative trade. What would happen to the reputation of this country? To catch a glimpse of what would happen, look at the situation in the

Netherlands. Most people, when asked what comes to mind when they think of Amsterdam, talk not of tulips, canals, windmills, clogs or Anne Frank but of drugs, especially cannabis. Is this really the sort of reputation that we want for our country? Indeed, in 2005, responding to pressure from other European Union members that disapprove of the Dutch approach to cannabis, the coalition government adopted a more conservative stance, resulting in a 50 per cent decline in the number of permitted cannabis outlets in Amsterdam.

If any country were to decide to go down the road of fully legalising cannabis, then it needs to be clearly understood that it is a one-way road. Once legalised, the use of cannabis would, in our view, increase to such an extent that it would be impossible to try and recriminalise its use. This is not something that can be experimented with in order to see what would happen. If that step is taken, it will be irrevocable. There will be no going back.

Once the legalisation of cannabis were secured, what would be next? To believe that all of the supporters of cannabis's legalisation would then be satisfied is naive. Some would not be satisfied until all drugs are legalised. And where would that leave us?

Appendix I
Formulation of a Substance Misuse Policy

The following notes are intended to provide a checklist for anyone attempting to formulate a school or workplace substance misuse policy. It is recognised that such institutions vary greatly and may face different problems, but each point in the checklist will need to be considered if the policy is to be comprehensive.

1. A statement of the school or workplace philosophy towards the use of illegal substances, the misuse of legal substances and the provision of substance misuse education/training. *Consider:*

   - clear explanation of the policy to all those subject to it, both internally and externally

   - possession and/or use of illegal drugs, solvents, tobacco, alcohol, prescribed medicines and other legal but undesirable substances

   - whether any particular incident will be considered as a disciplinary or welfare matter.

2. A clear definition of where, when and to whom the policy applies. *Consider:*

   - physical boundaries of the site in which the policy applies

   - students, staff, ancillaries, contractors, etc.

   - outside journeys/visits, including foreign trips

   - visitors to the site

   - vehicles of students, staff, ancillaries, contractors and visitors when on site.

   - official vehicles

   - students, staff, ancillaries or contractors revisiting the site out of hours, either authorised or unauthorised

   - individuals away from site but in uniform or still identifiable as part of the school or institution

   - individuals when not connected with the school or institution, i.e. in own time.

3. Statement of sanctions/interventions that can be applied to breaches of the policy. *Consider:*

   - level of offence, such as possession for own use, encouragement of others to join in substance misuse, supply, or possession with intent to supply

- exclusion/suspension/dismissal as first or last option
- referring on for expert help.

4. Involvement of parents/students/staff. *Consider:*

   - provision of opportunities for parents/students/staff to comment on the proposed policy
   - notification of parents when substance misuse by students is suspected
   - feedback to parents/students/staff on implementation of the policy
   - provision of awareness-raising sessions for parents/students/staff.

5. Liaison with the police/other authorities. *Consider:*

   - involvement of police, social services, etc. when substance misuse is suspected or confirmed
   - potential outcomes of involving outside authorities
   - your statutory duties in law.

6. Liaison with other bodies that use the site.

7. The circumstances in which members of staff may carry out searches of individuals and/or the site, including vehicles, lockers, desks, cupboards, personal possessions, etc.

8. Will the school admit pupils who have been excluded from another school following an incident of substance misuse?

9. The appointment of a dedicated member of staff who will coordinate all enquiries into substance-related incidents.

10. Training of staff in the recognition and management of substance-related incidents.

11. Liaison with the media. *Consider:*

    - whether all media enquiries should be dealt with by a named person(s)?
    - the position with regard to reporters who may wish to interview staff or students, either on or off site
    - appropriate responses from management if parents or others make comments to the press

12. Liaison with other agencies, such as drug misuse services, local doctors, hospitals, health promotion units, etc.

Appendix 2

Useful Organisations

The following national organisations may be of help to anyone seeking further information, help or support for a drug or substance problem.

UK

Alcoholics Anonymous
PO Box 1 Stonebow House
Stonebow
York YO1 7NJ
Tel: 01904 644026
For local branches, consult your telephone directory.
Website: www.alcoholics-anonymous.org.uk

Childline
Help line: 0800 11 11
Free confidential 24-hour help line for children in trouble or danger.
Website: www.childline.org.uk

Citizens' Advice Bureau
For local branches, consult your telephone directory.
Website: www.citizensadvice.org.uk

DrugScope
Formed by the amalgamation of ISDD (Institute for the Study of Drug Dependence) and Scoda (Standing Conference on Drug Abuse). Provides expert information, training and resources.
Website: www.drugscope.org.uk

Narcotics Anonymous
UK Service Office
202 City Road
London EC1V 2PH
National help line: 020 7730 0009 (10 a.m. to 10 p.m. daily)
Email: ukso@ukna.org
Website: www.ukna.org (gives details of international contacts)

National AIDS Helpline/Sexual Health Line
Tel: 0800 567 123
Free confidential 24-hour service.

National Drugs Helpline/Frank
Tel: 0800 77 66 00
Free confidential 24-hour service to users, their families and friends.
Website: www.talktofrank.com

Northern Ireland Council for Voluntary Action
61 Duncairn Gardens
Belfast BT15 2GB
Tel: 028 9087 7777
Details of drug services in Northern Ireland.
Website: www.nicva.org then follow links to Community NI.

Parentline Plus
UK registered charity that offers support to anyone parenting a child.
Free help line: 0808 800 2222
Website: www.parentlineplus.org.uk

Rape Crisis
Provides counselling, advice and support to survivors of rape or sexual assault.
Website: www.rapecrisis.org.uk (gives contact details of local services)

Release
388 Old Street
London EC1V 8LT
Administration tel: 020 7729 5255
Help line: 0845 4500 215
24-hour advice, information and referral on legal and drug-related problems for users, their families and friends.
Website: www.release.org.uk

Re-Solv
Works to reduce and prevent solvent abuse.
30a High Street
Stone
Staffordshire ST15 8AW
Tel: 01785 817885
Help line: 0808 800 2345
Free confidential 24-hour service to users, their families and friends.
Website: www.re-solv.org

Samaritans
National Lo-call number: 08457 90 90 90
For local branches, consult your telephone directory.
Website: www.samaritans.org.uk

Scottish Drugs Forum
5 Waterloo Street
Glasgow G2 6AY
Tel: 0141 221 1175
Details of drugs services in Scotland.
Website: www.sdf.org.uk

For details of other voluntary and statutory agencies in your area that may be able to offer help, advice or information, look in your local telephone directory under 'Help and Advice'.

Australia

National Drugs Campaign
Tel: 1800 250 015 freecall
Drugs information
Website: www.drugs.health.gov.au/youth/index.htm

National Drugs Strategy Committee
GPO Box 9848
Canberra
ACT2601
Tel: 02 6288 1555
Drugs education website: www.nationaldrugstrategy.gov.au

Canada

Canadian Centre on Substance Abuse/National Clearing House on Substance Abuse
112 Kent Street
Suite 480
Ottawa KIP 5P2
Tel: 613 235 4048
Information and advice concerning substance abuse.
Website: www.ccsa.ca

Republic of Ireland

The Department of Health
Hawkins House
Dublin 2
Republic of Ireland
Provides details of services available.
Website: www.tcd.ie/community_health

The Netherlands

Netherlands Institute of Mental Health and Addiction

PO Box 725
3500 AS Utrecht
Tel: 030 297 11 00
Fax: 030 297 11 11
Provides advice and literature on drug matters.
Website: www.trimbos.nl/default37.html

New Zealand

National Society on Alcohol and Drug Dependence (NSAD)

PO Box 9183
Wellington
Tel: 04 385 1517
Provides advice and literature on drug matters.
Website: www.nsad.org.nz

New Zealand Drug Foundation

PO Box 3082
Wellington
Tel: 04 499 2920
Fax: 04 499 2925
Provides advice and literature on drug matters.
Website: www.nzdf.org.nz

USA

National Clearinghouse for Alcohol and Drug Information

PO Box 2345
Rockville
MD 20852
Information and advice concerning substance abuse.
Website: www.health.org

Cocaine Helpline

Tel: 800 C.O.C.A.I.N.E.
24-hour free and confidential help regarding cocaine use.

National Institute on Drug Abuse

Hotline: 1 800 662 H.E.L.P.
24-hour free and confidential help and referral for people with drug problems. Provides advice and literature on drug matters.
Website: www.nida.nih.gov

Index